KU-300-638

CAE Result

Student's Book

Kathy Gude & Mary Stephens

CENTRE	Lincoln
CHECKED	Jad ✓
ZONE	Black
CLASS MARK/ SUFFIX	428.24 GUD
LOAN PERIOD	1 month

Lincoln College

3000138

OXFORD

UNIVERSITY PRESS

3000138
£26.00

Exam Overview

Introduction

Cambridge English: Advanced corresponds to Level Four in the Cambridge ESOL five-level system. It also corresponds to the Association of Language Teachers in Europe (ALTE) Level Four (Competent User), and Council of Europe level C1 (Effective Proficiency).

There are five papers in the examination, each worth 20% of the total marks. To achieve a passing grade (A, B or C) candidates must gain approximately 60% of the total marks available, or above. Candidates' grades are based on the total score from all five papers and there is no pass or fail grade for individual papers.

Paper 1 Reading (1 hour 15 minutes)

This paper has four parts, with a range of text types and comprehension questions on each one. There are 34 questions in total.

The texts may consist of several short pieces, and the length of texts in each part is between 550–850 words.

The texts are taken from newspapers, magazines, journals, fiction and non-fiction books, leaflets, brochures, etc.

Part	Task type	Number of items	What you do	What it tests	How to do it
1	Themed texts	6	Choose the best answer from four-option multiple-choice questions	Understanding of a text and opinions or details expressed	page 34
2	Gapped text	6	Decide where paragraphs belong in a text	Understanding of text structure and development	page 22
3	Multiple choice	7	Choose the best answer from four-option multiple-choice questions	Understanding of a text and opinions or details expressed	page 10
4	Multiple matching	15	Match prompts to sections in a text	Understanding specific information, opinion and attitude	page 106

Marks
- Two marks for each correct answer in Parts 1, 2 and 3.
- One mark for each correct answer in Part 4.

Paper 2 Writing (1 hour 30 minutes)

This paper has two parts. The Part 1 question is compulsory and is based on input information. In Part 2, you choose one question from five.

Answers for Part 1 should be 180–220 words in length and answers for Part 2 should be 220–260 words in length.

The task types for Parts 1 and 2 include the following: articles, contributions to leaflets and brochures, letters, reports, proposals, reviews, essays, competition entries, set texts, memos.

Examples of Paper 2 questions types can be found in the Writing Guide on pages 155–165.

Part	Task type	Number of items	What you do	What it tests	How to do it
1	Compulsory contextualised task based on one or more texts and/or visual prompts	One compulsory task	Read the input information and complete the task given.	Ability to evaluate and select information, express opinions, hypothesise and persuade.	page 43 page 150
2	Contextualised task	One from a choice of four tasks	Select one question from a choice of five and complete the task given.	Ability to follow instructions and write in the correct style, layout and register in order to have a positive effect on the reader	page 18 page 43 page 165

Marks
* Parts 1 and 2 have equal marks.

Paper 3 Use of English (1 hour)

This paper has five parts, and a total of 50 questions.

The testing focus is on understanding and controlling elements of language, e.g. grammar, lexis, word formation, lexical and grammatical transformations, and spelling.

Part	Task type	Number of items	What you do	What it tests	How to do it
1	Multiple-choice cloze	12	Fill gaps in a text of about 200 words from multiple-choice options	Phrases, collocations, idioms, phrasal verbs, linkers, used to complete a text with the correct meaning and grammatical context	page 40
2	Open cloze	15	Fill gaps in a text of about 200 words with one word per gap	Awareness and control of grammatical and lexico-grammatical items	page 28
3	Word formation	10	Form appropriate words from the stems of words to fill gaps in a text of about 130 words	Ability to form parts of speech correctly	page 16
4	Gapped sentences	5	Complete gaps in a set of three sentences using the same word in each gap	Awareness and breadth of lexical knowledge	page 17
5	Key word transformations	8	Transform information from one sentence to another using three to six words including the word given	Awareness and control of grammatical structures and lexical items	page 29

Marks
- One mark for each correct answer in Parts 1, 2 and 3.
- Two marks for each correct answer in Part 4.
- Up to two marks for each correct answer in Part 5.
- All spellings must be correct.

Paper 4 Listening (approx. 40 minutes)

This paper has four parts and 30 questions.

The recorded texts may include the following:

- monologues: announcements, radio broadcasts, telephone messages, speeches, talks, lectures, anecdotes.
- conversations between two or more speakers: interviews, discussions, radio broadcasts.

The testing focuses on understanding specific information, gist, attitude, opinion, context, main points and detail.

Each Part is heard twice.

The speakers will have a variety of accents. There may be some background sounds, before the speaking begins, to give contextual information. There may also be some subdued reaction from audiences to talks, speeches, etc.

Part	Task type	Number of items	What you do	What it tests	How to do it
1	Short extracts	6	Choose the best answer from multiple-choice questions on three unrelated short extracts with interacting speakers	Ability to understand topics, opinions and specific information	page 26
2	Sentence completion	8	Write a word or short phrase heard in the monologue to complete gaps in sentences	Understanding of specific information and stated opinion	page 50
3	Multiple choice	6	Choose the best answer from multiple-choice questions on conversations with two or more speakers	Ability to understand attitude and opinion	page 122
4	Multiple matching	10	Select the correct answer from a list of eight options on five short theme-related monologues	Ability to understand gist, attitude, main points and context	page 14

Marks
- One mark for each correct answer.
- In part 2, spelling must be correct for common words and those considered easy to spell.

Paper 5 Speaking (15 minutes)

This paper has four parts.

The standard format is two candidates and two examiners, one acting as interlocutor and assessor, the other acting as assessor only. If there is an odd number of candidates, three candidates sit the test together at the end of the examining session.

Part	Task type	Length	What you do	What it tests	How to do it
1	Two-way conversation between candidates and interlocutor	3 minutes	Ask and answer 'personal' questions	Ability to use general interactional and social language	page 15
2	Individual long turns and brief responses	4 minutes	Talk about two out of three pictures based on visual and written prompts for one minute	Ability to describe, speculate, compare and comment during a longer and organised discourse	page 27 page 39
3	Two-way interaction between candidates	4 minutes	Discuss a problem-solving task based on visual and written prompts	Ability to interact and exchange ideas, express opinions, agree or disagree, evaluate and reach a decision by negotiation	page 50 page 62
4	As Part 1	4 minutes	Discuss issues related to the Part 3 task	Ability to talk about wider issues and express and justify opinions on them	page 62

Marks

- Candidates are assessed on their performance throughout the test in the following areas:
  - Grammar Resource – range and control.
  - Vocabulary Resource – range and control.
  - Discourse Management – ability to express ideas in coherent, connected speech without undue hesitation.
  - Pronunciation – individual sounds, stress and intonation.
  - Interactive Communication – initiating, responding and developing the interaction.
- The assessor marks according to detailed Analytical Scales, and the interlocutor gives a mark on a Global Scale, which is less detailed.

What are you like?

Lead in

1 What is your ideal job? Make a list of useful qualities for that job, e.g. *imagination*, *sensitivity*. Which do you possess?

2 Do the personality quiz below, then look at page 153 to discover the best career for you. Do you think the quiz is accurate? Why/Why not?

Head or Heart?

1 If your friend started dating someone you disliked and asked what you thought, would you … ?
   a be brutally honest
   b be tactful but truthful
   c tell a lie if necessary

2 If you are with friends and an argument breaks out, do you … ?
   a leave them to get on with it
   b take the side of the person you agree with
   c try to find a compromise

3 Which pair of words best describes you?
   a logical and mature
   b decisive and motivated
   c caring and sensitive

Extrovert or Introvert?

4 When out with a group of your friends, how much of the talking do you do?
   a hardly any
   b quite a lot
   c almost all

5 What do you tend to do when you meet new people socially?
   a stick with the people you know
   b worry about how to keep the conversation going
   c mingle with as many new people as possible

6 Which pair of words best describes you?
   a cautious and thoughtful
   b inquisitive and independent
   c lively and energetic

Facts or Ideas?

7 You buy a piece of furniture which you have to assemble yourself. Do you … ?
   a follow the instructions exactly
   b scan the instructions then set them aside
   c leap in, only referring to the instructions if you get stuck

8 When giving directions to your home, do you … ?
   a provide a step-by-step list of instructions
   b draw a rough map
   c just give general directions

9 Which pair of words best describes you?
   a practical and efficient
   b realistic and enthusiastic
   c inventive and imaginative

Reading   Part 3 Multiple choice

how to do it

- Read the text quickly for general meaning.
- Read the question or stem but not the options.
- Find the part of the text that relates to the question; remember, the questions are in order.
- Read the options and eliminate any that are clearly wrong.
- Choose the option that answers the question fully and accurately.

tip

Remember that there will be seven questions in the exam.

1 Read the text opposite and note down the main idea of each paragraph.

2 Choose the correct answer (A, B, C or D) to questions 1–5, and say why the other options are wrong. Question 1 has been done as an example.

Example

1 What reason is given in the first paragraph for the increased use of personality testing?

   A It is used by 50% of managers. ✘

   50% of managers are selected on the basis of these tests.

   B It has been accepted by educational bodies. ✘

   Personality tests <u>may</u> be used by universities in the future.

   C Research has justified its use. ✔

   See lines 4–7

   D The tests are now available on the Internet. ✘

   This is true but not the reason given for the increased use of personality tests.

2 What does the writer imply about the test she tried out herself?
- A It didn't come up with the right result.
- B It was psychologically challenging.
- C It was a tedious way to spend her time.
- D It was too personal for her liking.

3 The Myers-Briggs Type Indicator is based on the belief that
- A character traits are largely inherited.
- B certain personality traits are universal.
- C character is largely decided from birth.
- D some personality types are better than others.

4 What is the problem with personality tests, according to Dr Gill?
- A They can have a negative effect on takers.
- B People can easily lie about their true abilities.
- C The results could be counter-productive for employers.
- D Employers often find their results to be unreliable.

5 What final conclusion does the writer reach about the value of personality tests?
- A They are not really worth doing.
- B They may encourage greater realism.
- C They are of doubtful value to employers.
- D They can strengthen our self-image.

finding

Psychometric testing for recruitment – assessing personality traits as an indicator of performance in a certain role – has mushroomed as studies
5 show their results to be three times more accurate in predicting your job performance than all your previous
10 work experience combined. These tests are now included in virtually all graduate recruitment and in the
15 selection of more than 50 per cent of managers. Similar tests may be used in future as part of university applications, dating agencies swear by them, and they have been used to match pets to owners. Meanwhile online personality tests make the
20 Top 3 of Internet hits. We're living in the age of the personality test. So does your personality meet the grade? Would you rather have a strong will or strong emotions? And if you had to choose between being shipwrecked or lost in the jungle, which would you prefer?

25 For the purposes of research, I decided to try out one of these tests. At one particular site I was informed of my career personality and the number one job that matches it statistically. This is a key part of the appeal of online tests: the premise that there is a perfect job, a perfect mate, and
30 a perfect you, and all you have to do is unlock your subconscious inner self and they will materialise. These tests are also the perfect self-discovery vehicle for our alienated hi-tech age: intimate but anonymous. It is incredibly compulsive; when you get hooked on a test,

3 Match a–f with meanings 1–6, using the text to help you.

a indicator (l.2)   1 argument
b emotion (l.22)   2 disadvantage
c row (l.49)   3 sign
d insight (l.53)   4 feeling
e downside (l.73)   5 typical behaviour
f tendency (l.99)   6 understanding

4 Have you ever taken a test like this? How useful or interesting was it?

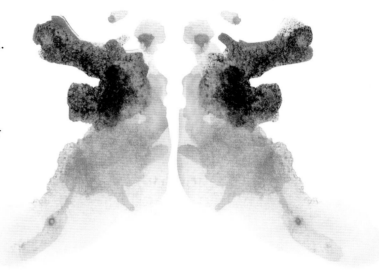

the real you

you're there for hours. And there is no aspect 35
of life too mundane or frivolous to test for.
After 40 minutes of diligently recording my
reaction to a series of ink blots (Is the
mood of this picture sad,
nostalgic, happy, violent or 40
neutral? Can you find the
chicken in this picture?
Can you find your wife's/
husband's mother?) I
discovered I am mainly 45
motivated by peace. I might
have been more convinced
about this if I hadn't just had a
blazing row with my partner (my fault entirely).

If the tests were only amusing it wouldn't account 50
for their massive popularity. In fact, a large number
are decidedly unfunny, and seduce with promises of
genuine insight. This is true of the most popular personality
test in the world: the Myers-Briggs Type Indicator, which
spans the gulf between the cult of personality testing and 55
its science. Widely used in major corporations around the
world, it is based on the theory that we are born with a
predisposition to one personality type which stays more or
less fixed throughout life. You answer 88 questions and are
then given your 'type': Introvert or Extrovert, Thinking or 60
Feeling, Sensing or Intuitive, and Judging or Perceiving. If
you're Introverted, Intuitive, Feeling and Perceptive, you'll
probably find it harder to do work where you're required to
entertain, or persuade lots of people, such as a job in sales
or public relations. 65

Critics of testing mutter darkly about the 'social engineering'
aspect of personality tests, which often seem to be looking

for the same kind of person. Dr Colin Gill, a psychologist
specialising in personality testing, agrees that 'too many
organisations always want people with the same traits: 70
extrovert, agreeable, conscientious and open to new
experience.' But, he warns, these 'popular' personality traits
have their downside. 'An extreme extrovert tends to be a
selfish 'get on' type, who may walk over others. Overly-
conscientious people are prone to burn out and people who 75
are extremely open to new experience can be butterflies,
going from one big idea to the next without mastering any
of them.' All the same, the psychometric test is here to stay
– which may be why a whole sub-industry on cheating
personality tests has sprung up. 'It's possible to cheat', 80
admits expert David Bartram, 'but what's the point? Why try
to pretend you're an ambitious extrovert
if you're a more thoughtful introvert?
Having to fake the person you are at work
will be exhausting and 85
miserable and
probably
short-lived.'

Our obsession with
personality now invades every 90
aspect of our lives. If you ask an
expert for advice on your wardrobe or the sort of diet
you should go on, you'll probably be quizzed about your
personality. But it isn't all self-centred navel gazing. If
personality tests have any value to us (rather than 95
employers) perhaps it is this: to disabuse us of the illusion
that all of us are full of potential, and remind us of what we
are. If that happens to be an averagely ambitious introvert
with controlling tendencies (as my test results showed), then
so be it. As they say in one test when they ask for your age: 100
pick the one you are, not the one you wish you were.

Vocabulary Character adjectives

1 Match character adjectives a–j with meanings 1–10.

a	mature	1	curious
b	decisive	2	outgoing
c	motivated	3	adult
d	sensitive	4	aiming high
e	inquisitive	5	keen
f	ambitious	6	withdrawn
g	independent	7	wanting to do things well
h	conscientious	8	self-reliant
i	introverted	9	firm
j	extrovert	10	aware of people's feelings

2 Which of the adjectives in 1 are generally positive and which negative? Give examples.

3 Read the dictionary entry for words similar in meaning to *honest*. Use this information to complete sentences a–c below.

> **WHICH WORD?**
>
> **Honest** and **frank** refer to *what* you say as much as *how* you say it: *a(n) honest/frank admission of guilt*. They are generally positive words, although it is possible to be *too* frank in a way that other people might not like. **Direct**, **outspoken** and **blunt** all describe sb's manner of saying what they think. **Outspoken** suggests that you are willing to shock people by saying what you believe to be right. **Blunt** and **direct** often suggest that you think honesty is more important than being polite. **Open** is positive and describes sb's character: *I'm a very open person.*

Oxford Advanced Learner's Dictionary, 8th edition

a I hope you don't mind me being .... , but that dress really doesn't suit you.

b Some journalists are deliberately .... – they don't care who they upset, they just want a good story.

c You should ask Nick's opinion. You can trust him to tell you the truth, he's so ....

4 Discuss questions a and b.

a Which five character adjectives do you think a friend would use to describe you?

b Do you think we are born with certain character traits, or is our character formed as we grow up?

Grammar

Review of tenses GR p166–169

1 Match the verb forms in the sentences below with these tenses.

Present Simple	Present Perfect Continuous
Present Continuous	Past Simple
Future Simple	Past Continuous
Future Continuous	Past Perfect Simple
Present Perfect Simple	Past Perfect Continuous

a Since I moved here, I've *been learning* to drive.
   Since I moved here, I've *learnt* to drive.

b Carla's *playing* the guitar very well.
   Carla *plays* the guitar very well.

c It *started* raining when I left the house.
   It *had started* raining when I left the house.

d I'*ll be getting* the dinner ready when you arrive.
   I'*ll get* the dinner ready when you arrive.

e When we got to her house, she *cried*.
   When we got to her house, she'*d been crying*.

f My brother *always tells* me what to do.
   My brother's *always telling* me what to do.

g We *were having* a party when my sister announced her engagement.
   We *had* a party when my sister announced her engagement.

2 Explain the difference in meaning between the pairs of sentences in 1.

3 Complete sentences a–i using the correct form of the verbs in brackets.

a His back was aching because he .... (dig) in the garden all day.

b .... (your father/work) abroad at present?

c Maria left college early today because she .... (have) a dental appointment an hour ago.

d As soon as it stops raining, we .... (take) the dog for a walk.

e My neighbour couldn't stop because his bus .... (leave) and he didn't want to miss it.

f For the past six weeks, I .... (have) singing lessons.

g I can't phone you at that time because I .... (travel) on the underground.

h The photocopy machine .... (break down) twice already and it's not even lunchtime!

i As a rule, we .... (spend) part of each summer at my parents' house.

4 Correct any verbs in a–h which are not normally used in a continuous form.

a These gloves aren't mine – are they belonging to you?

b My girlfriend doesn't like perfumes that are smelling of flowers – she prefers something more exotic.

c Our teacher said we were all deserving a great deal of praise for our exam results.

d Are you thinking what I'm thinking – that this new outfit just doesn't suit me?

e I've always been hating getting up early in the morning, even in the summer.

f This manual is containing all the information you need to run your new computer software.

g At the moment I feel that you really aren't putting in as much effort as you could with your studies.

h The hockey club we're belonging to is always on the lookout for new players.

5 Say which of these verbs are a) never used in a continuous form, or b) can be used in a continuous form but with a change in meaning.

like	believe	know	remind
detest	hear	understand	belong
contain	taste	prefer	mean

6 Match a–j with a suitable ending from 1–10 and explain how the verb tense changes the meaning.

a My favourite actor is appearing …
b I'm afraid the video appears …
c The manager is having …
d Celine has …
e Everyone thinks …
f She's thinking …
g Working as a wildlife guide really appeals …
h Our local school is appealing …
i I am seeing …
j I see …

1 … a career adviser tomorrow to get advice on working in IT.
2 … a lot of experience in working with children.
3 … a meeting to discuss the new proposal.
4 … for funds for a new building.
5 … in a new musical in London's West End.
6 … Jose will get the job.
7 … of buying a car in the near future.
8 … to be broken.
9 … to me.
10 … nothing but fields when I look out of my bedroom window.

7 Complete sentences a–e with the correct form of the verb.

a If you .... (feel) that I'm being unreasonable, please say so.

b Sandra .... (smell) the blossom on her cherry tree when she was stung by a bee.

c Even though you've explained it three times now, I still .... (not see) what you mean.

d Since I was a young boy, I .... (have) a fear of heights.

e .... (you/think) you could give me a hand lifting this equipment?

8 Read this extract from an email which was sent to an online penfriend agency, and correct any errors in tenses.

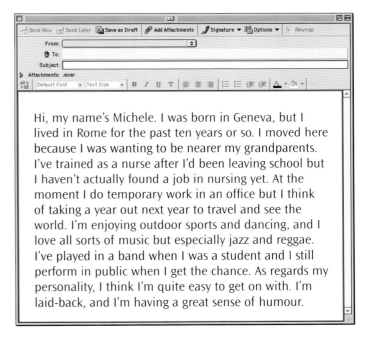

Hi, my name's Michele. I was born in Geneva, but I lived in Rome for the past ten years or so. I moved here because I was wanting to be nearer my grandparents. I've trained as a nurse after I'd been leaving school but I haven't actually found a job in nursing yet. At the moment I do temporary work in an office but I think of taking a year out next year to travel and see the world. I'm enjoying outdoor sports and dancing, and I love all sorts of music but especially jazz and reggae. I've played in a band when I was a student and I still perform in public when I get the chance. As regards my personality, I think I'm quite easy to get on with. I'm laid-back, and I'm having a great sense of humour.

9 Write your own email introducing yourself to a penfriend, using the corrected version in 8 as a model.

Listening

1 Why might someone decide to take up the hobbies and pastimes shown?

2 🎧 In **3** you will hear five people talking about their hobbies. First, listen and match the phrases they use (1–7) with the meanings (a–g).

1	....b.....	a	We all had different interests.
2	....	b	I became really inspired by it.
3	....	c	I was completely taken aback.
4	....	d	I'd lost my job.
5	....	e	I was chattering away about how busy I was.
6	....	f	I'd had some difficulties with my job.
7	....	g	I didn't have much to occupy myself with.

how to do it

- Use the time allowed to read both tasks quickly.
- Remember there are two questions for each speaker.
- On the first listening, answer as many questions as you can from <u>both</u> tasks.
- Use the second listening to answer any questions you missed.

3 🎧 Read the how to do it box, then listen twice and do the exam task.

For 1–5, choose the people's reasons for taking up their new interest (A–H).

A to recover from an accident
B to please a relative
C to be more independent
D to broaden their horizons
E to fill in time
F to take some exercise
G to express their feelings
H to relieve the pressure of work

Speaker 1 ☐ 1
Speaker 2 ☐ 2
Speaker 3 ☐ 3
Speaker 4 ☐ 4
Speaker 5 ☐ 5

For 6–10, choose the outcome of the speakers' new interests (A–H).

A It's enabled me to win an award.
B It's inspired me to be more competitive.
C It's turned out to be quite profitable.
D It's become a kind of obsession.
E It's restored my faith in human nature.
F It's made me more critical of myself.
G It's revealed a new aspect of my personality.
H It's made me feel less dejected.

Speaker 1 ☐ 6
Speaker 2 ☐ 7
Speaker 3 ☐ 8
Speaker 4 ☐ 9
Speaker 5 ☐ 10

4 Tell a partner about your hobbies and interests and why you enjoy them.

Speaking Part 1

1 In pairs, take it in turns to answer questions a–f. Try to use some of the phrases below.

    a Where were you born?
    b How long have you been studying English?
    c Have you always been interested in languages?
    d What's your favourite time of the year?
    e How would you describe your character?
    f What are your plans for the future?

> ### Answering personal questions
>
> Well, actually …
> That's a difficult question but …
> I've never given it much thought but …
> As a matter of fact …

2 🎧 Listen to five students answering an examiner's questions. What different mistakes with tenses do they make?

3 In pairs, ask each other about the subjects in a–e. Use the phrases below to help you.

    a your favourite TV programme
    b your ideal job
    c a day out you have enjoyed
    d subjects you enjoyed learning at school
    e the kind of music you listen to

> ### Asking for personal information
>
> So, tell me what … is.
> Could you tell me about … ?
> I'd like to know what … is/would be.
> What would you say … is/would be?
> Could you describe … ?

4 🎧 Listen to the next exam task and how two candidates answered it. Suggest three ways in which they could improve their performance.

how to do it

In Speaking Part 1 you may be asked to talk about a variety of topics, e.g. your past experiences, present circumstances or future plans, travel, education. Make sure you use the appropriate tenses.

5 In pairs, answer questions a–d giving reasons. Use the phrases below to help you.

    a Would you like to spend some time working in another country?
    b Do you think that having a lot of free time is a good or a bad thing?
    c How necessary is it to have good friends?
    d Which is more important: money or health?

> ### Expressing personal views
>
> In my opinion, …
> I think it's essential to …
> I strongly believe that …
> As far as I'm concerned …

6 🎧 Listen to a candidate expressing a personal view and decide if her attempt is successful. Explain why.

Use of English Part 3 Word formation

1 Look at the title of the text below. Do you think it is possible to be 'born lucky'? Why/Why not?

2 Read the text and the how to do it box. Decide which part of speech belongs in gaps 1–10 in the text.

3 Complete the text using the words in CAPITALS in the correct form. Use the tip box to help you.

how to do it

☐ Decide what parts of speech you need.

☐ You may need to form words with negative meanings, or plurals.

☐ You may need to make more than one change to the word given.

☐ Check your spelling carefully.

☐ Read your completed text for overall sense.

Born Lucky?

Research shows some **0** ....*noticeable*.... differences in the **1** .... attitude and behaviour of lucky and unlucky people. If genes affect one's **2** .... and behaviour, as they no doubt do, then you can be born lucky.

Lucky people tend to create opportunities for good fortune by being extrovert, sociable and using open body language that gets people to respond to them. They are relaxed and **3** .... and, therefore, they may be more receptive to new opportunities. They also like change and **4** .... They might, for instance, alter their routine by thinking of a colour on their way to a party and then speaking to people wearing that colour. This brings about new **5** .... and the prospect of new friends.

Lucky people also have positive **6** .... of life. A famous experiment illustrates this. Psychologists told American high school teachers certain children in their class were especially **7** .... In fact, there was nothing **8** .... about them. The teachers, however, showered them with praise and **9** .... and the children responded by producing better schoolwork than others. The study shows the power of positive thinking.

Yet the converse is also true. Finnish researchers divided 2,000 men into 'negative', 'neutral' and 'positive' groups, depending on their outlook on life. Over a six-year period, those in the 'negative' group were **10** .... more susceptible to illness and accidents.

0	NOTICE
1	PSYCHOLOGY
2	PERSONAL
3	APPROACH
4	VARY
5	POSSIBLE
6	EXPECT
7	GIFT
8	EXCEPTION
9	ENCOURAGE
10	DENY

tip

The 10 missing answers in this text include:
- three singular nouns
- two plural nouns
- four adjectives
- one adverb

Part 4 Gapped sentences

4 Read the dictionary entry for *create* below and match each definition (1–3) with sentences a–c.

> **cre·ate** 0— **AW** /kriˈeɪt/ *verb*
> **1** 0— ~ **sth** to make sth happen or exist: *Scientists disagree about how the universe was created.* ◇ *The main purpose of industry is to create wealth.* ◇ *The government plans to create more jobs for young people.* ◇ *Create a new directory and put all your files into it.* ◇ *Try this new dish, created by our head chef.* ⊃ SYNONYMS at MAKE **2** 0— ~ **sth** to produce a particular feeling or impression: *The company is trying to create a young energetic image.* ◇ *The announcement only succeeded in creating confusion.* ◇ *They've painted it red to create a feeling of warmth.* **3** to give sb a particular rank or title: ~ **sth** *The government has created eight new peers.* ◇ ~ **sth + noun** *He was created a baronet in 1715.*

Oxford Advanced Learner's Dictionary, 8th edition

a This soft lighting really helps to create a romantic atmosphere.
b The council have decided to create a new position for a deputy mayor.
c We need to create an educational system which gives equal opportunities to all.

5 Read questions a and b below and think of one word only which can be used appropriately in all three sentences. The how to do it box will help you.

how to do it

- Read the three sentences carefully and make a quick list of words that could complete each of the gaps.
- Look for one word that appears in all three lists, then try it again in each sentence.
- If the word doesn't fit each sentence, try other words from your lists.
- Remember that the word must be <u>exactly</u> the same for every sentence.

a There is no .... whatsoever in my mind that this is the only course of action to take.

   If in .... , always go for the easy option.

   The evidence showed beyond any .... that the accused was innocent.

b The holiday may .... much less relaxing than we anticipate.

   Sally's determined to .... she has been right in her judgement.

   The trouble with this job is that you feel you have to .... yourself all the time.

Vocabulary

Expressions with *luck*

1 Discuss the meaning of these expressions and match them with 1–8, then use them to complete a–h.

> with any luck   beginner's luck
> the luck of the draw   push your luck
> take pot luck   no such luck
> be out of luck   by a stroke of luck

1 rely on continuing good luck
2 fortunately and unexpectedly
3 success at your first attempt
4 risk the outcome
5 decided by chance
6 unfortunately not
7 if things turn out well
8 not be lucky this time

a 'Did you manage to fix your car?' ' .... It's a complete write-off.'
b You shouldn't .... You haven't been caught speeding yet but you might be!
c You may win the lottery – you may not. It's quite simply ....
d The only problem with this cheap package holiday I've arranged is you can't choose your accommodation; you just have to ....
e You .... , I'm afraid. I've just sold the last copy of that particular book.
f I've just realised I've forgotten my house key, but .... my wife might be at home.
g Jane missed the last bus but .... a friend was passing and gave her a lift.
h Robert won his first professional tennis match but modestly said it was just .... !

2 When was the last time you were very lucky or unlucky? What happened?

Writing Part 2 A formal letter WG p155

1 Read the writing task below and answer questions a and b.

  a Who are you going to write to? For what purpose?

  b What are the three things you must include?

> A friend of yours is applying for a job as a holiday representative with an international holiday organisation. The company has asked you to provide a character reference for your friend. The reference should indicate how long you have known the person. It must also include a detailed description of the person's character and the reasons why he or she would be suitable for the job.
>
> Write the **reference** in approximately **220–260** words.

2 Make notes on questions a–c.

  a What sort of things might a holiday representative have to do?

  b What skills might be needed?

  c Which personal qualities might be needed for the job?

3 The two references opposite, A and B, were written by two different people. Read them and decide which person did not make a plan before starting to write. Give examples of the effect this has had on the organisation of the reference.

4 Read the references again and do tasks a–c.

  a List the linking words in A and B (*so*, *because*, etc.). Which writer makes better use of them?

  b Identify the purpose of each paragraph in B.

  c Identify any useful phrases for references in general.

5 Read the question below, then write your reference. The how to do it box and tips will help you.

> One of your friends has applied for a job teaching English abroad. They will also supervise pupils aged 10–16 outside school and organise games and activities. You have been asked to provide a character reference for your friend.
>
> You should say how long you have known your friend and include a detailed description of their character. You should also give reasons why he or she would be suitable for the job.
>
> Write your **reference** in 220–260 words.

tip

Describe two or three things the person has done which show the qualities/abilities that make them right for the job.

tip

Start a new paragraph for each complete change of topic but avoid one-sentence paragraphs.

Try to include a topic sentence summarising the main idea of the paragraph. Expand on that idea and/or give examples in the rest of the paragraph.

how to do it

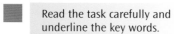 Read the task carefully and underline the key words.

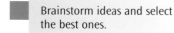 Brainstorm ideas and select the best ones.

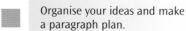 Organise your ideas and make a paragraph plan.

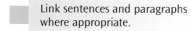 Link sentences and paragraphs where appropriate.

A

Dear Sir or Madam,

I am writing to you on behalf of Juan Fernandez.

I have known Juan for three years. We're in the same tutorial group at college.

He is very popular at college and certainly knows how to enjoy life.

Juan is very fit and healthy. He's good at sports.

Juan doesn't lose his temper very often. He'd be good at dealing with difficult customers and their complaints.

Juan's a complete extrovert. He loves being the centre of attention. He'd enjoy entertaining people in your resorts. In his free time, Juan likes to keep fit. He goes down to the gym most evenings and he swims and plays football. He's got lots of friends. He won't have a problem getting on with his clients.

Juan speaks fluent English. He will deal easily with different nationalities in the holiday destination. He's quite a laid-back person and he doesn't panic in difficult situations. You can rely on him to stay cool, calm and collected.

Juan works in a local bar on Saturdays and knows how to deal with difficult people. He doesn't lose his temper. He's prepared to listen, but he can be quite firm when it's necessary, too.

I am sure Juan will be a good holiday representative. I have no hesitation in recommending him for the post.

Yours faithfully,

Sylvia Garcia

B

To whom it may concern

Reference for Paola Gianni

I have known Paola for approximately six years. She is a very bubbly, down-to-earth character and gets on well with people of all ages, so she would be very popular with holiday groups. Paola helps run the local youth club in our area so she is very used to dealing with young people. The organisational and leadership skills she has learnt in this work should serve her well as a holiday representative. In times of crisis, Paola is an excellent person to have around because she is dependable and not inclined to panic or lose her temper. Although never bossy, she can take control of difficult situations without upsetting anyone. For this reason, I believe she would definitely be able to cope if things went wrong in a holiday situation.

When it comes to entertaining people, Paola is very talented, which might come in very useful in her role as a holiday representative. As well as singing and dancing, she plays the guitar and often takes part in performances at the youth club.

In addition to performing, Paola is an accomplished sportswoman. She is a strong swimmer and a qualified lifeguard. Her favourite sports include scuba-diving, windsurfing and waterskiing, at which she has reached competition level. With her enthusiastic, commonsense approach, she would ensure holidaymakers have safe access to a full range of beach activities.

In my opinion, Paola would make an excellent holiday representative. I have no hesitation in recommending her to your company.

Yours faithfully,

Antonio Calanducci

Review

1 Match character adjectives a–h with their opposite meanings 1–8.

a introvert   1 uninterested
b decisive   2 careless
c sensitive   3 outgoing
d inquisitive   4 thick-skinned
e mature   5 unmotivated
f independent   6 childish
g conscientious   7 helpless
h ambitious   8 vague

2 Complete the adjectives defined in a–h.

a diplomatic about what you say   ta _ _ _ _ _
b rational and reasonable   lo _ _ _ _ _
c concerned or interested in others   ca _ _ _ _
d helpful and considerate   th _ _ _ _ _ _ _ _
e hesitant about your actions   ca _ _ _ _ _ _
f excited or passionate   en _ _ _ _ _ _ _ _ _ _
g sensible and realistic   pr _ _ _ _ _ _ _
h creative and imaginative   in _ _ _ _ _ _ _

3 For questions a–c, think of one word only which can be used appropriately in all three sentences.

a Everyone wished her the best of .... at university and hoped she would enjoy it.

Jenny won the competition at her first attempt – perhaps it was beginner's .... !

There is no such thing as .... , we are capable of creating our own good fortune.

b If you ask Colin for advice, he will always give you his .... opinion.

To be .... , I thought Susan's advice was terrible.

I don't think Brian's ever done an .... day's work in his entire life.

c The waxwork looked so .... that I thought it was an actual person.

With so much strong competition, we have to be .... about our company's long-term chances of survival.

Do you think, in .... terms, we really can afford to go travelling next year?

4 Complete the expressions with *luck* in a–h.

a I broke my grandmother's favourite vase but, by a .... of luck, I found an identical one in a shop down the road.
b Some things in life you have no choice about – it's just the luck of the ....
c Sorry, you're .... of luck! We sold the last newspaper five minutes ago.
d We aim to set out early and, ... any luck, we should arrive before dark.
e I thought I might get the job but .... such luck. They gave it to someone else.
f Let's just .... pot luck and see where we can book a last minute holiday to.
g Helen managed to get a film part after her first audition but she said it was just .... luck!
h I know everything seems to be going swimmingly at the moment but just remember – you shouldn't .... your luck!

5 Fill in missing words 1–14 in this job reference.

I am writing to you on .... 1 of Belinda Morris, who has .... 2 to be a trainee manager in your restaurant. Belinda is a very lively, ... 3 to earth character who .... 4 on well with people of all ages. She has worked as a waitress during the summer holidays in our hotel, so she's .... 5 to dealing .... 6 all kinds of customers. The organisational skills she has learnt should .... 7 her well .... 8 a restaurant manager. In .... 9 of crisis, she is an excellent person to .... 10 around because she doesn't panic. When it .... 11 to making people feel at ease, Belinda is an expert. What's .... 12, she has a great sense of humour. In my .... 13, she would make an excellent manager. I have no .... 14 in recommending her.

Customs and traditions

Lead in

1 Discuss the following questions.
  a What annual festivals or celebrations take place in your country?
  b When do they happen and what do they involve?
  c What do you know about their origins?

2 What do you imagine happens at the festivals shown in the photos?

3 🎧 Listen to two people talking about the two festivals shown and choose the best answer to questions 1–4.
  1 The Kattenwoensdog festival dates back to a time when
    a local people began to breed cats in the town's Cloth Hall.
    b local cats had been unsuccessful in ridding the town of rodents.
    c local people decided that the town cats had outlived their usefulness.

  2 What happened when the speaker visited the Kattenwoensdog festival?
    a Everyone taking part in the parade was dressed as a cat.
    b The bad weather failed to spoil the carnival atmosphere.
    c Spectators rushed to buy a toy cat from the jester.

  3 What is one of the rules of La Tomatina?
    a You must be a member of a team to join in.
    b The tomatoes must be crushed before you throw them.
    c Tourists are not allowed to hit locals.

  4 What happens at the end of La Tomatina?
    a Trucks arrive to clear away all the mess.
    b Free tomato juice is given away.
    c You can wash in specially provided showers.

4 Tell a partner about any festivals that you have been to or would like to go to.

La Tomatina

Kattenwoensdog

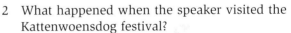

festival in the desert

There's little beyond the remote Malian town of Timbouctou but a vast expanse of desert. Most people consider it the end of the Earth, and even its residents rarely venture north into the Sahara. But
5 for one day in January, a host of musicians, politicians, tourists and technicians gather in the town's market place, preparing to head north into the dunes. As people fill their jeeps with diesel and supplies and travellers send quick postcards home,
10 it's hard not to get swept up in the excitement and anticipation of the remotest music festival on Earth.

1

The Tuareg, a nomadic group who inhabit the Sahara, have *a more appropriate form of transport*, arriving on white camels from every direction. In all,
15 there are 1,800 of them at the festival. It isn't surprising, *because the event grew out of an annual Tuareg get-together*.

2

As the Tuareg cook over campfires, the tourists settle into their tents and explore the festival site. But
20 soon everyone is beating a path towards the concreted stage, a strange sight in the middle of scrub and sand. The sun goes down and charcoal braziers light up the dunes. Then bands from Mali and neighbouring countries like Senegal, Niger and
25 Mauritania take the stage, playing calabashes, lutes and talking drums. There's a group of dancers from Niger decorated with beads and covered in body paint. There are Western performers too, although *some are not to everyone's taste*. As one group hit
30 their electric guitars and yell into the microphones, an old Malian lady claps her hands over her ears and scuttles off.

3

As a tourist attraction, the festival is still in its infancy. There are no more than 500 foreigners

35 present, most of whom feel lucky to be witnessing something 'authentic'. Beyond the odd soft drinks stall there is *little sign of the sponsorship or the profit motive* that underpin most World Music festivals.

4

A music festival may seem an odd mechanism for
40 kick-starting tourism all year round, but this is the intention. In the eyes of Ndiaye Bah, Mali's minister of tourism and handicrafts, Malian music is already one of the country's main draws, making the festival an obvious place to start. She is convinced that the
45 north contains enough potential to support year-round tourism. In fact most people agree that tourism growth is the only way forward for the Tuareg. The north of Mali is the poorest part of the country. As Bah explains, there are few opportunities
50 for the Tuareg. They need people to come and buy handicrafts and stay in local hotels, to bring employment and development to the region.

5

But this sort of envy only exists between the Tuareg because the festival is seen to be a good thing. In
55 fact, for now, *the event enjoys almost universal support. And similar events are springing up in neighbouring countries* like Mauritania too, with the Tuareg organisers of the Festival in the Desert fast becoming consultants.

6

60 The Tuareg dance and sing, Dicko explains, and afterwards they talk about their problems. He is studying to be a doctor in Timbouctou and his village is far away. At the festival he can meet his family and other people from his village for the first
65 time in two years. Perhaps it's to people such as Dicko, who've given up the nomadic lifestyle to live in towns such as Timbouctou, that the festival brings the greatest pleasure.

Reading Part 2 Gapped text

1 What music festivals are there in your country? Who goes? What happens?

2 Read the article about a music festival in the Sahara, and match paragraphs A–G with gaps 1–6. There is one extra paragraph. Find links in the text and use the words in italics to help you.

how to do it

- Read the main text for general meaning.
- Look for grammar and vocabulary links before and after each gap and in the paragraphs.
- Fill the easiest gaps first to reduce the number of options.
- Then try the extra paragraph in each gap again.
- Read the complete text again for grammar and overall sense.

A *With such obvious popularity*, who knows what the
70 future may hold for the Timbouctou festival. But for now, at
least, it still retains its original purpose as a get-together for
the Tuareg people themselves.

B But *despite this lack of commercialism*, there's no doubt
that the benefits of tourism are there for local people.
75 The Tuareg stroll between the tents setting out purses,
compasses and swords for tourists to buy or offering camel
rides. Dicko, my young Tuareg friend, explains that cash
spent by tourists filters back into the Sahara. The Tuareg, it
seems, bring with them jewellery and handicrafts made by
80 people in their villages. They sell these at the festival and
use the money to buy maize, sugar and millet in
Timbouctou which they take back to the villages.

C In fact, as the event's organiser Manny Ansar explains,
Tuareg have been meeting at this oasis for centuries. In this
85 spot they have traditionally arranged marriages, swapped
news, raced camels and made music. They decided to open
the music festival to enable their musicians to mix with
others and because they felt it was time for their
community to get in touch with the outside world.

90 **D** *Meanwhile*, the sustainability of the festival itself has
been called into question. Westerners say that if the festival
gets too big, it will lose its authentic feel. And anyway it
appears to have reached capacity already – tempers got so
frayed that a Dutch woman who was queuing for one of the
95 two small ferries struck a driver for jumping the queue.

E To get as far as Timbouctou, I spent three days driving
from Mali's capital, Bamako, and four hours queuing for a
small ferry over the River Niger. But as the convoy of four-
wheel drives headed into the dunes, chucking up dust behind
100 it, it became clear that the final stretch was the trickiest part
of the journey. The track was soon lined with jeeps which had
overheated or were stuck in deep sand. One group of tourists
told me that their jeep had broken down within earshot of
the music, but they hadn't dared venture on foot into the
105 desert, preferring to sleep *in the vehicle*. The next day they
found that the festival site was just ten minutes away from
where they had been sleeping.

F There are few concerns about the environmental impact
of the festival. Every single plastic bottle is taken away by the
110 Tuareg for use in the desert. But conflict between Tuareg
could be more of a problem. An elderly man complains that
the festival started out as a moveable event with a different
site each year, bringing benefits to different parts of the
Sahara. But for the past two years it has been held in the
115 same place because it is easier to build a permanent stage
in the dunes here. '*Why can't we have a festival where I come
from?*' he asks.

G But *while rock groups might not produce the desired effect
on everybody* at the festival, Tuareg bands do, and they
120 feature more prominently than any others. Their Tuareg fans
watch from the seats of their camels. From the ground, it's
hard to see over the hundreds of indigo turbans that are
standard attire for the tribesmen. This is clearly a Tuareg
event, but there is little sense of being an outsider. As I shovel
125 sand to try to gain some height, my Tuareg neighbours usher
me forward for a better view. The sense of intimacy and
respect among the small crowd is remarkable.

3 Complete the phrases in a–h with 1–8, then rephrase the sentences in your own words.

a The claim that the festival will remain authentic has been *called into* .... 1 draws
b We sat at the back of the crowd but just *within* .... *of* the music. 2 earshot
c There was a long delay before the concert began and *tempers got very* .... 3 impact
d As the bands began to play, we all *got* .... *up in* the excitement. 4 frayed
e One old lady's reaction showed clearly that rock music was *not to her* .... 5 question
f The festival only started a few years ago so it's still *in its* .... 6 infancy
g Traditional music is *one of the country's main* .... 7 swept
h There are few concerns about *the environmental* .... of the festival. 8 taste

4 What positive and negative effects might tourism have on traditional festivals like this?

Vocabulary

Easily confused words (1)

1 Choose the correct verbs in a–h to complete the collocations.

 a I wasn't enjoying myself so I .... *an excuse* and left. (did / put / made)

 b The director promised my sister a part in the film and he'd better .... *his word.* (keep / hold / take)

 c We're planning to .... *a party* to celebrate Tina's good news. (make / throw / do)

 d He .... *a lie* when the police interviewed him and now he's in big trouble. (told / said / spoke)

 e The first chapter of a book usually .... *the scene* for what happens later. (lays / puts / sets).

 f Everyone else was furious when one man .... *the queue* for tickets. (overtook / jumped / missed)

 g That film was so complicated – I didn't .... *a clue* what was going on! (follow / get / have)

 h It's very hard to .... *a living* as an actor. (earn / get / gain)

2 Read the dictionary entry below to find the adverb that collocates best with *disappointed*. Then choose the most suitable word in sentences a–c. Check your ideas in your dictionary.

> **dis·ap·point·ed** O━┓ /ˌdɪsəˈpɔɪntɪd/ *adj.*
> upset because sth you hoped for has not happened or been as good, successful, etc. as you expected: **~ (at / by sth)** *They were **bitterly disappointed** at the result of the game.* ◊ *I was disappointed by the quality of the wine.* ◊ **~ (in / with sb / sth)** *I'm disappointed in you—I really thought I could trust you!* ◊ *I was very disappointed with myself.* ◊ **~ (to see, hear, etc.)** *He was disappointed to see she wasn't at the party.* ◊ **~ (that...)** *I'm disappointed (that) it was sold out.* ◊ **~ (not) to be...** *She was disappointed not to be chosen.*

Oxford Advanced Learner's Dictionary, 8th edition

 a Amanda's (highly / fully) competitive with her more successful older sister.

 b It was (immediately / clearly) obvious that there was no way we could reach the airport in time.

 c She is an extremely strict teacher and expects (whole / total) obedience from her pupils.

3 Complete questions a–c, using your answers from 1 above, then discuss each question.

 a Do you generally queue in your country? What happens if you .... the queue?

 b How would you most like to .... a living?

 c Has anyone ever not .... their word to you? What happened?

Grammar

Gerunds and infinitives GR p171–172

1 Put these verbs into three columns as shown below.

avoid	want	like	deny	promise
enjoy	expect	fancy	hope	risk
offer	prefer	deserve	begin	continue
practise	threaten	manage	miss	love
refuse				

followed by gerund	followed by infinitive + *to*	followed by gerund or infinitive
avoid	*expect*	*like*

2 Which of the verbs in 1 can also be immediately followed by a *that* clause?

3 Complete these sentences with an appropriate verb in the correct form.

 a Our football team deserves .... because they have trained so hard.

 b One of the suspects has denied .... part in the robbery.

 c My sister is hoping .... a job as a stewardess with our national airline.

 d We lost the car keys but we managed .... the car by turning a piece of wire in the ignition!

 e I'm disappointed that my favourite group have refused .... at the festival.

 f Since my grandmother moved to another town, I really miss .... her every day.

 g What time is the President expected .... at the airport?

 h Armed police threatened .... the gunmen if they did not release the hostages.

4 Match each verb (in both the gerund and infinitive form) with definitions a–j.

　　stop　try　remember　regret　mean

 a do something to see what happens as a result
 b be sorry for something you've done
 c intend to do something
 d not forget that something must be done
 e stop something you've been doing
 f involve or require something
 g be sorry about something you're going to do
 h stop one thing to do something else
 i not forget something which has already happened
 j see if it's possible to do something

5 Use the verb in brackets to complete a–e in two ways: first with the gerund and then the infinitive.

a I didn't remember (invite) my neighbour to my barbecue so …

b I wish for once you'd stop (think) about …

c I like our neighbours, but I regret (say) that …

d My six-month-old nephew has just tried (eat) …

e … meant (get) my hair cut.

6 Complete sentences a–h with one of the prepositions below and an appropriate gerund.

> on   at   for   to   of   in

a I'm not very keen .... when the sea is this rough but I'll come if you insist.

b Are you looking forward .... school and getting a job?

c In trying to take a shortcut across the fields, we only succeeded .... completely lost.

d I apologise profusely .... you waiting in the cold for so long.

e My classmates insisted .... me a birthday present even though I said I didn't want one.

f If you carry .... about people behind their backs, you'll soon end up with no friends.

g I've never been very good .... letters but I regularly telephone my grandparents in Australia.

h My brother is thinking .... abroad, maybe as a tour guide.

7 Cross out *to* where it is not needed with the infinitives in these sentences.

a I don't think politicians should be allowed to get away with the lies they tell.

b If you let that boy to do whatever he wants, you'll really live to regret it.

c Adults can rarely be made to do what they don't want to, but you can often make someone to do something through persuasion.

d That looks like a nasty cut – I'd advise you to get medical attention at once.

e My parents helped me to buy a small flat in the suburbs.

f You had better not to tell anyone what we've just been discussing.

g It's just typical that when someone's watching you to do something, you make a right mess of it.

8 Complete these sentences with an object and an infinitive with or without *to* as appropriate.

a When I was a child, my parents wouldn't let …

b The water in the resort wasn't clean enough to drink so our holiday rep advised …

c I woke up suddenly and thought I heard …

d I know it may sound unreasonable but I'd rather …

e I love sitting by the lake watching …

9 Complete 1–13 with an appropriate form of the verb in bold.

I've always wanted .... 1 **do** something really adventurous so when, in my final year at university, I was invited .... 2 **join** a wildlife expedition to the Amazon, I didn't stop .... 3 **think**. I just said 'yes'! I looked forward to .... 4 **explore** the forests and dreamt of .... 5 **discover** a species new to science. I also hoped .... 6 **film** a jaguar as these animals are of special interest to me. The trip would mean .... 7 **struggle** through thick jungle and I knew we risked .... 8 **be** bitten by insects and snakes. My girlfriend was so worried about me that she threatened .... 9 **burn** my plane ticket! In the event, I managed .... 10 **avoid** any kind of disaster. I watched a giant snake .... 11 **catch** a monkey, but that was the nearest I came to any danger. I really enjoyed .... 12 **see** such a huge variety of wildlife and I would like .... 13 **go back** to the Amazon again one day, that's for sure.

BEWARE! QUICKSAND

Listening Part 1 Short extracts

1 Read this quote and discuss how far you agree with these ideas.

> We want to preserve our identity, history, land, language and values for our children. Our children, who are our future, must understand our history so no one can say our culture is gone. If we do not preserve this, our lives won't belong to us any more.

2 Read questions 1–6 below before you listen to the three different extracts. Then listen and choose the best answer (A, B or C) for each question. The how to do it and tip boxes will help you.

how to do it

- Read the context and both questions for each extract to familiarise yourself with the topic.
- Try to answer both questions for each extract in the first listening.
- In the second listening, check your answers carefully.

tip

Remember that the extracts will be on <u>different</u> themes in the exam.

extract one

You hear part of an interview with a tour operator discussing a museum dedicated to Native Americans.

1 What criticism does the man make about the museum?
   A Native Americans were not consulted enough when setting it up.
   B Some exhibits do not capture the impact of Native American culture.
   C The museum project took far too long to conceive and set up.

2 The museum aims to
   A ensure that it will attract large numbers of local visitors.
   B demonstrate the lifestyle of Native Americans to visitors.
   C display objects originally in the possession of local communities.

extract two

You hear two people talking about a town fair.

3 What did the two speakers learn about the town fair from the newspaper?
   A Attendance was down on last year.
   B It had managed to attract a lot of outsiders.
   C There was a lack of atmosphere.

4 The two speakers agree that
   A the best thing about the town fair was the evening concert.
   B the quality of the items on sale at the town fair was excellent.
   C the town fair greatly benefits the local community.

extract three

You hear part of an interview with a woman who is a curator in a museum.

5 The woman disagrees with the interviewer about
   A what kinds of historical objects should be displayed in museums.
   B the role of historical objects in educating young people.
   C whether historical objects should be returned to where they came from.

6 How does the woman see her responsibilities as a museum curator?
   A She believes we should be aware of the history of our ancestors.
   B She is determined to preserve the past for future generations.
   C She wants to encourage people to read more about history.

Speaking Part 2

1 Answer questions a and b about photos 1–3.

  a What are the ceremonies shown?
  b What do ceremonies like these have in common?

> • How might the people taking part in the ceremonies be feeling?
> • How memorable might these occasions be for them?

2 Underline the key words in the task above the photos opposite.

3 🎧 Read the how to do it box below, then listen to someone doing the task in 2 and answer these questions.

  a Which adjectives does she use to describe the people's feelings?
  b Does she answer the whole task?

how to do it

> ■ Choose the two photos you want to talk about.
>
>   Make sure you answer both parts of the task.
>
> ■ Use a variety of words to show your range of vocabulary.
>
>   Remember to compare, not simply describe the photos.

4 Fill the gaps in a–h with 1–8 below to form sentences about the photos.

  a It looks as if these people are .... in a degree ceremony.
  b The .... in this ceremony appear to be feeling very proud.
  c This ceremony is .... in a huge stadium.
  d I think the degree ceremony would be .... than the opening ceremony.
  e You would probably have lasting .... of all these occasions but for different reasons.
  f People .... occasions like these for the rest of their lives.
  g Photos like these .... us of important events in our lives.
  h Some occasions in our lives are simply ....

1	more memorable	5	remind
2	taking place	6	unforgettable
3	remember	7	taking part
4	memories	8	participants

5 In pairs, do the task in 2. Student A compares photos 1 and 2, and Student B compares photos 2 and 3. The how to do it box and phrases below will help you.

> ■ Speculating
>
> It looks like / looks as if it is …
> It seems to be / appears to be …
> They might be / could be …
> They probably / perhaps / may be …

Use of English   Part 2 Open cloze

1 When do young people 'come of age' in your country? How do you celebrate this event?

2 Read the text below quickly and answer these questions.

   a Who are the Xicrin?
   b Who takes part in the ceremony?

3 Read the text again and think of the word which best fits gaps 1–15. The how to do it and tip boxes will help you.

4 Do you think the Xicrins' traditions will survive? Why / Why not?

how to do it

- Read the text once for overall meaning, then again sentence by sentence.
- Look at the words before and after each gap.
- Don't always choose your first idea – consider some other options.
- Check your completed text for sense and grammar.

tip

The 15 missing answers in this text include:
- two linkers
- two pronouns (e.g. *It, This, One*)
- three prepositions
- three relative pronouns
- one auxiliary verb
- four words from part of a phrase

AN UNUSUAL COMING-OF-AGE CEREMONY

Living in the remote heart of the Brazilian Amazon, the Xicrin are one of a small number 0 ...*of*... tribes which have managed to retain their traditional customs and rites. 1 .... such ritual is part of an age-old ceremony which the young men of the Xicrin tribe have to endure in 2 .... to prove their manhood, and to gain the right to be called warriors. 3 .... entails climbing a tree and attacking a wasps' nest with their bare hands. This is just one of the many traditions 4 .... help to mark the coming of age of the young men and reflect the tribe's relationship 5 .... the natural environment.

I had been invited to witness this ceremony 6 .... of my support for the Indians over many years as they tried to 7 .... to terms with outside culture. 8 .... a period of several days and nights, the villagers had been preparing for the event, dancing and listening to music which is distinctive and pulsating. The young men, 9 .... are aged 14 to 18, had been listening to the myths and legends which recount the tribe's history and were also 10 .... taught hunting and survival skills. 11 .... they were ready for the final test, they were led to the spindly, latticework ladder which they 12 .... to climb up to fulfil their objective. The men nervously stood their ground 13 .... close to the tree as they dared, whilst the women hid themselves 14 .... the undergrowth of the surrounding forest. The ordeal, which always results in stings for the young men, proves 15 .... bravery, ability to withstand pain, and willingness to face dangerous situations.

Part 5 Key word transformations

5 Look at the example key word transformation exercise below. Which part of the first sentence has been replaced by the key word? Do both sentences have a similar meaning?

Example

Do you think I could disturb you for a moment?
WONDERING
I **was wondering if I** could disturb you for a moment.

6 Read the answers given to a–e and say which ones are correct. Then correct the ones that are wrong. The how to do it box will help you.

how to do it

- Find which part of the first sentence needs to be replaced by the key word.
- Think carefully how this will affect the grammar of the second sentence.
- Write between three and six words, including the key word given.
- Never change the key word.
- Read your completed sentence and check it has a similar meaning to the first sentence.

a The actor's autobiography was published last week.
CAME
This <u>is the actor whose autobiography comes</u> out last week.

b I'm so sorry we have to endure this dreadful journey.
PUT
If only we did <u>not put up with</u> this dreadful journey.

c Pam will never accept the fact that what she believed was a lie.
TERMS
Pat will never <u>come to terms with</u> the fact that what she believed was a lie.

d Mosquito bites are nowhere near as painful as wasp stings.
FAR
Mosquito bites are <u>less painful than</u> wasp stings.

e Will the elections be a massive victory for the opposition party?
RESULT
I wonder <u>if the results will be</u> a massive victory for the opposition party.

Grammar

Relative clauses GR p172–173

1 Complete sentences a–j with clauses 1–10.

a You may decide to enrol for our courses online, ...

b My grandfather, ... kept chickens in the garden.

c Paris is a city ... .

d The house was full of famous paintings, ...

e We ventured further afield to explore the remote, uninhabited islands, ...

f I eventually finished writing my essay at midnight, ...

g The popular foothills ... were often cut off in winter.

h Have you ever had one of those days ... ?

i Give me one reason ... .

j Initially, you will be placed in a class of ten students, ...

1 by which time I had missed my favourite TV programme

2 all of which were worth a small fortune

3 none of whom has ever studied another language before

4 where we went climbing in the summer

5 about which very little is known

6 when everything seems to go wrong

7 whose love of the outdoors was his passion,

8 whose art galleries are one of its biggest attractions

9 in which case, the following instructions must be followed

10 why you don't want to go out tonight

Writing Part 2 A proposal WG p162

1 Look at the photos and answer questions a–c.

   a Which country is this?
   b What different aspects of culture are shown?
   c What else do you know about this country's culture?

2 Read this exam task and answer questions a–c.

> You are on the planning committee representing your country for an international cultural festival in London. Write a proposal for the festival organiser suggesting what should be included in the festival to represent the culture of your country and explaining why you think the aspects you have chosen would be of special interest.
>
> Write your proposal in 220–260 words.

   a Who is your target reader?
   b What type of text should you write?
   c What two main points should you include in your answer?

3 Read the model answer and decide if statements a–g about proposals are true or false.

  a They begin in the same way as a letter.
  b They focus on a future event.
  c They are informal in register.
  d They are divided into sections with clear headings.
  e They aim to inform and persuade the target reader.
  f They do not need an introduction or conclusion.
  g They give suggestions and/or recommendations.

4 List the different ways the writer suggests for showing his ideas, e.g. *a live performance*.

5 Which verb forms cannot be used in a–d? Read the proposal to check your answers and find other ways of making suggestions.

  a I suggest *we show/to show/show/showing* a film about our national history.
  b It would be a good idea *teach/teaching/to teach/that we teach* people one of our local dances.
  c I recommend *invite/to invite/inviting/we invite* one or two of our national celebrities to appear.
  d I propose *putting on/put on/we put on/us to put on* a special display for children.

6 Find phrases in the proposal which mean the same as a–e below. Why is each equivalent phrase in the model more suitable?

  a Nobody else has a culture like theirs.
  b a group of people from our past
  c make our past seem more real
  d Visitors would think the animals were great.
  e Why don't we go for Kylie Minogue?

7 Write your proposal. Plan your answer first by doing a–c.

  a Think of all the aspects of your country that are culturally significant.
  b Choose the ones you could show at a festival, and decide how you would show them.
  c Decide on three main headings, and select the best items from your ideas in b). Remember to include a separate introduction and conclusion.

Introduction

This proposal contains my suggestions for our country's contribution to the international festival in London.

Our national history

Aboriginals were the only inhabitants of Australia and their culture is completely unique. I recommend a live performance of traditional dances and music. Visitors might also enjoy a photographic display of aboriginal cave and rock paintings and of Uluru, their sacred red rock. We could follow that with a procession of historic characters in costume, which should bring our history alive.

Outdoor life

I suggest we show a video so visitors can appreciate how thrilling it is to surf and swim off our fabulous beaches. Scuba diving is very popular too, so I suggest having a display showing people diving at the Great Barrier Reef. We could also have photos showing people trekking in the rainforest. Visitors would be amazed and captivated by the huge variety of wildlife to be found.

Contemporary arts

The Sydney Opera House is world famous and I am sure visitors would enjoy a live performance by one of our celebrated opera singers. I propose we also ask singers from our thriving rock scene to contribute. Kylie Minogue would be an obvious choice. Another aspect of the arts scene that would definitely interest visitors is our film industry, so we could show clips and stills from films, featuring our most famous actors, such as Russell Crowe and Nicole Kidman.

Conclusion

My proposal would give visitors a real taste of Australian culture, past and present, and I hope it meets with your approval.

Review

1
Rearrange the words in bold so that they fit the correct definitions a–e.

a **Parades** are days or periods of celebration.
b **Traditions** are formal public occasions celebrating a particular event.
c **Rituals** are public processions.
d **Ceremonies** are customs or beliefs handed down to future generations.
e **Festivals** are a prescribed order of performing rites.

2
Rewrite the second sentence in a–c keeping the meaning the same. Use three to six words including the word given.

a There have been serious doubts about Sam's professionalism after his recent behaviour.
QUESTION
Sam's professionalism ....
after his recent behaviour.
b We don't want any criticism to be overheard by the event's organisers.
WITHIN
Be careful not to say anything ....
the event's organisers.
c Everybody is affected by the excitement of a carnival.
UP
It's impossible not ....
in the excitement of a carnival.

3
Complete the following sentences with a suitable verb or adverb to match the meaning of the words in brackets. The first letter of the word is given.

a One of the main motivations in many people's lives is to e............ a living (make money).
b If you read the programme, you will find a paragraph at the beginning which s............ the scene (gives the background) brilliantly.
c A first child can often be f............ (extremely) competitive with younger siblings.
d Ted's p............ (strongly) interested in archaeology. He's been on hundreds of digs.
e I would like to say how d............ (very) grateful I am for all that you have done.
f One thing politicians rarely admit to is b............ (going back on) their word.
g We were a............ (completely) furious to hear that Paula had missed the train again.
h Would you be b............ (terribly) disappointed not to be offered the job?

4
Use the verbs in brackets in their correct form to complete sentences a–f.

a We would like to thank you for your invaluable .... (contribute) to the event.
b At the entrance to the museum, there is an impressive wooden .... (carve) of a buffalo.
c The .... (reveal) that someone had robbed her of her most treasured possession was devastating.
d You should let the airline know of any special dietary .... (require) in advance.
e After the initial .... (form) of the company, the business rapidly went from strength to strength.
f Clearly confused, she looked at me with no sign of .... (recognise) on her face.

5
Complete the sentences with a word connected with remembering. The first letter of the word is given.

a Which do you think is more m............ as you grow older – your childhood or your teenage years?
b Souvenirs can bring back happy m............ of special events.
c The chairman has asked to be r............ in good time about the annual meeting.
d My first day at work was u............ for a number of very interesting reasons.
e Please don't f............ to phone your aunt. It's her birthday tomorrow.

6
Number sentences a–e in the best order (1–5) to form a proposal suggesting what to include in an international exhibition about France.

a To accompany this, we could also have a small gallery of photographs showing the many islands off the French coast. ....
b Another aspect would, of course, be an exhibition outlining the country's history. I am sure this would be popular with visitors. ....
c As well as showing people the geography of France, it would be an excellent idea to have a section devoted to traditional French cuisine, as well as a section with examples of traditional crafts. ....
d My suggestions would give visitors a taste for French culture and I hope they meet with your approval. ....
e I would recommend initially showing a video of France's impressive mountains. ....

Looking ahead

Lead in

1 Answer these questions.

a Look at the photos and talk about different situations in which people make predictions.

b What kind of jobs involve people making predictions?

c Who relies on the information provided by their predictions?

d What can happen if the predictions turn out to be inaccurate?

2 What changes are you likely to see in the following areas in your lifetime? The expressions in the language box below will help you.

- work
- holidays
- transport
- entertainment

Making predictions

There's no likelihood of …
It's unlikely that …
There's absolutely no way that …

As likely as not …
There's a good chance that …
The chances are that …

… seems inevitable.
… is bound to …
There's no doubt that …

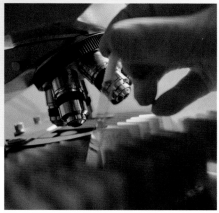

3 If you could find out any three things about the future, what would they be?

Reading Part 1 Themed texts

1 Quickly read the three extracts below and opposite, which are all concerned in some way with the future. Then think of a suitable title for each one.

2 Read the three extracts again and the two questions below each one. Then choose the best answer (A, B, C or D). The how to do it box will help you.

Space tourism is already grabbing the headlines and terrestrial travel has entered the space age. So what lies in store for tomorrow's holidaymakers?

Plans to build a new fleet of 'spaceliners' are currently
05 underway so in the not-so-distant future we may all be heading out into space as a matter of course. According to present estimates, it won't be cheap and in fact you'll be in true space for just three minutes. But for the thousands of aspiring astronauts who are expected to sign up, none
10 of that matters.

And just consider what may be on offer by 2020, when it is predicted that space hotels will be open for business. Holiday brochures already claim that their hotels are out of this world. These exaggerated claims of excellence could
15 become mere statements of fact if plans for space hotels take shape! An American tycoon has reportedly committed millions of dollars to developing an orbiting hotel, and another company plans to build one using space junk. At present the sums are prohibitive, but investors hope costs
20 will decrease in time.

For those who prefer holidaying nearer home, there is another possibility. Futurologist Ian Pearson claims 'active skin' technology will be widespread by the year 2050. Computer chips smaller than skin cells will be hooked
25 up with nerve endings to make electronic records of sensations, which can then be replayed. 'Tiny transmitters attached to your fingertips, toes, and face could enable you to enjoy the sensations of a holiday – walking on a beach or enjoying a holiday romance,' says Pearson. But
30 will a virtual holiday be as enjoyable as a real one? And if this is the future, do we really want it?

how to do it

- Read the first extract quickly and look at the two questions.
- Eliminate any options that are clearly wrong.
  Choose the option that fits best.
- If you are unsure of any question, move on to the next question/extract, and try again later.

1 The extract suggests that in the future hotels in space
   A might be an impossible dream.
   B may be as good as ones on earth.
   C could cause environmental damage.
   D may become cheaper to build.

2 What appears to be the writer's attitude towards 'active skin' technology?
   A confused
   B sceptical
   C optimistic
   D scared

IF YOU'RE BORED WITH THIS BUSINESS WORLD, TRY YOUR HAND IN ANOTHER BUSINESS WORLD

... IN VIRTUAL SPACE.

35 **Second Life** (SL) is an Internet-based virtual world where you can interact and do business with a whole new community. You can create objects, sell them, and make real money. Our virtual world has a real economy, with its own currency – the Linden $.
40 Real-life businesses can flourish in SL!

And very soon retailers may be able to place a 'door' to a SL store from their website, inviting people to jump from two-dimensional browsing into a three-dimensional shop. For example, an avatar (a virtual
45 person) with a customer's measurements could even try clothes on. The current Internet has forced us into a cramped two-dimensional space that doesn't capture the way humans window-shop. SL can bring us back to the three dimensions where we belong.

50 The news is travelling fast. Our members now include senior representatives of some of the best-known companies in the world. Several world-leading companies have built replicas of their conference rooms in SL, where distant
55 employees can meet and exchange information. Other companies are looking at using SL for their corporate training. And it has also become the perfect way to get to know colleagues after a stressful day in the virtual office.

60 **Nanotechnology** was born in the 1980s and describes the advanced capabilities of assembling molecules with atomic precision. In layman's terms, it means that we may have the ability to place one atom at a time in a specified place – it's molecular
65 manipulation at the very finest level. This is a huge advance in technology and it has enormous possibilities for every aspect of our lives. Hence substantial government funding in this area and the vast number of nanotech companies already in existence.

70 **Intended Uses**

There are some that doubt it will be possible to manipulate molecules in the way nanotechnology claims it can. But others claim that it will soon be possible to make tiny devices like 'nanobots', which are microscopic robots small
75 enough to travel in our bloodstreams, destroy cancer cells, or repair faulty heart valves. They hope that the technology can also be used in other areas of our lives, such as to generate cheap electricity and to purify water.

Potential Drawbacks

80 There are rumours that there could be dangerous unintended consequences, such as self-replicating robots destroying the world. Problems are actually more likely to be similar to those people associate with nuclear energy and genetically modified foods. That is, some of the tiny
85 units could damage cells and be an environmental danger. And whilst there is a legal requirement to inform the public, this could also pose risks if nanotechology were to fall into the wrong hands, such as activist organisations, and be used to harm innocent people. Openness on technological
90 issues is essential but regulation is also important.

3   Why might shopping in Second Life (SL) be better than current ways of shopping on the web?

   A   There would be more retailers to choose from.
   B   Customers can do more than just look at items.
   C   A retailer could select and advise on products.
   D   It would be a quicker way to pay for clothes.

4   Businesses are using SL because it

   A   broadens people's social lives.
   B   allows them to advertise their buildings.
   C   lets people work and socialise together.
   D   offers new job opportunities.

5   Interest in the potential benefits of nanotechnology is evident from

   A   financial investment from the state.
   B   the support of surgeons worldwide.
   C   the design and manufacture of robots.
   D   widespread public support.

6   What concerns does the writer voice about nanotechnology?

   A   Assessments of its safety might be incorrect.
   B   The usual tests have not been carried out on it.
   C   Dangerous groups may get hold of it.
   D   It could be more dangerous than nuclear energy.

Vocabulary GR p182–183

Phrasal verbs with *up* and *down*

1 Complete a–e with phrasal verbs formed from these verbs plus *up* or *down*.

    break   set   put   bring   turn

  a If you haven't got enough room, we can .... your relatives for the night.

  b His intention is to use the inheritance to .... his own business.

  c Protesters are threatening to .... the government if their demands aren't met.

  d Police .... the demonstration by firing tear gas into the crowd.

  e It was the thought of commuting every day that made me .... the job offer.

2 Use your dictionary to answer these questions.

  a In which phrasal verbs in 1 could you put the object between the verb and the particle?

  b Turn the objects of the phrasal verbs in a–e into pronouns. Then rephrase the sentences.

Example

a If you haven't got enough room, we can put them up for the night.

3 Replace the underlined verbs in a–d with new phrasal verbs formed from the verbs in 1 plus *up* or *down*. Check your answers in your dictionary.

Example

  It's best if you don't <u>mention</u> the subject of Mark's resignation, as it's a rather sensitive matter.

  bring up ....

  a The key witness <u>lost control and started crying</u> in court.

  ....

  b You shouldn't have <u>made him look stupid</u> in front of his friends – no wonder he was upset.

  ....

  c Could you <u>increase the sound on</u> the radio a bit – I can hardly hear what the newsreader's saying.

  ....

  d Students are expected to respect the college rules as <u>written down</u> in the official handbook.

  ....

Grammar

Future forms GR p167–169

1 Name the verb forms used to express the future in a–g, then match them with functions 1–7.

  a Our train leaves at 4 o'clock tomorrow morning.

  b I'm having my hair cut tomorrow.

  c By this time next year, I'll already have left school and found a job.

  d I'm tired. I think I'll go to bed.

  e I'll be lying on a beach this time next week.

  f We're going to move house next year.

  g By the end of this week, they'll have been travelling for a year.

  1 an appointment/definite arrangement

  2 a spontaneous decision

  3 a timetable or travel plan

  4 an action completed before another future time

  5 an action happening for a continuous period before a future point

  6 a personal plan

  7 an action that will be in progress at a certain future time

2 Choose the correct verb forms to complete the dialogue.

A: Have you heard? Anna and Mark (1) *are going to get/will get* married.

B: Surely not! Anna (2) *will start/is starting* university next week.

A: Well she must have changed her mind. Her parents (3) *are going/will go* crazy when they find out.

B: You're not joking! Are you absolutely certain?

A: Quite certain. I'll tell you what, (4) *I'm going to/I'll ring* her right now and she can tell you herself. She (5) *will have/is having* some friends over for dinner tonight so she should be at home.

B: Good idea! I hope it's not just a rumour. I think (6) *they'll make/they're making* a perfect couple.

3 Put the verbs in brackets into an appropriate future form.

a Do you think most office workers .... (work) from home by 2020?

b .... space tourism .... (become) widespread within the next five years, in your opinion?

c How likely is it that ordinary people .... (use) robots to do domestic tasks in their houses in the very near future?

d Do you think scientists .... (clone) a human being by next year?

e Where do you think most people in your country .... (live) in 50 years' time; in rural or urban areas?

4 Discuss your opinions of the completed questions in 3.

5 Underline the time conjunctions in a–c and match the verb forms which follow them with 1–3.

a We'll be going to the beach as soon as the rain has stopped.

b When space flights become cheaper, we'll all want to try them.

c News reporters will be taking photos while the President is speaking.

1 emphasises the continuous nature of the action
2 emphasises that one action will be finished before another begins
3 simply states a fact

6 Complete sentences a–e with your own ideas and say which tenses could follow the time conjunctions.

a Make sure you phone me from the airport as soon as …

b I'm sure you will be in a better mood once …

c I usually feel really tired after …

d Do you think you'll still enjoy clubbing by the time …

e One of our assistants will help you the minute …

7 Correct the tense errors in a–d. There may be more than one possible answer.

a My brother is planning to travel round Europe with his girlfriend next year, but now she's changed her mind.

b The celebrity who is to open the new hospital has pulled out at the last minute.

c She is about to take a mouthful of wine when she noticed the wasp in her glass.

d I hadn't realised my mother-in-law will stay until the end of the month.

8 Complete the sentences in an appropriate way.

a They were going to order dessert …

b We were about to leave the house …

c If I had known my boss was going to …

d I knew that my decision would …

9 Ask a partner or partners about a–e.

a What they're doing for a holiday this year.

b Whether they hope to be living in the same place in five years' time.

c Whether they think that something significant will have happened to them by this time next year.

d Which film they think they'll see next.

e What the next big purchase they're about to make is.

Listening Part 3 Multiple choice

1 What can be done to preserve places like the ones in the photos for future generations?

2 🎧 Read quickly through the questions, then listen twice to two conservationists, Bob and Carrie, talking about plans for the future of ancient monuments, and choose the best answer for 1–6.

1 What does Bob say about building a tourist centre near ancient monuments like Stonehenge?

A Facilities like these are essential for encouraging tourism.
B It's difficult to find architects willing to take on projects like these.
C Finding the right design for centres like these is problematic.
D The cost of building projects like these is incredibly high.

2 What suggestion does Carrie make regarding Stonehenge?

A Existing visitor facilities should be updated.
B The standing stones should be removed from the site.
C There should be a maximum number of visitors allowed.
D The site should go back to how it looked in the past.

3 Bob feels that Carrie's plan for Stonehenge

A would not be environmentally friendly.
B would result in a huge loss of income.
C might be popular with the authorities.
D might lead to an increase in tourism.

4 What comment does Carrie make about the planned redevelopment of Petra?

A It will be designed to blend in with the landscape.
B The new building work will destroy the atmosphere of the place.
C The idea has been welcomed by many local people.
D It will restrict the entrance of large groups of tourists.

5 In Bob's opinion, the Petra building project will

A prove to be too ambitious.
B go over budget.
C be educational.
D make Petra even more beautiful.

6 According to Carrie, many people believe places like Stonehenge and Petra should

A be visited by as many people as possible.
B provide a relaxing experience for tourists.
C receive more publicity in the future.
D be allowed to keep their air of mystery.

3 Match a–e with 1–5 to make phrases about the future from the recording.

a on the   1 in store
b in the   2 cards
c what lies   3 run
d you never know   4 pipeline
e in the long   5 what's around the corner

4 Use some of the phrases in 3 to talk about things you expect to happen in the future where you live.

Speaking Part 2

1 Talk about your ambitions for the future using some of the phrases below.

Talking about the future

I'm not really sure what …	I doubt if I'll …
I wouldn't be surprised if …	It's unlikely that I'll …
I think I'll probably decide to …	

2 Put these expressions into three groups: 'success', 'failure' or 'making an effort'.

a come up with something original
b lack the talent to do something
c have the determination to do something
d make it to the top
e beat the competition
f make your mark
g put your heart and soul into it
h make (a lot of) sacrifices
i lack the necessary ambition
j give it everything you've got

3 Look at the two pairs of photos and the task above them and make some notes about how you could answer these questions.

4 🎧 Read the how to do it box, then listen to how one candidate began the task in 3, and say how suitable their answer is and why.

how to do it

- Don't talk about more than two out of the three photos.
- Keep talking for one minute.
- Use a range of structures and vocabulary.

5 Now do the exam task in 3 with a partner.

6 Take it in turns to look at your partner's photos and answer this follow-up question:

'Which of these ambitions do you think would be the most difficult to achieve?'

tip

For the follow-up task, give only a brief answer (no longer than 30 seconds) for the question about your partner's photos.

- What ambitions might the people have for the future?
- How difficult might it be to fulfil their ambitions?

Use of English Part 1 Multiple-choice cloze

1 How accurately can you tell someone's age by looking at them? What else gives you clues to how old people are?

2 What do you think the difference is between your 'calendar age' and your 'biological age'? Read the text in 3 quickly to check.

3 Read the how to do it box then complete gaps 1–12 with the best option (A, B, C, or D).

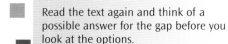

how to do it

- Read the text quickly for general sense, ignoring the gaps.
- Read the text again and think of a possible answer for the gap before you look at the options.
- Try each option in the gap to check your choice.

As old as you feel

It might after all be true that you are only as old as you feel. A British clinic is 0 ....C.... new high-tech tests to calculate the 'real' biological age of patients 1 .... on their rate of physical deterioration.

Information on every 2 .... of a patient's health, fitness, lifestyle and family medical history is 3 .... into a computer to work out whether they are older or younger than their calendar age suggests.

The availability and increasing accuracy of the tests has 4 .... one leading British gerontologist to call for biological age to be used to determine when workers should retire. He 5 .... that if an employee's biological or 'real' age is shown, for example, to be 55 when he reaches his 65th birthday, he should be 6 .... to work for another decade. Apparently most employers only take into 7 .... a person's calendar years, and the two may differ considerably.

Some of those prepared to pay substantial sums of money for the examinations will be able to smugly walk away with medical 8 .... showing that they really are as young as they feel, giving them the confidence to act and dress as if they were younger. Dr Lynette Yong, resident doctor at the clinic where the tests are offered claims that the purpose of these tests will be to motivate people to 9 .... their health. The concept of 'real age' is set to become big 10 .... in the USA, with books and websites helping people work out 11 .... their body is older or younger than their years. Others firmly believe that looks will always be the best 12 .... of age.

0	A working up	B working off	C carrying out	D carrying through
1	A based	B decided	C arranged	D established
2	A position	B prospect	C attitude	D aspect
3	A supplied	B fed	C provided	D planned
4	A projected	B prodded	C provoked	D prompted
5	A debates	B argues	C discusses	D enquires
6	A encouraged	B supported	C incited	D promoted
7	A interest	B detail	C account	D importance
8	A grounds	B signs	C demonstration	D evidence
9	A progress	B improve	C gain	D increase
10	A trade	B pursuit	C business	D concern
11	A whether	B unless	C in case	D so that
12	A notice	B indicator	C figure	D token

4 Try these tests to find your biological age. How accurate do you think they are?

A Stand on your left leg, with your right leg bent behind at 45 degrees and hands on your hips. Close your eyes. Time how long it is before you lose your balance. Take the best score from three.

biological age:	20	30	40	50	60
seconds:		70+	60	50	40

B Hold a ruler out below your eye. Hold a business card at the end of the ruler, and slowly move it towards you until it blurs. Measure the distance at which you can still read it.

biological age:	20	30	40		50	60
centimetres:		10	20	30	40	50	60

C Get someone to hold a 45cm ruler above your open dominant hand. Catch the ruler as quickly as possible when dropped. Measure where you catch it and take the average of three scores.

biological age:	20–30	30–40	40–50	50–60
centimetres:	5	10	15	20	25	30	35

Vocabulary

Expressions connected with age

1 Match the expressions in italics in a–h with the meanings 1–8.

a My 90-year-old grandfather has only recently begun to *feel his age*.

b The children shouldn't have acted so irresponsibly. They are *old enough to know better*.

c Some people say that the secret of staying young is to remain *young at heart*.

d *The youth of today* seem so different from when I was a youngster.

e My aunt may be 60 but she certainly *doesn't look her age*.

f When I was a lad, anyone over 40 seemed *as old as the hills*.

g Tim's only 14 but very mature. He *has an old head on young shoulders*.

h We should take every opportunity because we're *not getting any younger*.

1 be mature enough to act in a more sensible way
2 young people
3 be more mature than is expected for someone so young
4 growing older
5 look as old as you really are
6 still feeling and behaving as you did when you were younger
7 extremely old
8 be physically aware of your real age

2 Discuss the following questions.

a Do you have similar expressions about age in your language?

b Do you agree with the saying 'You're never too old to learn'? Why/Why not?

Writing   Part 1 A formal letter   WG p155

1 Read the writing task and input texts and say

    a what the Principal is planning to do and why.

    b who you have to write to.

> Your student committee at an international college has received a memo from the Principal, announcing future cuts to the transport facilities. You have been asked to write a letter to the Principal, telling him that you will be opposing the cuts and giving reasons. Use the Principal's memo with your comments, to write your letter in 180–220 words.

To   The Student Committee

From   P Simpson, Principal

Review of transport facilities

The college has run into debt and has had to consider various ways to save money in future.

Wrong – nearly all students use them at least twice a week!

My colleagues and I have been discussing the university transport facilities. In our view, these are underused. It seems that only a small number of students use the student car park and the free buses run half empty.   *Full in winter!*

Not enough spaces?!

We have therefore decided on some immediate changes. Firstly, we intend to make the car park available to the general public during the day, and to charge a fee. Secondly, we will be terminating the free bus service. More bicycle stands will be provided to encourage students to cycle to college.   *Dangerous cycling in city!*

No, we'll fight it!! — I trust the committee will support our decision.

P Simpson

Principal

2 Which of a–g would be appropriate for your letter? What is wrong with the others?

Example

Take it from me, your idea of cutting our transport facilities is right out of order. (Too informal – rather aggressive)

a Yours sincerely
b If you let outsiders use the car park, how on earth are we going to find spaces?
c I have to inform you that after careful consideration we have decided to oppose these drastic measures.
d Hi Mr Simpson
e For a start, what you say about students not using the buses is just plain wrong.
f I am writing on behalf of the student committee in response to your recent memo regarding financial cutbacks at the college.
g It's crazy expecting us to cycle to college when the traffic's so awful.

3 Rewrite a–e in a more formal style.

Example

the buses are half empty – the buses are not used to full capacity

a we've just done a survey
b what you say is wrong
c the changes you want to bring in
d we can't agree to this
e it's so unfair

4 List the points from the Principal's memo to include in your answer to the exam task. Add comments in your own words.

Example

college transport facilities underused – we believe that …

5 Use some of these linking words to join your notes from 4 into sentences.

however   nevertheless   although
in spite of/despite   because (of)

6 Make a plan of four paragraphs for the exam task. Decide where the sentences in 2 should go. Use the how to do it box to help you write your letter.

tip
You will generally need to write about four paragraphs for a letter.

how to do it

Read the task carefully.

Read all the input information, then read the task again.

Make notes for all the points you must include.

Decide on the correct format and organise your notes accordingly.

Check that you have covered everything in the task and input information.

Write your answer in your own words in the appropriate register.

van

Review

1 Correct the mistakes with the phrasal verbs in a–g.

a On hearing the sad news, Sally broke up and wept.

b It's an international organisation helping those in crisis, and was set off last century.

c If you get more guests than you bargained for, we have plenty of space, so can easily put up some.

d Who finally put up the subject of money during the negotiations?

e It's extremely unprofessional to turn someone down in front of their colleagues.

f The rules and regulations for the procedure are set up in this document.

g Only after several shops had been robbed did the authorities break down the riot.

2 Write the missing words in the phrases in a–e.

a Following a spell of poor weather, forecasters say that high temperatures are just .... corner.

b Although I've applied for a number of jobs, I have nothing definite .... pipeline yet.

c Initially, this may seem an expensive investment, but .... run, it will prove good value for money.

d If we'd known what .... store for us that day, we would never have gone on the excursion.

e Everyone hopes it won't happen, but it's .... cards that the factory will close.

3 Correct any mistakes in the underlined expressions in a–h.

a Despite <u>putting it everything we'd got</u>, we still lost yesterday's match.

b Only by analysing their strengths and weaknesses can we hope to <u>knock the competition</u>.

c It seems that nowadays you need very little talent to <u>do your mark in life</u>.

d After years without success, John finally accepted that he <u>wanted the talent</u> to become a star.

e Few celebrities realise the pressures involved in <u>getting it to the top</u>.

f You could see from the children's faces that they were <u>putting their head and soul</u> into the performance.

g At the end of the day, I wasn't prepared to <u>create the sacrifices</u> needed in my personal life for the sake of my job.

h To be a successful inventor, you've got to <u>come up to</u> something original at the right time.

4 Choose the correct word to complete sentences a–f.

a Our marketing strategy is *decided/based* on a tried and tested system.

b Many senior citizens have contacted us to *enquire/discuss* about the new tax.

c We always take an *interest/account* in a prospective employee's ambitions.

d In *sum/addition* to government grants, private finance has funded this project.

e Campaigners against the international arms *trade/concern* have presented a petition.

f We can't help you *unless/so that* you are prepared to confess to the robbery.

5 Circle the correct word in sentences a–g.

a We should make the most of life because none of us are *coming/going/getting* any younger.

b Some people stay young at *head/soul/heart* all their lives.

c For many people, it isn't until they hit retirement that they begin to *be/seem/feel* their age.

d Sam has always had an old head on young *neck/shoulders/body*.

e What outrageous behaviour! You're old enough to know *well/better/best*.

f It's amazing how some elderly famous people don't *seem/look/show* their age!

g Teenagers consider anyone over 30 to be as old as the *valleys/rivers/hills*.

6 Use a–g to complete part of a letter about the results of a survey.

a I therefore recommend   e in your survey
b in your view   f firstly
c I trust   g the results show
d in addition

.... 1, you asked students how often they use the vending machines in the college. Apparently .... 2 that they are used by most students only about once a week. .... 3, these machines were grossly underused. While I agree with the results of the survey, I would be reluctant to see all the vending machines disappear. .... 4 making the following changes. .... 5, it would be advisable to relocate the most popular vending machines nearer to the catering facilities where they would be seen by everybody. .... 6, those machines which are hardly ever used should be removed from the premises completely. .... 7 you will take my views into consideration.

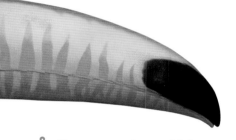

Into the wild

4

Lead in

1 For each part of the body below, name two creatures which have them.

mane	scale	beak	hide
flipper	antenna	hoof	tusk
fin	claw	horn	paw
wing	shell		

2 Name a creature which:

a is generally feared.
b might be found repulsive.
c has human characteristics.
d is thought of as man's friend.
e has sinister associations.
f is exotic.
g is endangered.

3 Say which creatures are described in a–d and explain the words in italics.

a Most members of this species are very *agile* climbers and swing through the trees at great speed. They are highly *sociable* and spend hours *grooming* each other.

b They're *intelligent*, playful creatures with fins but no scales, and are a favourite with sailors.

c They're tall, extremely *graceful* animals with long necks and very small horns.

d They're *fierce* hunters with large paws. They *stalk their prey* and can run faster than all the other big cats.

4 Write brief descriptions of three more wild animals and see if a partner can guess what they are.

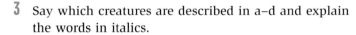

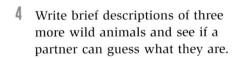

Reading Part 2 Gapped text

1 Do you know any stories, real or fictional, in which animals help humans?

2 Quickly read the main text and summarise what it says about the relationship between humans and dolphins.

3 Look at lines 1–8 and lines 9–12. Which of a–c below is most likely to summarise the first missing paragraph? Match a–c with paragraphs from A–G.

   a   other similar incidents about dolphins
   b   a theory of animal behaviour
   c   what led up to this situation

4 Complete the text with the remaining paragraphs, using the highlighted words and the tip box to help you find links. There is one extra paragraph.

5 Say how the clues helped you match the paragraphs.

Example

The word drama *in paragraph G summarises the events of the first paragraph.*

6 Do you agree that humans are purely motivated by self-interest? Can you think of any examples of people acting unselfishly?

As the dolphin hurtled through the water straight at him, Rob Howes, a burly 38 year-old lifeguard, wondered if he was about to be killed. A stone's throw from him across the choppy ocean waters, his 15-year-old daughter Niccy and her friend Karina were
5 terrified. The girls had been surrounded by six highly agitated dolphins and were being held hostage in a maelstrom of flashing fins and swerving bodies. The seventh dolphin was charging Howes, seemingly intent on driving him back to the other captives.

1

Believing the advancing dolphin was going to ram him from
10 beneath, Howes turned to his right in anticipation of where it was going to surface. But as he turned, what he saw in the water was not a dolphin, but something much worse – a great white shark.

2

So were the dolphins really trying to protect their human 'hostages'? It isn't the first time these creatures have apparently
15 saved humans from disaster. Greek mythology tells how Arion, a musician, was carried to land on the backs of dolphins after sailors had thrown him from their ship. The fact that the myth centres on dolphins indicates that, even then, humans believed this species to be brighter and possibly kinder than other beasts.

3

20 The near-fatal attack was witnessed by diver Matt Fleet. He and his crew were anchored nearby when he saw the dolphins circling. He grabbed his camera and jumped into the water, hoping to get some pictures. But the first thing he saw as he surfaced was not a dolphin but the vertical fin of a great white.
25 Had it not been for his boat's underwater rescue team, he too might have come under attack.

4

Such questions are extremely difficult for scientists to answer. In fact, biologists have argued for years over whether even humans are capable of altruism – many believing that every apparently
30 kind act has some self-interest behind it.

5

According to these scientists, all the apparently benevolent acts seen in nature – wolves sharing their kill with the rest of the pack, adult birds risking their lives to protect their young against predatory hawks, and primates feeding the offspring of others in
35 their group – are explained by the idea of kinship. The theory is that kindness is offered only to relatives of the same species who carry many of the same genes as the giver. By helping them, it is suggested, the seemingly unselfish giver is improving the chances of his or her own genes surviving.

tip

For this task think about

- lexical links, e.g. nouns and pronouns.
- time references, e.g. earlier, later.
- the order of events in the story.

the seas

6

40 Whatever the answer, these creatures have little reason to be thankful to humans; thousands are killed each year by tuna fishermen using drift nets. And Howes is still uncertain whether two dolphins found slaughtered by poachers near Whangarei harbour were members of the group that saved him. The thought leaves him
45 distraught. 'This is how we repay them for their help,' he says. 'I'd like to give the men responsible a taste of their own medicine.'

A

The modern version of this debate has its origins in the 1975 publication of Edward O Wilson's book *Sociobiology* and, a year later, of Richard Dawkins's *The Selfish Gene*. Wilson believed
50 animal and human behaviour is rooted entirely in our genes. Dawkins described human and animals as 'lumbering robots', whose minds and bodies are entirely controlled by selfish genes.

B

So do incidents like that witnessed by Fleet prove that dolphins really are the good guys of the deep, always ready to extend a
55 flipper to humans in distress? And if they are genuinely altruistic, what makes them that way?

C

Such a belief would appear to be justified by other, real-life events. In 1996 Martin Richardson, a 29-year-old traveller, was mauled by a shark while swimming in the Red Sea. He credited bottlenose
60 dolphins with chasing away the predator as it closed in for the kill.

D

This may explain altruism within species but why should dolphins help humans, as in the Whangarei incident? Were they following an ethical code? Or had they simply mistaken the human swimmers for other dolphins?

E

65 Howes had often spotted these fearsome predators in the course of his work, but this was one of the biggest he had ever seen. Had the dolphin not intentionally diverted the shark with its charge, he contends, he would almost inevitably have been attacked and killed.

F

It could be that they mistook the shape of a human in the water
70 for a sick dolphin. The dolphin sonar system can create a three-dimensional picture of any living object and the air spaces, internal organs, and other human features may have looked very similar to those of a dolphin.

G

The drama had started some minutes earlier. Howes and the girls
75 were swimming in Whangarei harbour, off New Zealand's North Island. They had been diving from rocks, and were swimming across open water when the group of dolphins appeared and started herding them up, circling tightly. This is very unusual behaviour for dolphins, which normally show little aggression to
80 humans.

saviours of the sea

Vocabulary

Expressions with animals

1 Complete sentences a–f with these words. Explain the meanings of the expressions with animals.

water   dinner   work   time   grass   bag

a Although we didn't think we'd enjoy ourselves, we ended up having a whale of a ....

b I can't believe I did my homework so badly – I made a real dog's .... of it!

c Next week's party was meant to be a surprise but Sonya's just let the cat out of the ....

d Tom had always lived in the country and felt like a fish out of .... in the city.

e My last boss was a real snake in the .... – you couldn't trust a word he said.

f When we decorated our house, my husband helped me choose the paint but left me to do the donkey ....

2 Complete sentences a–e appropriately to illustrate the meaning of the expression. Use your dictionary to look up any expressions that are new to you.

a I wish you'd stop rabbiting on about football – you know I ... .

b I've got butterflies in my stomach because this time tomorrow, I ... .

c Brian usually eats like a horse but ... .

d Poor David's going to be in the doghouse. He's just ... .

e If Jane's having a hen party, it must mean ... .

3 Answer these questions.

a When was the last time you were in the doghouse? What had you done wrong?

b Can you remember the last time you felt like a fish out of water? How did you cope?

c Do brides-to-be in your country usually have a hen party? What do they do?

d Have you ever let the cat out of the bag about something important? What happened?

Grammar

Past tenses GR p166–167

1 Name the tenses in italics in a–i.

a After the football match, we *went* to a bar, *had* a few drinks and *celebrated* our win.

b By the time the fitness trainer finally turned up, we *had been waiting* for half an hour.

c So *you've been on* the Atkins diet? How was it?

d Inspector Lomas looked out the window. It *was snowing* and the streets *were becoming* icy.

e Karen*'s put* on a lot of weight recently.

f That's the best film *I've seen* in a long time.

g As the skier *was racing* downhill, his ski hit a stone and threw him off balance.

h Heavy fog delayed us and by the time we reached the airport, our plane *had taken off*.

i Farmers *have been campaigning* for more support from the government for years.

2 Look again at the verbs in 1 and complete the grammar description below.

a .past simple. : for a series of separate past events

b .... : for events in the recent past, which are not completed, or connect to the present.

c .... : for an event that finished before another past event or time.

d .... : for a continuous past action that finished before another past event or time.

e .... : for an interrupted past event or a background event.

f .... : for the first, second, etc. time we do something, and with superlatives.

3 Put the verbs in brackets in a–g into the past simple or present perfect simple. Identify any time expressions or other clues that help.

a I (study) in Paris for six years until my parents moved to Rome.

b This isn't the first time I (taste) shark meat.

c As a child, I (excel) at sports.

d Ouch! I (twist) my ankle.

e It was a long time before I (dare) tell my parents I had a tongue stud.

f I (resist) eating a single piece of chocolate for the past six weeks.

g Many of the plays that Shakespeare (produce) have been made into films.

4 Put the verbs in brackets into the present perfect simple or continuous.

a He .... (play) for the national football team three times so far this season.
b I .... (work) on the computer since 8 a.m. but I'm going to have a break in a minute.
c So far I .... (phone) Jim five times this morning but I haven't managed to catch him yet.
d If you .... (read) the book I lent you, can I have it back now?
e Opera singer Pavarotti .... (travel) round the country all summer giving performances.

5 Write two sentences about yourself for each of a–c, using the present perfect simple, present perfect continuous, or the past simple, as appropriate.

a challenging things at work or school

Example

I've been working on a fascinating project./I gave an important presentation last week.

b disappointing/exciting experiences
c free time activities

6 Explain how the sentences in each pair below differ in meaning.

1a A policeman stopped the motorist because he was breaking the law.
 b A policeman stopped the motorist because he had been breaking the law.
2a Most students were taking their exam when the fire bell rang.
 b Most students had taken their exam when the fire bell rang.

7 Correct any errors with tenses in these sentences.

a I knew she had cried because her eyes were red and puffy.
b Last week they were killing a great white shark which had been menacing swimmers for weeks.
c I was washing my car and my flatmate repaired his motorbike when our landlord turned up.
d As our plane had been landing, one of the engines caught fire and we had to make an emergency landing.
e When I last saw Bill he sat on the river bank, throwing stones into the water.
f The reason the DVD player wouldn't work was because you weren't plugging it in!

8 Put the verbs in italics (1–17) into the correct form.

Most of us .... 1 *see* gorillas on TV but few people .... 2 *ever/observe* one in the wild. I .... 3 *be* fascinated by these creatures since I .... 4 *be* a child. So imagine my delight when, a few weeks ago, I .... 5 *get* the chance to go to Rwanda to track wild mountain gorillas. The trip was not without danger. An armed soldier .... 6 *accompany* us to scare off the buffalo which .... 7 *attack* a previous group. Our guide .... 8 *cut* a path through the undergrowth and we .... 9 *follow*. When we .... 10 *find* what looked like claw marks in some trees, we realised that gorillas .... 11 *feed* there recently. Suddenly, we .... 12 *catch* sight of them – a whole family of gorillas! The adults .... 13 *sit* in the sun watching the youngsters, who .... 14 *play* in the trees. One of the adults .... 15 *stare* at me, ... 16 *scratch* his head, and .... 17 *yawn*. For me, it was love at first sight!

9 Using your imagination, make up a story about the events that led up to this scene, using a variety of tenses.

Listening

Part 2 Sentence completion

1 Discuss what wildlife photographers do and what skills or training they might need.

2 🎧 You will hear Clare Martin talk about wildlife photography. Read the how to do it box and correct the wrong answers given for 1–8.

how to do it

- Use the sentence context and structure as clues to the answers.
- Don't be too quick to put an answer; it may be a distractor.
- You usually only need to write one or two words.
- You listen twice, so if you miss an answer, concentrate on finding it the next time.
- Check your answers for spelling, grammar and sense.

Wild about animals!

Clare has just returned from an assignment in
South Africa **1**

Most of her correspondence comes from
young schoolchildren **2**

Earning a living as a wildlife photographer isn't easy because of the many really good quality pictures **3** operating in the field.

The bird photographer Arthur Morris was originally a
teaching .... **4** by profession.

One university in Britain offers a degree in
Biography .... **5** Imaging.

Clare suggests working as a travel guide or
conversationist .... **6** to establish yourself.

You need to bring in compensation **7**
to cover your expenses.

She recommends studying creative subjects **8**
if you want to become a full-time photographer.

Speaking Part 3

1 Read the examiner's question below, then use the information to complete the exam prompts.

'Imagine you are writing an article about the importance of animals in people's lives. Here are some photos you are considering using to illustrate the article. Talk to each other about how important the animals are to the people in these pictures, then choose two photos which you think would best illustrate the article.'

- How .... 1 are the .... 2 to the .... 3 in these .... 4 ?
- Which .... 5 photos would best .... 6 the article?

2 Talk about the photos by completing the gaps in a–e with 1–5 and finishing the sentences appropriately.

1 companionship	4 entertainment
2 independence	5 resource
3 responsibility	

a Horses are a valuable .... for the police. They can be used …

b The old couple probably like having a cat for .... I expect they …

c Having a pet like a hamster when you're young gives you a sense of .... The animal relies on you …

d If you're blind or partially sighted, a guide dog can be vital for your .... Without one …

e These fish are a form of .... They attract visitors because …

3 🎧 Read the how to do it box, then listen to two students do the task in 1 and answer these questions.

a What initial mistake does the female student make?

b What does the male student do right?

c What does he do wrong?

how to do it

- Answer all parts of the question.
- Give reasons for your ideas to show your range of language.
- Encourage your partner to speak.
- Make negative comments and disagree politely with your partner, if you wish.

4 Do the task in 1 in pairs, using the tip box
and phrases below to help you.

■ Inviting your partner to speak

Do/Don't you think this one … ?

Personally, I (don't) think this one … .
What about you?

I think … , don't you?

Would(n't) you agree that … ?

What do you think about this one?

How about you, what would you say?

How do you feel about this one?

tip

Remember
to show your
ability to
interact in
Part 3.

Use of English

Part 2 Open cloze

1 Look at these pictures of imaginary creatures and discuss which real creatures they resemble.

2 Read texts A–D, ignoring the gaps, and match them with the pictures and these names.

> The Toraton   The Ocean Flish
> Snowstalker   The Megasquid

a This fearsome creature will be one **1** .... the most ferocious predators of the next Ice Age. In order to adapt to the blizzards that will bury northern Europe **2** .... several metres of ice, it will have a thick coat, and sturdy legs with large flat paws. It will travel **3** .... miles in pursuit of its prey – sheep-size rodents called 'shagrats'.

b This amazing creature will be like no other. Heavier than an elephant and almost as large, it will push its way **4** .... the dense forest on eight tree trunk-size legs. It will walk **5** .... elongating each of its legs in turn, and then compressing them again.

c This will be the largest animal ever to walk the planet but will evolve **6** .... something as small as the humble tortoise. Grazing on more than half a ton of vegetation every day, it will be **7** .... home in the huge swamps formed when the east coast of Africa collides **8** .... the south coast of Asia. These massive creatures won't have many predators to fear.

d These creatures, so called because they can fly and swim, will replace the birdlife which will previously have been wiped **9** .... They will develop from cod-like creatures and grow elongated fins that serve as wings, enabling them to make their escape from predators in the sea **10** .... the safety of the birdless sky.

3 Read texts A–D again and complete gaps 1–10 with these prepositions and particles.

> with   for   out   into   under
> through   by   of   from   at

4 Read the text below to find out more about these creatures, and complete gaps 1–15 with one word each. These questions will help you with 1–10.

1 What does the verb *be around* mean here? What tense should it be in?
2 Which word can collocate with *to* meaning *in their opinion*?
3 Which word is missing from this conditional sentence?
4 Which phrasal verb with *finish* means *to destroy* or *to end*?
5 What collocates here to mean *helped by*?
6 Which preposition is missing here?
7 What can collocate with *as* to mean *like* or *similar to*?
8 What can collocate with *of* to mean *from*?
9 What can collocate here to mean *plenty of*?
10 What collocates with *look* to mean *resemble*?

5 Use your imagination to think of other creatures which might evolve in the future, taking characteristics from two or more of these creatures.

| kangaroo | leopard | eagle | snail |
| giraffe | shark | chameleon | swan |

OUt OF thIs WORld?

We humans pride ourselves on **0** ..being.. the masters of the earth, but modern man **1** .... only been around for 200,000 years of the planet's four-and-a-half billion year history. And **2** .... to many scientists, the long-term outlook for us isn't rosy. **3** .... our tendency to get rid of each other doesn't finish us **4** ...., then our propensity for destroying the environment could. So what might replace the human race? Here, **5** .... the aid of the latest computer graphics, are some **6** .... the fantastic creatures that experts believe could emerge as our inheritors. Creatures **7** .... as these might look like something **8** .... of a science-fiction film, but experts claim that there are **9** .... than enough clues to predict what future inhabitants of the earth might look **10** .... We know the continents are moving and that the Atlantic is widening **11** .... about the rate our fingernails grow. So with the right computer modelling, we can calculate **12** .... the continents will end up. Ecologists can then predict what habitats might exist, and **13** .... types of animals that might live in them. The good news is that this species upheaval **14** .... about three million years away, so there is **15** .... need for us to lose sleep over it just yet!

Writing Part 2 A contribution WG p156

1 Name the animals in the pictures. Say which of them live in the wild in your country and what else you know about them. Talk about:

- their habitat
- what they eat
- their characteristics and behaviour.

2 Underline the key points in this exam task. Two have been done for you.

> A publisher is bringing out <u>a guide to wildlife</u> in your country. You have been asked to <u>write a contribution</u> on one wild animal found in your country that might interest visitors. You should include details about the animal and advice on how to observe it in the wild. Write your answer in 220–260 words.

3 Read the model contribution and answer a–c.

a Why is the contribution in two sections?
b What different kinds of information are given about the otter in the first section, e.g. *size*?
c What does the second section say about when, where and how to see an otter?

The Otter

GENERAL INFORMATION

One of the most appealing animals found in this country is the otter. These attractive creatures live near rivers or by the sea and are perfectly adapted for life in the water, having waterproof fur and a streamlined body. They live on a diet of fish and are particularly fond of salmon, eels and shellfish. As well as being skilful swimmers, they are playful creatures and love rolling and tumbling in the water. Their homes are made from piles of branches, often by the roots of a tree. Otters are solitary creatures and it is rare to see a male and female together. However, cubs stay with their mothers for about a year before they leave to fend for themselves.

OBSERVING OTTERS

Catching sight of an otter in the wild is quite a challenge as they are rather secretive animals. Those that live by rivers are mostly nocturnal, which makes it very difficult to see them. Those that live by the sea, on the other hand, often venture out during daylight hours, and can be seen hunting in pools along the rocky shore. The best place to see an otter in this country is on the west coast. Set out early one morning and drive slowly along the coastline until you find a likely spot. Then sit quietly on the beach somewhere where they cannot detect your scent. If you are fortunate, you will be rewarded with a sight of these fascinating creatures.

4 How does the writer rephrase the following information to avoid starting each sentence in the same way?

a Otters are attractive creatures that live near rivers.
b Otters are skilful swimmers.
c Otters live in piles of branches.
d Otters are quite difficult to see.
e Otters that live by rivers are nocturnal.
f Otters in this country are best seen on the west coast.

5 Sentences a–g are too informal for a contribution. Rewrite them in a more formal style as shown, then compare your answers with the model.

a Otters are really at home in water.
Otters are perfectly .... for life in the water.
b They eat fish.
They live .... diet of fish.
c They really like eels.
They are particularly .... of eels.
d They like playing.
They are .... creatures.
e They like being by themselves.
They are .... creatures.
f They don't like being watched.
They are .... animals.
g They mainly come out at night.
They are mostly ....

6 Rewrite sentences a–d to keep the same meaning.

a It is extremely difficult to find an eagle's nest.
.... is extremely difficult.
b Giraffes are easily spotted because of their height.
.... spot giraffes because of their height.
c It is an amazing experience to see a lion at close quarters.
.... is an amazing experience.
d It will alert animals to your presence if you wear bright colours.
.... will alert animals to your presence.

7 Choose an animal you could base the exam task on. Make notes and use the information in this section to help you write your contribution. Remember to:

• include one paragraph about the animal
• write a separate paragraph on how to observe it
• keep your language fairly formal
• vary your sentence structure.

tip

You do not always need to write an introduction or conclusion.

Review

1

Match the parts of the body in 1–12 with creatures a–f.

a	fish	1	flipper	7	scale
b	bull	2	hide	8	hoof
c	eagle	3	beak	9	fin
d	lion	4	shell	10	horn
e	tortoise	5	wing	11	mane
f	dolphin	6	claw	12	paw

2

Complete the dialogues in 1–5 with suitable phrases based on these animals.

rabbit   butterfly   dog   hen   horse

1 A Are you going go out to celebrate with your girlfriends before the wedding?
   B Yes, my bridesmaid's organising a .... for me.

2 A How did you feel about performing in front of such a large audience?.
   B I have to confess I .... in my stomach just thinking about it!

3 A I can't believe I forgot to go to that meeting this morning.
   B You'll be .... for the rest of the week then!

4 A Do you fancy watching the new chat show on television tonight?
   B No way. I can't stand programmes with so-called 'celebrities' .... about themselves.

5 A Do you think I've bought enough food to go round at the barbecue?
   B However much you buy it will get eaten – everyone we know eats ....

3

Circle the correct animals to complete the phrases in a–e.

a The ageing president felt like a *fish/whale* out of water when he attended the music awards.
b I don't mind doing all the *goat/donkey* work as long as I get paid for it.
c We had a *butterfly/whale* of a time on the last night of the sales conference last year.
d I once tried my hand at painting but the result was a real *cat's/dog's* dinner.
e The controversial new traffic scheme was supposed to be kept under wraps, but someone let the *rat/cat* out of the bag.

4

Complete gaps 1–8 in these newspaper extracts using suitable prepositions or particles.

It is a widely held theory that the dinosaurs were wiped .... 1 by a giant meteor which collided .... 2 the earth. It is possible, however, that there is another explanation for what finished .... 3 the dinosaurs.

Some .... 4 the most adaptable creatures on earth can survive in extremely inhospitable places. For example, the camel is so .... 5 home in the desert that it can journey .... 6 miles without water.

According .... 7 experts, the pace at which global warming is developing might be more serious than we thought. It seems that the world is warming up .... 8 an alarming rate.

5

Rewrite this paragraph in a more formal style for part of an information leaflet about toucans.

You can find toucans in South and Central America. There aren't any wild ones in the UK, but you can see lots of them in zoos. You can recognise these creatures easily. They've got a really big beak. Their beaks have very bright colours. Their body is about twice as long as their beak. They really like fruit, seeds and insects. They don't like being on their own. In fact, they live in groups.

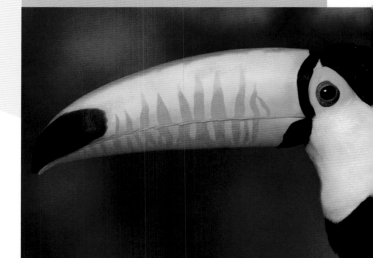

Health matters

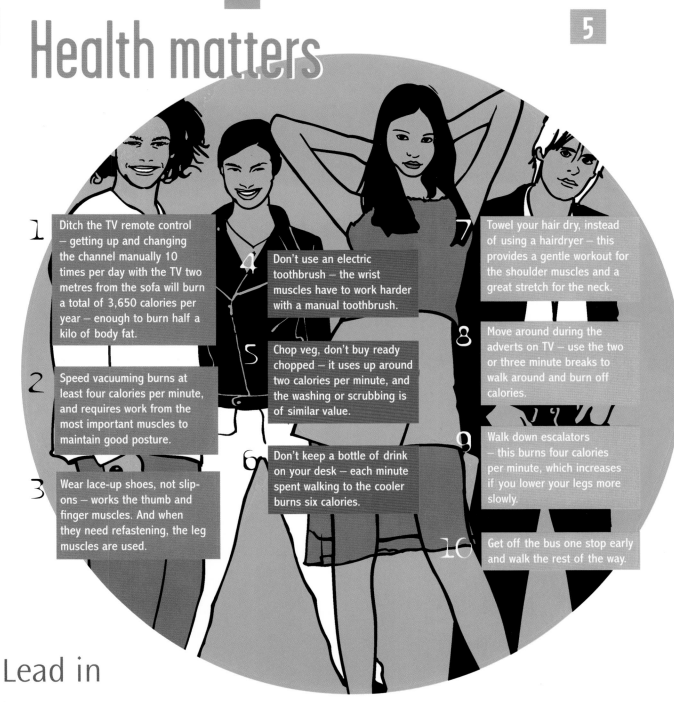

1. Ditch the TV remote control – getting up and changing the channel manually 10 times per day with the TV two metres from the sofa will burn a total of 3,650 calories per year – enough to burn half a kilo of body fat.

2. Speed vacuuming burns at least four calories per minute, and requires work from the most important muscles to maintain good posture.

3. Wear lace-up shoes, not slip-ons – works the thumb and finger muscles. And when they need refastening, the leg muscles are used.

4. Don't use an electric toothbrush – the wrist muscles have to work harder with a manual toothbrush.

5. Chop veg, don't buy ready chopped – it uses up around two calories per minute, and the washing or scrubbing is of similar value.

6. Don't keep a bottle of drink on your desk – each minute spent walking to the cooler burns six calories.

7. Towel your hair dry, instead of using a hairdryer – this provides a gentle workout for the shoulder muscles and a great stretch for the neck.

8. Move around during the adverts on TV – use the two or three minute breaks to walk around and burn off calories.

9. Walk down escalators – this burns four calories per minute, which increases if you lower your legs more slowly.

10. Get off the bus one stop early and walk the rest of the way.

Lead in

1 Read the ten simple ways to get fit. Which three do you think would be most effective? Which three could you build into your daily routine?

2 Can you add any similar simple suggestions for getting fit? Think about:

   shopping   housework   getting ready for school/work   getting around

3 What advice would you give to a teenager and an elderly person for leading a healthy lifestyle? Think about:

   diet   sleep   physical exercise

Reading Part 3 Multiple choice

1 What do you think is the best form of physical exercise? What is the minimum and maximum amount of exercise you think you should do each week? How much do you do?

2 Read the text opposite quickly to find out what unexpected thing happened to explorer Ranulph Fiennes and why it may have happened.

3 Read the text again and use the clues to help you with question 1. Ask yourself similar questions for options A–D to help you choose the best answer to questions 2–6.

tip

Make sure <u>all</u> the information is correct in the option you choose.

1 What does the writer say in the first paragraph about Fiennes' obsession with diet and health?

  A It was unreasonable even for an explorer.
    What does the phrase 'comes with the territory' in line 10 tell us?
  B It had become more intense with time.
    How long has Fiennes been 'fine-tuning' his body'?
  C It contributed to his collapse.
    Does the writer state this in the first paragraph?
  D It makes subsequent events hard to believe.
    What 'came as something of a surprise' to the writer?

2 On the question of who will live longest, it seems that

  A genetic make-up is the main factor.
  B there is no clear explanation why some people outlive others.
  C lifestyle choices play little part.
  D family history is not as significant as once thought.

3 According to the text, one of the positive effects of taking regular exercise is that it

  A speeds up the heart rate.
  B strengthens blood vessels.
  C quickens the pulse.
  D reduces heart exertion.

4 What does health expert Len Almond imply?

  A Our bodies can cope with intense physical stress.
  B We should allow a long period of recovery after any physical exercise.
  C There is more to learn about the effects of physical stress.
  D Taking part in endurance sports is harmful in the long term.

5 Experts in sports medicine have

  A studied the effects of altitude on various types of athletes.
  B questioned the wisdom of taking part in extreme sports.
  C found a common factor among competitors in extreme sports.
  D discovered an enzyme which causes heart attacks in cyclists.

6 What final conclusion about exercise does the writer reach?

  A It makes life more enjoyable.
  B It may not be worth the effort.
  C It should be done in moderation.
  D It ought to be a priority.

4 'It's not how long life is, but how good it is, that matters.' How far do you agree?

The *Guinness Book of World Records* describes Ranulph Fiennes as the world's greatest living explorer. His expeditions include the first polar circumnavigation of the Earth and the first unsupported crossing of the Antarctic continent on foot. He has been up the White Nile in a hovercraft, and parachuted onto Europe's highest glacier. An obsession with diet and fitness comes with the territory, and for years Fiennes has fine-tuned his body

vegetables and reduced levels of saturated fat helps prevent obesity and stops fatty deposits forming in the arteries and blocking them. Smoking, incidentally, has the opposite effect, as nicotine increases the heart rate and makes the blood clot more easily. Exercise is highly beneficial as it reduces both the pulse rate and blood pressure so minimising strain on the heart as it pumps blood round the body. It also helps

could have had an effect, or there may be genetic predisposition and an event could have made it worse,' says Almond. 'We haven't done enough research in this area.'

This is changing though. There is growing interest in sports medicine, a field that arguably began as long ago as 490BC when the first person to run the marathon ran the 26 miles from the town of Marathon to Athens with news of a

an unhealthy obsession

to cope with the most inhospitable of environments and the most stressful situations of physical hell. So when I read that this model of physical fitness had gone and suffered a heart attack – not while planting a flag in a no-man's-land, but while boarding a plane – it came as something of a surprise.

Given what happened, lesser mortals like myself might be forgiven for wondering whether the benefits of following a healthy lifestyle are all they're cracked up to be. Why bother exerting all that effort if in the end survival turns out to be a lottery? Of course fitness and diet are only part of the story. 'Some people live a healthy lifestyle and still succumb to heart problems,' health expert Alison Shaw explains. Genetics and family history also play a crucial role in determining who will achieve longevity. 'It could all be a question of genes', she says, 'but then some people never have a trace of the disease even though their family history would seem to make them prime targets.'

Whether or not some people are genetically programmed to have a higher chance of heart disease, there are steps they can take to reduce their risks. A healthy diet with plenty of fruit and

to keep the artery walls more elastic. 'Whether you've got a family history of heart disease or not, everybody should be living a healthy lifestyle,' Shaw says. 'We wouldn't want people to stop looking after themselves.'

But can you look after yourself too much? On the subject of exercise, the standard recommendation is to take five sessions of 'moderate' exercise a week, where moderate is a little more than brisk walking. 'We need to be very careful when we're doing extreme sports or endurance events,' says health expert Len Almond. 'Extreme physical stress can impose almost impossible demands on the body's ability to recover. The strain of endurance events such as exploration force biochemical changes in the human body. The physiological response to that kind of activity will be extreme … and how the body overcomes that is bound to leave some kind of legacy.' So could Fiennes' love for exploration and endurance events have contributed to his condition? 'It

victory over the Persians. The man, a soldier called Pheidippides, collapsed as soon as he arrived, and the cause of his sudden demise is not known. However, scientists are using athletes like him to answer questions about the effects of extreme exercise on the heart. One group, at the University of Innsbruck in Austria, studied cyclists taking part in a race called the Tyrolean Otztaler Radmarathon, a one-day event that covers 230km with an altitude change of 5,500m. They were interested in one particular enzyme, high concentrations of which are found in those who have suffered a heart attack. The scientists found that levels of this chemical increased in 13 of the 38 cyclists who completed the race. The largest increases were seen in the youngest, fastest cyclists who had trained the hardest. Similar increases in the chemical have been found in competitors in the Hawaii Ironman triathlon and in cross-country skiers.

Most of us will never put our bodies to such severe tests. But if when you hear about someone like Fiennes you ask whether exercise is worth it, I advise you to consider your own priorities. Personally, I subscribe to this adage sent in by a reader to a local newspaper: 'Run not to add years to your life but to add life to your years.'

Vocabulary

Health and fitness

1 Put the parts of the body in a–p under the appropriate headings.

a thigh	e rib	i hip	m ankle
b elbow	f chin	j wrist	n calf
c shoulder	g skull	k palm	o cheek
d heel	h thumb	l waist	p shin

arm and hand	
leg and foot	
face and head	
torso	

2 Which of a–p in 1 can you harm in these ways?

a break/fracture   c sprain
b twist   d dislocate

3 Read the dictionary entry below for synonyms of *disease*. Use this information to complete sentences a–d.

> **Disease** is used to talk about more severe physical medical problems, especially those that affect the organs. **Illness** is used to talk about both more severe and more minor medical problems, and those that affect mental health: *heart/kidney/liver illness* ◊ *mental disease*. **Disease** is not used about a period of illness: *she died after a long disease*.
>
> **infection** an illness that is caused by bacteria or a virus and that affects one part of the body: *a throat infection*
>
> **condition** a medical problem that you have for a long time because it is not possible to cure it: *a heart condition*
>
> **ailment** (*rather formal*) an illness that is not very serious: *childhood ailments*
>
> **bug** (*informal*) an infectious illness that is usually fairly mild: *a nasty flu bug*

Oxford Advanced Learner's Dictionary, 8th edition

a There's a nasty *condition/bug* going round college. I had it last week, but I'm feeling much better now.

b My sister has always been prone to chest *infections/ailments* and seems to catch them quite often.

c Whilst there appears to be no cure for his heart *condition/infection*, he can still lead an active life.

d More *conditions/ailments* are reported during the winter months than at other times of the year.

Grammar

Direct and indirect speech   GR p173–175

1 Rewrite statements a–e as direct speech.

Example

Sailor Ellen MacArthur said she'd been preparing for her trip for months so she was feeling optimistic.

'I've been preparing for this trip for months so I'm feeling optimistic.'

a Critics said it was likely that the new Harry Potter film would break box-office records.

b My doctor told me I'd feel much better if I did some exercise.

c The manager told them they could all play in the final but that they had to attend all the practice sessions the next day.

d The boss told me that I didn't need to work over the weekend.

e My physiotherapist says my shoulder is responding well to treatment.

2 Use the sentences in 1 to help answer these questions about direct speech.

a What do you normally need to change when rewriting reported statements as direct speech?

b When do you not need to change the verb tense?

c Which modal verbs change form, and which stay the same?

3 Choose the most appropriate reporting verb to complete the sentences in a–h as shown.

admit	boast	complain	explain
mention	protest	realise	warn

a 'This beach isn't safe for swimming off today.'
   One of the lifeguards .... us that ...

b 'Oh no! I've left the car keys in that café.'
   John suddenly .... that ...

c 'By the way, Alice and I are thinking of trading in our motorbike and buying a car.'
   My brother .... that ...

d 'The reason I want this job so much is because it will allow me to travel.'
   At his interview he .... that ...

e 'Yes, it's true. I've been lying.'
   The prime suspect .... that ...

f 'I'm a million times better than anyone else in the team.'
   Our club's top scorer .... that ...

g 'It's ridiculous – there's never anyone at the reception desk when you need them.'
Some of the hotel guests .... that …

h 'But honestly, I really didn't cause the accident!'
The driver .... that …

4 Correct any mistakes in the reported questions in a–g.

a Reporters asked the climber how long had he been training to climb Everest.
b Fans wanted to know whether Kylie is playing at last night's concert.
c In the interview Fiona was asked had she ever worked abroad.
d Our neighbours were keen to find out when were we going on holiday.
e Union leaders enquired whether the deal would go ahead or not.
f The taxi driver asked would I like a hand with my luggage.
g Mum wanted to know did the postman deliver the package she'd been expecting.

5 For a–g circle the word in italics which correctly completes the sentence.

a My boss *suggested/begged* me to reconsider.
b Health experts *advise/recommend* us to eat five portions of fresh fruit or vegetables daily.
c The celebrity model has *denied/refused* selling her story to the press.
d Haven't your parents ever *forbidden/warned* you not to do something?
e Are you *proposing/threatening* going to the police about this?
f Your boss shouldn't *ask/promise* you to do something that's impossible!
g Sergeant Smith *ordered/reminded* his soldiers that they had to polish their boots every day.

6 Rewrite the sentences in 5 using the word in italics not circled.

7 Complete a–e with your own ideas.

a Parents should always warn teenagers …
b Recently, my friend foolishly suggested …
c Politicians always promise …
d My dad once threatened …
e I usually need to be reminded …

8 Complete sentences a–f, using one of the prepositions below and an appropriate gerund.

| on | from | of | for |

a Staff are blaming one of the pupils …
b Maria accused her boyfriend …
c Bystanders praised the heroic firefighter …
d The accident wouldn't have happened if you hadn't insisted …
e An effective way of discouraging children …
f The millionaire footballer has apologised …

9 Underline the correct structure in a–f from the pairs in italics.

a My mother suggested *my friends and I going/that my friends and I should get* away for the day.
b Enrico rang and asked if *we were going/we are going* to last night's birthday celebrations.
c I was shocked when the policeman accused me *to shoplift/of shoplifting*.
d Mark wanted to know what *was I planning/I was planning* after work.
e His wife proposed *they go out/them to go out* for dinner.
f Terrorists threatened *blowing up/to blow up* major government buildings.

Listening   Part 1 Short extracts

1   Discuss these questions which relate to the extracts in 2.

   a   How can poor eyesight be improved?
   b   How can you ensure a good night's sleep?
   c   What techniques can help your memory?

2   🎧 Read questions 1–6 below before you listen to the three different extracts. Then listen and choose the best answer (A, B or C) for each question.

Extract one
You hear part of an interview with a health expert.

1   What does the interviewer say happens to people after a bad night's sleep?
   A   They wake up feeling exhausted.
   B   They often sleep badly the next night as well.
   C   They lack energy later on in the day.
2   Some children fail to sleep well because they
   A   use their computer too much.
   B   read for too long before going to sleep.
   C   have too many late nights.

Extract two
You hear two people talking about how to improve brain power.

3   What do they disagree about?
   A   whether the size of the brain can be increased
   B   how easy it is for some people to forget things
   C   the usefulness of doing activities like crosswords
4   What does the woman suggest the man can do to improve his brain power?
   A   take some physical exercise once a week
   B   try to think more about what he's doing
   C   take up a hobby like dancing

Extract three
You hear a doctor and a patient talking about laser eye surgery.

5   How does the doctor feel about laser eye surgery?
   A   It has had a very low success rate to date.
   B   It works better if your eyesight is very poor.
   C   It has dramatically changed the treatment of poor eyesight.
6   What warning does the doctor give the patient?
   A   Even after surgery, eyesight will still get worse with age.
   B   He may never be able to wear ordinary glasses again.
   C   An experienced eye surgeon could still make mistakes.

Speaking   Parts 3 and 4

1   Imagine the photos opposite appear on a government leaflet. Discuss with a partner:
   a   what the leaflet might be about.
   b   what the exam task might be.

2   🎧 Listen to the exam task and write the two questions in the box below. How does it compare with your ideas in 1?

> • ....
> • ....

3   Read some of the things two students said when doing the task in 2, and correct any mistakes.
   a   I'm thinking she's just about getting on her bike. It's a healthy activity.
   b   How about this one in a café – in the No Smoking area? I'm sure the message is seeming clear in this one, don't you?
   c   This picture might be encourage students to eat healthy food. The food is looking quite tempting, isn't it?
   d   And here, they're being in a gym. This should encourage people taking more exercise.
   e   This picture of visit a dentist gives an important message to young people.
   f   She seems to be drink mineral water. It's vital drinking water when you exercise.
   g   So are we agree that this picture would be the best for the cover of the leaflet?

4   With a partner, do the task in 2, then tell another pair of students which photo you chose and why.

5   Answer these Part 4 questions, using the prompts and how to do it box to help you.
   a   How else can you keep fit and healthy? (What do your friends or family do?)
   b   Should smoking be banned in all public places? (How would you feel as a a smoker and a non-smoker?)
   c   Some people say that fast food restaurants promote an unhealthy diet. Do you agree? (Don't be afraid to say if you don't agree, but explain why.)

how to do it

- Quickly correct any mistakes, but don't interrupt your flow of talking.
- Don't give one-word answers; try to develop the discussion as much as possible.

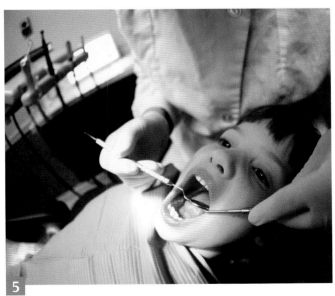

Use of English Part 3 Word formation

1 Read the text quickly, ignoring the gaps, and choose the best heading (a, b, or c).

    a Life-threatening illnesses.
    b Looking after your health.
    c A disease we can avoid.

2 Read the text again carefully and decide which part of speech belongs in each gap. Check your ideas with the tip box opposite, then complete gaps 1–10 with words formed from those below.

> **tip**
>
> The 10 missing answers in this text include
> - two plural nouns
> - two singular nouns
> - one adverb
> - three adjectives
> - two adjectives with a prefix

Rising temperatures and a hotter climate? Well, if you are 0 ....unfortunate.... enough to live in a country with a 1 .... climate, it sounds great, doesn't it? But there is a dark side. This climate might bring with it visitors of a particularly 2 .... kind – anopheles mosquitoes, 3 .... of malaria. Despite the fact that no one has caught malaria from a British mosquito for several decades, 4 .... believe that this tropical disease may become more widespread.

It seems that malaria in our modern world would be much more endemic if any 5 .... by the authorities were to occur. The disease breeds in countries with particular 6 .... conditions. Nevertheless, there are many parts of the world where malaria would exist were it not for 7 .... by the authorities to keep it in check and prevent it from spreading. In spite of their warm climate, places such as Italy and Spain do not have problems with malaria because they have 8 .... managed their medical resources. It is important to remember that malaria is not an 9 .... disease providing it is dealt with promptly. So if you should come back from the tropics feeling ill, it is essential to receive medical 10 .... as quickly as possible.

0 FORTUNE	3 CARRY	6 ENVIRONMENT	9 CURE
1 MISERY	4 SCIENCE	7 INTERVENE	10 TREAT
2 HAZARD	5 MANAGE	8 EXPERT	

Vocabulary Word formation (1)

1 Change the form of the words in bold to complete the second sentence in a–d.

  a Jane's work is always **perfect**.
     Jane is a ....

  b I don't really **believe** in alternative medicine.
     I'm not a strong .... in alternative medicine.

  c The college has to **provide** career advice.
     The college is responsible for the .... of career advice.

  d You are required to **attend** the event.
     Your .... at the event is compulsory.

2 Fill in the missing parts of speech in the table below. There may be more than one possible answer.

	verb	noun (thing)	noun (person)	adjective	adverb
a		product			
b			perfectionist		
c			authority		
d	———	medicine			
e	provide			———	———
f		management			
g	believe				
h	———		expert		
i	———	fortune	———		
j	attend			———	———

3 Look up *product* and *perfect* in your dictionary. How does the word stress change with the different parts of speech?

4 Write adjectives ending in *-able* to match definitions a–h.

  a for _ _ _ _ _ _ _ _ (something you're unlikely to remember)
  b avo _ _ _ _ _ _ (something you can prevent)
  c tol _ _ _ _ _ _ (something you can bear)
  d acc _ _ _ _ _ _ _ (something satisfactory)
  e des _ _ _ _ _ _ (something wanted)
  f pre _ _ _ _ _ _ _ _ (something you are sure will happen)
  g agr _ _ _ _ _ _ (something pleasant)
  h ex _ _ _ _ _ _ _ _ (something you can explain)

5 Add prefixes to the words in 4 to give an opposite meaning, then use the words to talk about things that have recently happened to you.

Writing   Part 1 A letter WG p155

1 Read the writing task below and correct these statements.

    a You must write a memo to the manager of your fitness club.
    b You should only comment on the negative aspects of the visit.
    c You should say how the brochure could be improved.

> While studying in New Zealand you recently visited a health spa with your local fitness club. The visit was not as good as you expected. Read the brochure for the spa on which you have made some comments. Then write a letter of 180–220 words to the manager saying what was successful about the visit, and what wasn't, and including some suggestions for improvements.

LAKELAND SPA

ACCOMMODATION

All <u>rooms</u> are ensuite.

nice – good size and clean

CLOTHING AND EQUIPMENT

Please bring swimwear and appropriate clothing for any of the activities you wish to do. Our shop has <u>a range of clothing</u> for sale.

only small sizes   *very expensive!*

WHAT'S ON OFFER

Activities include exercise sessions in the gym and pool, aerobics and yoga classes. Just <u>sign up for one of the groups</u> on arrival. We also offer a range of therapies.

most groups full

EVENING ACTIVITIES

A <u>range of talks</u> on ways to improve your lifestyle as well as health and beauty demonstrations.

great – really helpful!

2 Discuss which of a–c in 1–4 gives the best advice for writing the exam task.

1 a Use the handwritten notes as examples but include only your own ideas.
  b Include all the input information.
  c Choose one or two of the handwritten notes, then comment on other parts of the brochure.

2 a Never use any of the words from the input information.
  b Copy long phrases from the input information.
  c Rephrase the information in your own words where possible.

3 a Write an informal letter.
  b Write a formal letter.
  c Write either a formal or informal letter as you prefer.

4 a Put all the points in a bulleted list.
  b Start a new paragraph for each separate point.
  c Group the points into suitable paragraphs.

3 Read the brochure with your added comments on page 66, then make notes on the positive and negative aspects of your visit.

Example

positive: *rooms nice, very big and clean*
negative: *clothes very expensive, limited range of sizes in stock*

4 Next to the negative aspects, write notes suggesting improvements.

Example

clothes very expensive – lower your prices

5 Expand your notes from 3 and 4 into full sentences using your own words.

Examples

We were pleased with our rooms which were extremely clean and spacious.

Perhaps you should consider lowering the prices in your shop and restocking more frequently.

6 Decide which of a–g would not be suitable to include in your introduction or conclusion and why.

a Dear Spa Manager
b I am writing with regard to the visit we made to Lakeland Spa last month.
c Don't worry, some aspects of your spa are all right.
d These were the positive aspects of our stay, but unfortunately there were some negatives too.
e The price of clothes and equipment in the shop is crazy.
f You must devise a better booking system.
g I hope this information will be of assistance.

7 Organise your notes into four paragraphs as below, then write your letter.

• introduction explaining why you are writing
• what was good about your visit
• what wasn't good and how things could be improved
• conclusion saying what you hope your letter will achieve

Review

1 Match parts of the body a–h with explanations 1–8.

a rib   d skull   g waist
b chin   e cheek   h shin
c wrist   f thumb

1 the bony casing that protects the brain
2 the joint that gives flexibility to the hand
3 the narrower middle part of the human figure
4 young children often suck this
5 used as a verb with 'up' it means 'climb quickly'
6 the fleshy part at the front of the jaw
7 parts of the face that blush if you are embarrassed
8 one of the curved bones that protect the lungs

2 Complete sentences a–h with suitable words in the correct form.

a Most of the children in school were off last week with a nasty stomach ....
b The lead singer had picked up a chest ...., so the opera had to be cancelled at the last minute.
c I fell down some steps and .... my ankle. Now I can hardly walk, it's so painful!
d The team's top striker will be out of action for weeks because of his .... leg.
e Lung .... is one of the major health risks associated with smoking..
f One of the Olympic gymnasts .... her shoulder in a fall and had to have it put back into place.
g If you suffer from a heart .... you should not take this medicine.
h Although the top tennis seed's wrist wasn't broken, it was so badly .... that she had to withdraw from the championship.

3 Use words 1–8 below in the correct form to complete sentences a–h.

1 survive   4 predict   7 threat
2 mechanic   5 technology   8 prevent
3 manage   6 intervene

a It's true to say of most illnesses that .... is better than cure.
b .... in the affairs of others is usually inadvisable.
c I'm afraid I'm not ....-minded enough to be able to fix the DVD player!
d Several supporters of the visiting football team were arrested for .... behaviour.
e Do you think this amount of work is .... in such a short space of time?
f Although the ship sank without trace, a rescue boat managed to pick up all the ....
g What are your .... for the next general election? Who would you say is going to win?
h My motorbike's at the garage as it's recently developed a serious .... fault.

4 Read this newspaper extract about a demonstration, then replace the words in brackets with adjectives ending in *able*.

> Yesterday's mass demonstration was 1 (likely to be remembered) .... for many reasons. The large turnout was 2 (not a surprise) .... and the atmosphere could be described as 3 (pleasant) .... at the start of the day, with the level of policing 4 (satisfactory) .... Unfortunately, for some 5 (impossible to explain) .... reason, events took a turn for the worse. Violence previously thought to have been 6 (possible to prevent) .... broke out and several incidents of vandalism took place which local residents found 7 (impossible to put up with) .... It was therefore considered 8 (wanted) .... to bring the demonstration to a halt before it reached its intended destination.

Would you believe it?

Lead in

1 Discuss whether these statements are true or false. The answers are on page 154.

a To see a full-length reflection of yourself in a mirror, it must be at least half as tall as you.

b The word 'news' is formed from the first letters of north, south, east and west.

c Of any group of 23 people, there is a 50% possibility that two of them will share a birthday.

d Chewing gum takes seven years to pass through the digestive system.

e The number of people alive today is greater than the number of people who have previously lived and died.

f Eating celery makes you lose weight.

2 Complete these sentences with *true* or *false*.

a I hope all your wishes come ....

b The tourist brochure had given a .... impression of the resort; our hotel was only half built.

c Obtaining money under .... pretences is a criminal offence.

d I'm sure something fishy's going on – Tim's explanation just doesn't ring ....

e The newspaper was sued for making accusations that weren't strictly ....

f Buying a cheap car is usually a .... economy, as you often end up spending more on it than you paid in the first place.

g Winning the lottery is a dream come .... for some and a nightmare for others.

h Installing smoke alarms can give a .... sense of security, as people forget to check them regularly.

3 Discuss the following.

a What things did you believe as a child that you now know aren't true?

b Do you wish any of them were true?

c Are there any you're glad aren't true?

d Is it right to let children believe things that aren't true?

Reading Part 4 Multiple matching

1 Match the 'superheroes' shown with the text headings A–E and name their special abilities. Quickly read the text to check your ideas.

2 Read the text again and the tip boxes. In which section (A–E) are 1–12 mentioned? The underlined words will help you find links to A–E.

a <u>substance</u> that <u>speeds up</u> a natural process	1 ….
a <u>substance</u> that <u>looks weaker</u> than it is	2 ….
a <u>system</u> that makes up for <u>limited vision</u>	3 ….
<u>someone</u> who takes refuge <u>away from his home</u>	4 …. 5 ….
a <u>substance</u> that enables <u>creatures</u> to <u>secure themselves</u> in place	6 ….
a <u>selfless act</u> with unforeseen consequences	7 …. 8 ….
<u>someone</u> given a <u>new identity</u> from a <u>young age</u>	9 ….
a <u>creature</u> that hides itself by <u>changing the way it looks</u>	10 ….
<u>someone</u> whose powers are the principle behind a <u>form of transport</u>	11 ….
<u>substances</u> that make physical <u>discomfort</u> <u>less noticeable</u> to the sufferer	12 ….

3 If you had the capability to do <u>one</u> of these things, which would you choose and why?

> **tip**
> Remember that there will be 15 questions in the exam.

> **tip**
> Remember that concentrating on one section at a time will be quicker than reading A–E for every question.

- become invisible at will
- fly
- see in the dark
- breathe underwater
- change your appearance at will

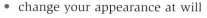

A SPIDER-MAN

Spider-Man acquired his superhuman abilities when, during a demonstration of radiation technology, a spider crept into the beam of radiation and bit his hand. As Peter Parker he works as a photographer for the Daily Bugle, but as Spider-Man he
5 fights evil in the dangerous, crime-ridden streets of New York. Spider-Man shoots and spins webs from small jets attached to his wrists and can stick to almost any surface, scaling skyscrapers with his bare hands. So how far can real science go in explaining his powers? Like our superhero, spiders can
10 adhere to almost any surface. Many do this by secreting sticky silk onto their feet, which anchors them in position. Others have millions of specially shaped microscopic hairs on their legs, that slip into nooks and crannies. As for Spider-Man's traps, anyone who has ever walked into a spider's
15 web knows that the silk is deceptively strong, despite its gossamer appearance. Dragline silk, which spiders use to crawl down from ceiling to floor, is the strongest of all; weight for weight it is actually
20 stronger than steel.

B SUPERMAN

As a child, Superman was forced to flee his doomed planet, Krypton, eventually landing on Earth where he was adopted under the name Clark Kent. He now works as a mild-mannered newspaper reporter but whenever danger calls, he's only a
25 quick-change away from saving the world … as Superman. He is faster than a speeding bullet, can fly, has superhuman strength, can leap tall buildings in a single bound and has X-ray vision. Superman's cells convert the sun's energy into incredible superpowers – but can scientific fact explain this? While animals
30 have to eat plants (or each other) to survive, plants can harvest their energy directly from the sun's light by photosynthesis, the chemical reaction that converts carbon dioxide and water into glucose and oxygen. Plants are full of a chemical called chlorophyll that accelerates this reaction. It is perhaps the most
35 important molecule in the world, because it traps all of the energy we need to live, storing it inside plants until the energy is released inside our bodies after eating. So perhaps Superman is using some form of photosynthesis to build up the tremendous reserves of energy that he needs for his superhuman feats
40 of strength. One thing's for sure – he's not using chlorophyll, because it would turn him bright green!

C DAREDEVIL

When Matt Murdoch saved a man from being hit by a truck, some of the radioactive waste inside it spilled into Matt's eyes, blinding him permanently. But Matt's other senses became more acute. He developed a radar sense, allowing him to 'see' the world   45 around him. He could smell the faintest odour or even 'read' a newspaper just by touching the print. After training as a lawyer, Matthew set up in practice and discovered that his new powers enabled him to tell when suspects are lying by listening to their heartbeat. When unable to bring criminals to justice by legal   50 means, Matt becomes Daredevil, employing his superpowers to help him. So is there any basis in real science for his fictional powers? Radar resembles sonar, which is used by dolphins and bats to construct an image of their surroundings. By emitting a high-pitched sound and listening for the echo as it bounces off an   55 object, they can tell how far away the object is, what it is made of, and how fast it is moving. But what about Daredevil's other senses? Scientists know that if the part of the brain responsible for seeing is underused, it may take over the processing of information from other senses, particularly hearing. This could   60 explain why blind people are good at judging where people are in a room just by listening to their breathing or the echoes produced by a voice.

heroes

D MAGNETO

Hunted by the X-Men, Magneto was born a
65 mutant in a world that feared and despised his kind. In response he isolated himself from humanity on Asteroid M, preparing for the time when mutants would rule the Earth. Magneto can create electromagnetic fields and
70 control them so that he can levitate all objects made of metal, project forcefields, and generate electricity. So can science explain his abilities? Iron and steel are magnetic, and are attracted to either the north or south poles of a
75 magnet. Electromagnets are used to make trains that float over the rails; these are easier to move forward than a conventional train, which loses a lot of energy through friction between
80 the rails and wheels. Most materials, including water, are 'diamagnetic', meaning that they are always repelled by both magnetic poles. Since animals are mostly water, scientists have found that if they use a strong
85 enough magnetic field, they could levitate a live frog without hurting it at all.

E THE INCREDIBLE HULK

As a nuclear physicist, Bruce Banner developed a new gamma bomb for the military. When a reckless teenager strayed onto the bomb test site, Banner saved him – but was caught in the middle himself and transformed into a   90 huge green monster, enormously strong and driven by fury. When angry, Banner now changes into the Hulk, acquiring superhuman strength – and turning green – but with decreased intelligence and an inability to control his temper. At times of stress, humans do   95 sometimes perform great feats of strength. This may be caused by the release of certain hormones into the body which boost the levels of oxygen and fuel available to muscles. Over time, they can even increase muscle   100 bulk. Other natural chemicals can mask the pain that over-stretching muscles may cause, allowing individuals to push their body beyond its natural limits. The Hulk's colour changes may be   105 related to the way animals use colour cells to alter their appearance; the cuttlefish uses this for camouflage, and may even be able to communicate using waves of colour.

Vocabulary

Verbs of moving and looking

1 Decide which word in each group a–e is not a verb of movement.

    a creep   glance   stumble
    b hobble   totter   gaze
    c limp   plod   glimpse
    d glare   stagger   limp
    e peep   trip   crawl

2 Which verbs of movements in 1 have similar meanings? Choose the best verbs to complete a-e below.

    a It was such a low tunnel that we had to .... on our hands and knees.
    b We got completely lost on our walk and had to .... through lots of wet, muddy fields.
    c I got home after midnight and slowly .... upstairs so I wouldn't disturb anyone.
    d Despite .... slightly after the first fence, the horse quickly recovered and won the race.
    e My mother is extremely prone to accidents and is always .... over things.

3 Read the dictionary entries for synonyms of *look*. Which verbs of looking from 1 are being defined?

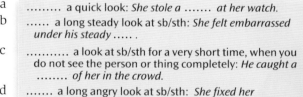

    a .... a quick look: *She stole a .... at her watch.*
    b ...... a long steady look at sb/sth: *She felt embarrassed under his steady ..... .*
    c .... a look at sb/sth for a very short time, when you do not see the person or thing completely: *He caught a .... of her in the crowd.*
    d .... a long angry look at sb/sth: *She fixed her questioner with a hostile ..... .*

Oxford Advanced Learner's Dictionary, 8th edition

Grammar

Modals GR p175–176

1 Underline the modal verbs in a–g and match them with their functions 1–7 below.

    a I could ride a bike by the time I was five years old.
    b Passports must be shown at the border.
    c We might arrive in time for the conference, but I doubt it.
    d The stewardess said we can unfasten our seat belts now.
    e You should put on overalls if you plan to paint the bedroom.
    f We don't need to get a visa to visit France.
    g Clare must be allergic to bananas – they always bring her out in a rash.

    1 obligation   5 possibility
    2 absence of obligation   6 ability
    3 permission   7 strong advice
    4 assumption/deduction

2 Look at the picture and decide whether the assumptions and deductions in a–g on page 73 are justified, giving reasons. Then make other deductions from the clues in the picture.

Example

The owners of the house can't be well-off. ✗
The owners of the house must be well-off because they've got a safe.

a The safe can't be burglar-proof.
b The burglars must have had a key for the flat.
c A neighbour might have called the police.
d There could have been more than one burglar.
e The burglars can't have taken any valuables.
f The police might have found a clue.
g The owners couldn't have gone out for the evening.

3 Use modal verbs of assumption or deduction, and the verbs in brackets, to complete the dialogue.

A: Oh no! I put my bag down by the door and it's gone! Someone .... (1 steal) it!
B: Don't be ridiculous. There's nobody here but us!
A: Yes, but we've been busy talking. Someone .... (2 come) in quietly, picked it up, and slipped out with it. It's possible, you know.
B: Are you sure you didn't leave it on the bus? I saw you put it down on the seat next to you. You .... (3 leave) it behind when you got off.
A: No, I .... (4 do), because I remember looking in it on the way here. I wanted to check I'd got my mobile.
B: Well, it's not here now.
A: Oh dear, I .... (5 be) more careful with it, I know. Thank goodness there wasn't much in it.
B: That's a relief! Let's just check at the police station anyway. You never know, someone .... (6 hand) it in there.

4 Complete a–g with an appropriate form of *can/able to*.

a Sorry I .... get out to meet you last night but I had to babysit for some friends.
b One day, we .... cure many common illnesses.
c It took a lot of work but in the end the mechanic .... get the car going.
d I .... go ice-skating for the past few weeks because I've injured my leg.
e Tom .... come to the phone at the moment but I'll take a message if you like.
f A child genius, he .... solve difficult fractions by the time he was three years old.
g I love .... stay in bed on Sunday mornings.

5 Complete a–f with an appropriate form of *don't need to* or *needn't* and the verb in brackets.

a Look, there's no one else on the tennis courts. We .... (bother) to book one in advance.
b Apparently there are still plenty of tickets left for this year's festival so we .... (worry) about getting hold of some.
c My work colleagues kindly took me out to dinner to celebrate my promotion and I .... (pay) a penny.
d My husband and I bought a dishwasher yesterday, so we .... (do) the washing-up ever again!
e You .... (apply) for a visa to travel round this country, as far as I know.
f It was much too cold to go swimming when I was on holiday so I .... (pack) my bikini after all.

6 Correct the modal verbs in these sentences.

a Surely you mustn't be retiring this year? You look so young!
b You mustn't make up your mind about the job offer yet if you don't want to.
c How lovely to see you Bill! And this should be your wife Betty?
d After many failed attempts, they could rescue the trapped miners.
e I've just seen the weather forecast and it could not be warm enough for a barbecue after all.

7 Match modals a–e with their meanings 1–5. Then explain to a partner the rules of the game or sport you know well, using a–e.

a You don't have to/need to …
b You shouldn't …
c Everyone has to …
d You ought to …
e You mustn't …

1 It's forbidden to do it.
2 The rules say so.
3 It isn't necessary to do it.
4 It's advisable to do it.
5 It isn't advisable to do it.

Listening Part 4 Multiple matching

1 Who would you include in a top five of today's best live performers? Discuss your choices.

2 🎧 Listen to part of a radio programme about a pop group to find out:

a   why Frank Farian was impressed by Rob and Fab.
b   what happened to Rob and Fab with Farian's help.
c   what Rob and Fab's secret was.
d   how their secret was exposed.
e   how the music world reacted.

3 🎧 You will hear five short extracts in which people are talking about pop stars miming or 'lip-synching'. While you listen, complete tasks 1 and 2 below. The tip box will help you.

> **tip**
>
> Remember that questions 1–5 and 6–10 refer to the <u>same</u> five speakers, so scan across the questions while you listen.

TASK ONE

For questions 1–5, choose from the list A–H what each speaker feels about the music industry today.

A   The only thing that matters nowadays is talent.
B   The industry creates music that follows what's fashionable.
C   Tickets for live shows should be offered to fans first.
D   The industry's too concerned about what artists look like.
E   It's not only professionals who can perform well.
F   It's a pity that a lot of talent is going to waste.
G   It's not always easy to obtain tickets for live concerts.
H   Many singers are second-rate live performers.

Speaker 1 ☐ 1
Speaker 2 ☐ 2
Speaker 3 ☐ 3
Speaker 4 ☐ 4
Speaker 5 ☐ 5

TASK TWO

For questions 6–10, choose from the list A–H each speaker's attitude towards artists lip-synching.

A   It would be unwise for some performers not to lip-synch.
B   No professional musician should need to lip-synch.
C   Most singers who lip-synch simply look awkward.
D   It's better to watch a recorded performance than artists lip-synching.
E   The press should give more coverage to the fact that artists lip-synch.
F   Lip-synching is acceptable if you know it's going to happen.
G   Lyrics aren't important any more so it doesn't matter if artists lip-synch.
H   If artists lip-synch, this is an insult to the audience.

Speaker 1 ☐ 6
Speaker 2 ☐ 7
Speaker 3 ☐ 8
Speaker 4 ☐ 9
Speaker 5 ☐ 10

4 Do you think artists should ever lip-synch?

Speaking Part 2

1 Match phrases a–e with the photos.

a (in) fancy dress   d (in) costume
b make-believe   e dressed up as
c putting on

2 Which of the people in the photos might be experiencing these feelings? Explain why.

- excited at the thought of something
- lost in a world of their own
- committed to what they are doing
- apprehensive about what might happen
- self-conscious about their appearance

3 With a partner, each choose a pair of photos to compare. Talk for a minute each about why the people have changed their appearance in these ways, and how they might be feeling.

4 Look at your partner's photos and tell your partner, in no more than 30 seconds, which change of appearance is the most necessary.

> **tip**
> For a follow-up question like 4, refer to the photo you have chosen and give a brief explanation for your choice.

Making decisions and giving reasons

I'd go for this one because …
It has to be this one because …
Definitely this one because there …
It's difficult to decide between these two, but …
I'm torn between them, but …

Use of English · Part 1 · Multiple-choice cloze

1 Discuss any tricks you have played on someone, or any good ones you have heard about.

2 Read the newspaper article below quickly, ignoring the gaps, to find out what trick a fast food chain played and who was fooled by it.

THE LEFT-HANDED BURGER

A well-known fast food chain recently published a full-page advertisement announcing that they were 0 ....B..... a new item to their menu – a 'Left-Handed Burger', 1 .... specifically for their left-handed customers. 2 .... to the advertisement, the 3 .... of the new burger were identical to those of the original burger, 4 .... were the ingredients. The difference was that the ingredients had been rotated by 180 degrees to 5 .... left-handed people to handle the burger without 6 ....

The following day, April 2nd, the fast food store 7 .... that the story had been invented as an April Fool's trick and the left-handed burger didn't exist. 8 .... , restaurants reported that they had been visited by several thousand customers 9 .... the new burger. Simultaneously, there were many other 10 .... customers who insisted that staff served them with their own right-handed 11 .... It just goes to show how readily people can be 12 .... , even on April Fool's Day.

3 Decide which answer (A, B, C or D) best fits each gap in the text in 2.

0	A establishing	B introducing	C initiating	D organising
1	A created	B imagined	C projected	D generated
2	A Relative	B Appropriate	C Corresponding	D According
3	A dimensions	B measures	C quantities	D portions
4	A while	B as	C since	D because
5	A enlist	B endure	C entitle	D enable
6	A difficulty	B issues	C problem	D damages
7	A conflicted	B confessed	C confided	D conformed
8	A Although	B Nevertheless	C Despite	D Whilst
9	A requesting	B calling	C attracting	D appealing
10	A involved	B concerned	C attentive	D disturbed
11	A figure	B form	C version	D adaptation
12	A trapped	B disappointed	C betrayed	D deceived

Part 5 Key word transformations

4 Match phrases a–d with the similar meanings in 1–4.

a to be taken in by someone
b to come up with (an idea)
c to get hold of (something)
d no point

1 not necessary
2 obtain
3 be deceived
4 invent

5 Rewrite the second sentence in a–d keeping the meaning the same. Use three to six words including the word given. Your answers from 4 will help you.

a Do you know whose invention this gadget was?
CAME
I wonder .... the idea for this gadget.

b Have you any idea where I can obtain a cheap, second-hand car?
HOLD
Where .... a cheap, second-hand car?

c I don't see why it's necessary to work so hard.
POINT
There .... so hard.

d Bob deceived me with his promises to invest capital in the business.
TAKEN
I .... Bob's promises to invest capital in the business.

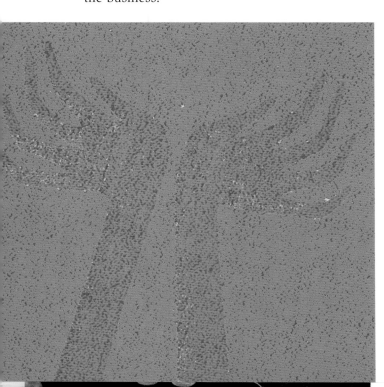

Vocabulary

Expressions with *right* and *left*

1 Choose the best explanation for the expressions with *right* in a–g below.

a I thought that film we saw last night was really violent.
Too right – not my kind of film at all.
(I completely agree/I think you're being unfair)

b John's just popped out to get a paper but he'll *be right back*.
(return eventually/return soon)

c *By rights* the children should be in bed by now.
(according to what is proper/only if necessary)

d The company started distributing advertisements for their products *left, right and centre*. (in three locations/everywhere)

e My colleagues in my new job were so friendly that I felt at home *right away*. (completely/immediately)

f Apparently our new manager is very friendly – if you manage to *get on the right side* of him! (get him to realise you exist/get him to like you)

g Paul didn't need to apologise because he knew he *was in the right*.
(gets answers right/has justice on his side)

2 Match the expressions with *left* with the most suitable sentence in 1–4 and discuss their meaning.

a The *left-luggage office* is on platform 3.
b David's *got two left feet*!
c There were a lot of *leftovers* from our meal.
d Sam *doesn't know his left from his right*.

1 So I don't need to cook anything new tonight.
2 He's the worst dancer I've ever seen.
3 We can leave our suitcases there.
4 That's why he's no good at giving directions.

3 Look up *left* and *right* in your dictionary. Which one has more idioms? How many new words can you find that derive from each one?

Review

1 Rewrite the second sentence in a–c keeping the meaning the same. Use three to six words including the word given.

a No one believed the accused's explanations about the illegal merchandise during the trial.
RING
The accused's explanations about the illegal merchandise .... to anyone during the trial.

b Tom deceived Sally when he married her as he already had a wife.
PRETENCES
Tom married Sally .... as he already had a wife.

c Buying poorer quality products at lower prices is not financially sensible.
FALSE
It is a .... poorer quality products at lower prices.

2 Circle the verb which matches the definitions in a–d.

a plod   limp   trip   = walk slowly with heavy steps
b totter   stagger   creep   = walk in an unsteady way
c hobble   stumble   crawl   = almost fall over
d glance   gaze   peep   = look steadily at

3 Match one of the words you did not circle in 2 to definitions a–e.

a look quickly then look away
b walk with difficulty when one leg hurts
c move on your hands and knees
d walk with difficulty when both legs hurt
e walk silently and slowly

4 Circle the correct preposition in each sentence.

a I remember being very self-conscious *with/ about/of* my appearance when I was young.
b If you want to succeed in life, you need to be committed *for/with/to* everything you do.
c What's the matter with Terry? He seems to be lost *in/for/to* a world of his own nowadays.
d Despite being understandably apprehensive *for/ of/about* her interview, it went off very well.
e The team were excited *with/for/at* the thought of meeting their opponents in the Cup Final.

5 Complete the comments in sentences 1–6 using a word or phrase with *right* or *left*.

1 A I don't suppose you know what's showing at the cinema this weekend?
  B I've no idea but I can find out ....

2 A I can't believe Tim hasn't passed his driving test yet.
  B It's no surprise to me, he doesn't know his .... from his .... !

3 A I'm sorry to hear that you were held responsible for the accident.
  B It was extremely unfair. I was definitely in .... and I intend to make an official complaint.

4 A What makes you think that Richard will never make a footballer?
  B Well, for a start, he's got two ....

5 A I'm starving. I don't suppose there's anything in the fridge to eat?
  B Only some .... from last night's supper, I'm afraid.

6 A How come you're working this Saturday?
  B .... I shouldn't have to work weekends at all, but I'm covering for a colleague.

6 Use the following link words to complete this text about the popularity of soap operas.

| although | after | on the other hand |
| despite | while | so that | as well as |

1 .... the fact that soaps come in for a lot of criticism, they remain one of the most popular forms of entertainment, 2 .... being moneyspinners for their producers. 3 .... , this does not necessarily mean that they are of a consistently high quality. Perhaps it is not quality but suspense that attracts so many ardent viewers. 4 .... being left on tenterhooks at the end of each episode, fans have no option but to tune in again next time 5 .... they can learn the characters' fate. In addition, 6 .... many people sneer at soaps, it is surprising how they enthusiastically participate in conversations based on their characters and storylines. The secret of their success may lie in the fact that fans identify with the characters 7 .... , at the same time, remaining detached from their trials and tribulations.

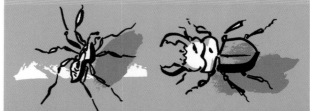

Traces of the past

Lead in

1 Look at the pictures and discuss these questions.

a Which periods of history are represented here?

b What do you know about each one? Think about the following aspects.

- art
- buildings
- medicine
- knowledge of the world
- technology
- writing and learning

c Where do we get our information about these different periods of history?

d What effect did these or other periods of history have on future generations? Use the phrases below to help you.

... led to ...
... resulted in ...
... was (directly) responsible for ...
... had an effect on ...
... was the source of ...

Reading Part 1 Themed texts

1 Look at photos a–c below and match them with the extracts opposite.

a

b

c

2 Read the extracts and choose the best answer (A, B, C or D) for questions 1–6. The tip box will help you.

tip

Use the question to decide 'how' to read, e.g. scan for specific detail (q.2) or understand a general opinion (q.4).

WANTED
ROMAN SOLDIERS!

Would you like to activate your understanding of the past? Then come and join us in The Roman Military Research Society. We are a research and re-enactment group and present living history displays of Roman life
05 at venues all over the country.

* As a member of our display team (males only) you will represent a Roman soldier of a Roman Legion. You will demonstrate the tactics, training, armour and equipment of the Roman army at public events.
10 Your duties will also include talking to members of the public, demonstrating equipment and eating authentically cooked Roman rations. You will speak Latin wherever possible and answer to a Roman name.

* Civilian members are both male and female. Like the
15 soldiers, they give information, answer questions and demonstrate the use of some of the items on display. These include aspects of domestic life or manufacturing and trade. Many of these provide opportunities for the public to gain 'hands-on'
20 experience under your guidance.

* Our society is a regular participant in films and television programmes. The society also runs weekend courses on Roman military life and many members give talks and presentations about various aspects of Roman history to
25 schools, colleges, clubs and societies.

WANT TO JOIN?

We are a welcoming and lively group with members from all over the world. Full Membership is £20 per annum for a family.

30 For those who wish to support the society's aims but who do not wish to participate in re-enactments, Associate Membership is available at £10 per annum.

1 What personal qualities are listed as necessary to become a soldier in this society?

A a qualification in Latin
B some previous military experience
C a willingness to deal with the public
D a moderate level of physical fitness

2 In order to take part in any of the display teams, you have to be

A a man.
B an Associate Member.
C a woman.
D a Full Member.

The first wave of humans moving across Eurasia consisted of Homo erectus, who left Africa almost
35 as soon as they emerged as a species. Over time these early humans further evolved into distinctive types, into Java man in Asia and Homo neanderthalensis in Europe. Neanderthals were nothing if not tough. For tens of thousands of years this early species of
40 hominid lived through conditions that no modern human outside a few polar scientists and explorers has experienced. During the worst of the ice ages, blizzards with hurricane-force winds were common. Temperatures routinely fell to minus
45 45 degrees Celsius. The Neanderthals naturally retreated from the worst of it, but even so they will have experienced weather that was at least as bad as a modern Siberian winter. They suffered, to be sure – but as a species they were magnificently
50 resilient and practically indestructible.

Then a smarter, lither species of creature – the ancestors of every one of us alive today – arose on the African plains and began to spread. For a long time, it was believed that the Cro-Magnons, as
55 modern humans in Europe became known, drove the Neanderthals before them as they advanced across the continent, eventually forcing them to the western margins of the continent, where they had no choice but to fall into the sea or go extinct.
60 In fact, it is now known that Cro-Magnons were in the far west of Europe at about the same time they were also coming in from the east. One curiosity of the Cro-Magnons' arrival is that it came at a time when Europe was plunging into yet another long
65 spell of punishing cold. Whatever it was that drew them to Europe, it wasn't the glorious weather.

Genealogy

INTRODUCTION

Genealogy is the study and tracing of family ancestries. This involves collecting the names of relatives, both living
70 and deceased, and establishing the relationships among them based on evidence and documentation. It can be a pleasantly addictive hobby or a professional undertaking.

RESEARCHING YOUR FAMILY HISTORY

Researching 'Family History' used to be regarded as
75 synonymous with genealogy, but it now applies to biographical research into one's ancestors – the aim being to produce a well-documented history of interest to family members and future generations. It involves putting flesh on the skeleton that is produced by
80 genealogy and considers the historical circumstances and geographical situation in which ancestors lived.

FIRST STEPS

When exploring family history it is advisable to work backwards from known information. Trying to work
85 forwards, e.g. seeking descendants of the famous historical figure that family legend claims as an ancestor, is rarely profitable. The best way to start is by consulting close relatives to establish basic facts, such as births, deaths and marriages. Collecting together family documents such as
90 letters and diaries will prove invaluable too.

SEARCHING THE ARCHIVES

Check published genealogies for a link to your family. However, do not put all your faith into a single lengthy document which apparently enables you to claim descent
95 from royalty (or a notorious criminal). Rather, take this as potentially valuable information whose accuracy you have to confirm carefully before you adopt it.

3 In the first paragraph, we learn that the Neanderthals were

A able to tolerate freezing conditions.
B part of a great number of species.
C accustomed to living in African regions.
D about to be defeated by the harsh environment.

4 The tone of the author's final comment is one of

A seriousness.
B appreciation.
C humour.
D disbelief.

5 According to the writer, 'Family History' differs from genealogy because it

A informs people about their descent from noteworthy figures.
B builds a detailed and thorough picture of the ancestors' situation.
C is a pastime rather than a serious academic study.
D means studying families for a longer time.

6 What advice is given about the process of exploring family history?

A avoid relying on information from relatives
B try not to feel too negative about your failures
C ensure your findings are well-supported
D only accept information from published genealogies

Vocabulary GR p182–183

Phrasal verbs with *off* and *in*

1 For each pair of sentences in 1–4, use the same verb, in the correct form, to make a phrasal verb with two different meanings.

1 a Even though we .... off relatively early, we still arrived extremely late.
  b When .... off fireworks, stand at arm's length and make sure children are supervised.

2 a After ten minutes trying to solve the puzzle, I .... in and looked at the solution.
  b The authorities refused to .... in to the ransom demand.

3 a Never .... off until tomorrow what you can do today.
  b Although he's really good-looking, I was completely .... off by his bad reputation.

4 a It's almost impossible for us to .... in statistics to do with our solar system.
  b His lies were so convincing that even his closest friends were .... in.

2 Match meanings a–h with the phrasal verbs as they are used in the eight sentences in 1.

a light   f make you dislike
b deceive   g agree to something
c postpone   you do not want
d understand   h admit defeat
e begin a journey

3 Use your dictionary to look up the different meanings of the phrasal verbs in a–d. Then complete the sentences appropriately.

a Our week in the mountains was ruined when .... *set in*.
b You wear a protective mask for this experiment as the chemicals used *give off* ....
c Although I specifically asked the hairdresser to *take off* just a few centimetres ....
d Whenever a member of staff leaves the firm, we all *put in* some money ....

Grammar

Participle clauses GR p177

1 Match the participle clauses in italics in a–f with functions 1–6.

a *Grown in the right conditions*, the plants will flower all summer.
b *Parking his car in a side road*, he strolled towards the town centre.
c A massive earthquake has hit parts of India, *leaving thousands of people homeless*.
d A group of archaeologists *exploring the island* have discovered the skeleton of a new species of human being.
e *Not having a mobile phone*, we were unable to ring our hosts and warn them we would be late.
f *Having finished his medical training*, my brother decided to work in Africa for a charity.

1 emphasising that one thing happened after another had finished
2 replacing a relative clause
3 showing that two actions happened within a short time period of each other
4 expressing a condition
5 expressing a reason
6 expressing a result

2 Rewrite the information in a–f using participle clauses.

a *The Scream*, which was stolen from the Munch Museum, is worth millions of pounds.
b If they are washed with care, woollen sweaters will retain their shape.
c They hoped to confirm the suspect's part in the robbery so the detectives arranged an identity parade.
d The winner crosses the finishing line and he raises his hands in triumph as he does so!
e The explorer will undergo final medical checks and then he will set out on his polar expedition.
f Because he didn't realise how dangerous the snake was, the toddler reached out towards it.

3 Give the present participles of verbs a–i.

a make   d offer   g travel
b build   e prefer   h argue
c stop   f lie   i occur

4 Give the past participle of these irregular verbs.

a bite   h leave
b bring   i meet
c catch   j prove
d drive   k sell
e fight   l set
f fly   m speak
g hide   n wake

5 Join the two sentences in a–e using the words in brackets and participles.

Example

I lost my purse. I was travelling to work. (while)
I lost my purse while travelling to work.

a A group of cavers have spent 10 hours trapped underground. They have finally been rescued. (After)
b I admit that driving at excessive speeds is dangerous. I don't accept we should have speed cameras everywhere. (While)
c He wasn't a local. He didn't know the area. (Not)
d Civilians heard that a peace treaty had been signed. They began celebrating in the streets. (On)
e The judge didn't agree with the defendant's actions. He said he did sympathise with her situation. (Although)

6 Say what is wrong with sentences a–f and suggest how they could be rewritten.

a Roaring ferociously, the girl fled from the lion.
b Two of the terrorists shooting the President have been caught.
c The man inventing the digital camera has won an award.
d Not wanting to spoil the fun, the wedding celebrations went on well into the night.
e Planted with care, novice gardeners will be amazed how easy it is to grow things.
f Passing his driving test, Gary became rather big-headed.

7 Rewrite the text below, replacing the underlined information with participle clauses, and making any other necessary changes.

After he had spent three days trapped on an ice floe, explorer Ben Miller was finally rescued last night. Because he wanted to become the first man to walk solo from Canada to the North Pole, he had set out last April, alone and unaided. He had no way of transporting possessions so he took very little with him apart from camping equipment, a mobile phone, and a shovel. He made good progress at first but he then experienced a number of setbacks. The longest day of the year was approaching, which meant that the temperature was starting to rise. The ice gradually started to melt around him with the result that he was prevented from going forward or back. Ben, who was now feeling desperate, searched around him. Because he didn't have any advanced technical equipment, he had to rely on common sense. He took out his shovel and he dug a runway in the ice. He then took a photo of the runway and sent it to a rescue team via his mobile phone. The pilot succeeded in landing on the narrow strip of ice, with the result that he saved Ben from almost certain death.

Listening Part 2 Sentence completion

1 Read the exam task in 2 and think of words or phrases with similar meanings to the underlined words.

2 🎧 Listen to a local historian talking about shipwrecks in a place in south-west England called The Lizard and complete sentences 1–8. The tip box will help you.

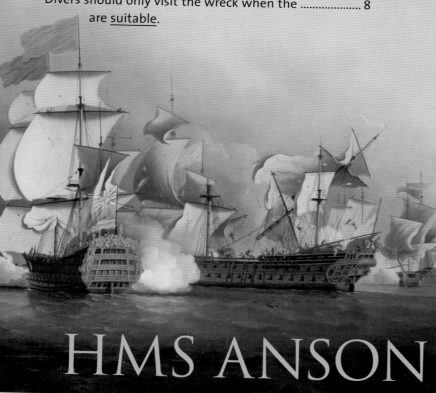

The Lizard is an <u>attractive</u> place for divers <u>due to</u> the many shipwrecks on the .... 1.

Divers may <u>come across</u> .... 2 in the treasure.

HMS Anson <u>left</u> the port of Falmouth on 24th December, ... 3.

The Captain had to <u>look for protection</u> from a full .... 4.

Sailors on the *Anson* thought the land they could see <u>in front of them</u> was the .... 5 into Falmouth.

The *Anson*'s <u>damaged</u> mast provided a type of .... 6 between the boat and the beach.

<u>Despite</u> being so close to .... 7, many of the <u>men on board</u> were lost.

Divers should only visit the wreck when the .... 8 are <u>suitable</u>.

> **tip**
> Remember that answers are no longer than three words in the exam.

HMS ANSON

Speaking Part 2

1 Look at the two sets of photos opposite and discuss what you might be asked to talk about in the exam.

2 Match these words and phrases with the photos.

a traditional crafts or skills
b personal reminders of the past
c an archaeological dig/excavation
d period costume
e documentary evidence
f early civilisations
g film footage
h medieval manuscripts
i battle re-enactment

3 In pairs, each choose one set of photos and do this exam task in one minute.

- What can these things teach us about the past?
- How successfully might they bring the past to life?

4 Look at each other's photos and say which way of learning about the past you think gives the most accurate information.

Writing

1 Using the prompts below, make a list of some of the key events of the twentieth century. Which do you think were the most significant? Why?

- technology
- sport
- entertainment
- politics
- science
- exploration

2 Read the exam task below, then read paragraphs A–C and say which major 20th century events they describe.

> You have seen this competition announcement on your college noticeboard and have decided to enter. Write your competition entry in 220–260 words.
>
> COMPETITION
>
> What do you consider to be the most important event of the 20th century?
> Briefly describe the event and explain its significance for our lives today. Competition winners will receive a set of encyclopedias.

B On November 9th, to everyone's amazement, the new government announced that all borders were to be opened. By midnight huge crowds had assembled. As the clock struck 12, they gave a huge cheer and crossed over in their thousands, and were greeted triumphantly by those on the other side. Many climbed to the top of the barrier where they danced, blew trumpets and celebrated in front of the television cameras. Soon people were breaking up the barrier with hammers and chisels, and carrying pieces off as souvenirs, while onlookers sprayed champagne and sounded their car horns. The celebrations lasted for days.

A When Neil Armstrong walked off the Apollo 11 capsule, he made history. Never before had man taken such a huge step. Watched by millions of TV viewers around the world, this momentous event inspired a generation. It was a huge achievement for mankind. It was also one of the most significant events of the twentieth century.

C The birth of Dolly was living proof that we can now create genetically identical animals. The significance of this for our society today is tremendous. While the technique may benefit farmers and those working in animal conservation, the danger is that scientists will be tempted to do the same with humans. That would challenge all our previous beliefs about what it means to be human.

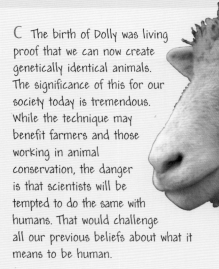

3 Answer these questions about paragraphs A–C.

a Which paragraph
- says why an event is still significant today?
- briefly describes an event?
- gives a detailed account of an event?

b Which would probably be the first, middle and last paragraph of a competition entry?

c What do you notice about the tenses used in each paragraph?

4 From your own knowledge, discuss the answers to a–f about the events in A–C.

a When and where did it happen?

Example

C 1996, Edinburgh, UK

tip

Make sure you know enough details before writing about a factual topic like this.

b Who was involved?
c Who was affected by it? How?
d How had things been before?
e How did things change afterwards?
f What effect does the event still have today?

5 Choose an event you could write about for the exam task. Make notes on it answering the questions in a–f above.

6 Decide whether adjectives a–j are positive, negative, or neutral in meaning.

a significant   f momentous
b beneficial   g catastrophic
c crucial   h unforeseen
d devastating   i grave
e inspirational   j severe

7 Complete sentences a–e using the adjectives from 6. There may be more than one possible answer.

a The Asian tsunami in 2004 had a(n) .... effect on the lives of thousands.
b One of the most .... sporting achievements of the last century was the first 'four-minute mile'.
c No one can deny how .... a development the Internet has been in our lives.
d Of the many .... incidents of the 20th century, Chernobyl's legacy has been one of the longest.
e A(n) .... consequence of the splitting of the atom was the development of weapons of mass destruction.

8 Write your competition entry, using your notes from 5 and some of the language in 6 and 7 where possible.

Review

1 Complete sentences a–e with the correct prepositions.

   a The industrial revolution resulted ………. dramatic changes to the structure of society.

   b It is essential for journalists to check the source ………. all the information they receive.

   c Overeating can lead ………. health problems in later life.

   d Within days of taking the antibiotics, there was a dramatic effect ………. her condition.

   e The authorities are keen to discover who was responsible ………. the destruction of the ancient monument.

2 Complete sentences a–h with phrasal verbs with *in* or *off* in the correct form.

   a There have been a number of cases of bogus doctors ………. in staff and patients and performing medical examinations.

   b None of the lights are working. Has someone ………. off the electricity?

   c At times we felt like ………. in but we carried on and managed to achieve our goal.

   d This year's festival will end with a display of fireworks to be ………. off at midnight.

   e The training centre isn't difficult to find – ………. off the road at the lights and follow the signs.

   f Please don't be ………. off by Bella's rather distant manner. She's very friendly once you get to know her.

   g What time will we have to ………. off to arrive in time for the ceremony?

   h It looks as if we shall have to ………. off our decision to relocate until we have found more suitable premises.

3 Find adjective forms of a–f which match definitions 1–6.

Example

a4 attractive

   a ~~attract~~   1 corresponding
   b signify   2 sensational
   c compare   3 widespread
   d extend   4 ~~pleasant to look at~~
   e perceive   5 important
   f drama   6 observant

4 For a–h, add a suitable negative prefix to make adjectives with the opposite meaning.

   a relevant   d moral   g suitable
   b legal   e capable   h logical
   c honest   f decisive

5 For a–e, use the correct word in brackets in its noun form to complete the sentence.

   a There was insufficient (accurate/evident) to convict the accused of the crime.

   b Our tennis coach says we must improve the (adaptable/accurate) of our strokes.

   c (Ambitious/Significant) is a quality politicians must have to achieve success.

   d Good drivers have an acute (aware/significant) of impending hazards.

   e The newly formed country gained its (independent/ambitious) only last year.

6 Replace the words in brackets with a suitable prefix.

   a Could you (an opposite action) ……….fasten this knot in my shoelace?

   b (with) …….operation between several countries meant that emergency aid arrived quickly.

   c The (across) ……….continental express is a luxurious way to travel.

   d If there's one thing I can't stand it's (too much) ……….cooked vegetables.

   e Police have been (wrongly) ……….informed about the whereabouts of the suspect.

   f London's Heathrow is one of the world's busiest (between) ……….national airports.

   g I think we have (too little) ……….estimated the strength of the opposition.

7 Complete this review using the words in brackets in the correct form.

> A free open-air concert on an international level, 'Live 8' was an 1 (inspire) ………. event. Its aim was to help counteract the 2 (devastate) ………. and 3 (catastrophe) ………. effects of world poverty, and to make a 4 (signify) ………. impact on its eradication. Some critics raised doubts about whether financial aid is actually 5 (benefit) ………. in the drive to stamp out poverty, claiming that it can often have 6 (foresee) ………. consequences. This made little difference to the millions who tuned in to watch the concert and to pledge their money.

The big issues

8

Lead in

1 Discuss why the issues below should concern us in the 21st century. Which are the three most burning issues? Why?

- privacy
- the Internet
- warfare
- an ageing society
- crime and terrorism
- globalisation
- the environment

2 For each of A, B, and C find one word which fits all three gaps.

A 1 'Governments should give as much foreign .... as possible to poorer countries.'

2 'In certain circumstances, emergency .... in the form of money should be sent immediately.'

3 'The most successful long-term .... programmes encourage self-help.'

B 1 'A lot of people only appreciate school after they leave full-time ....'

2 'State .... should be more academically based.'

3 'A practical .... makes it easier to change jobs later in life.'

C 1 'Few people could have predicted the huge impact of information ....'

2 'No matter how advanced .... becomes, machines will never be able to think like humans.'

3 'It's a waste of time for humans to do tasks that modern .... can do.'

3 🎧 Listen to three people talking about 2. Check your answers for A–C and tick the statement for the issues in each one that best reflects the speaker's point of view.

4 Do you share any of the views in 2? Why/Why not?

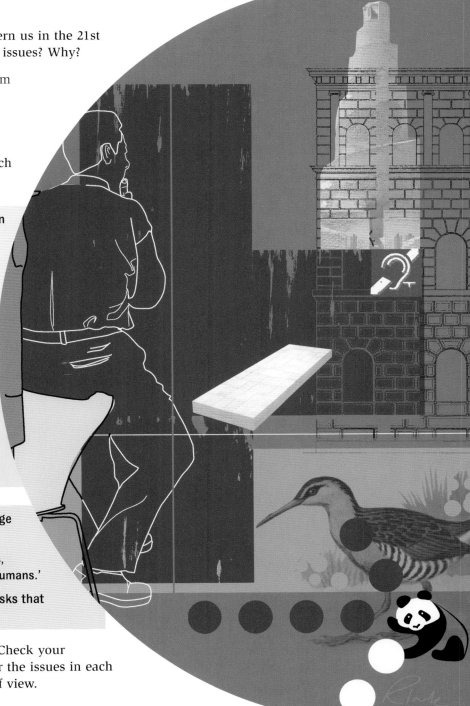

Reading Part 3 Multiple choice

1 What films or books do you know that feature robots? What relationship do these robots have with humans?

2 Match words a–f from the text opposite with meanings 1–6.

a gadget   d programming
b mechanism   e humanoid
c artificial intelligence   f robotics

1 a machine or creature with the appearance and characteristics of a person
2 a useful, usually small, piece of equipment
3 the science of designing and operating robots
4 a group of moving parts in a machine
5 the process of giving a computer instructions
6 the use of computers for human functions such as learning and making decisions

3 Read the text and discuss questions a–e.

a Why can't shoppers buy the domestic assistants mentioned in the first paragraph?
b How are Isaac Asimov's short stories different from those of his contemporaries?
c Why do experts think that protecting us from robots would be difficult?
d Why does the writer use the example of a robot taking food to Africa?
e What do many experts think about the dangers posed by the science of robotics?

> **tip**
> Before reading the options, see if you can answer the questions or complete the statements in your own words.

4 Read the text again and choose the best option (A, B, C or D) to complete 1–5.

1 Shoppers can't buy the domestic assistants mentioned in the first paragraph because they

A are not yet in the shops.
B can only be acquired online.
C don't actually exist.
D are only available to filmgoers.

2 Isaac Asimov's short stories differ from those of his contemporaries because they

A were influenced by Karel Capek.
B are less imaginative.
C describe a world ruled by robots.
D are more grounded in science.

3 Experts believe that protecting us from intelligent robots would be difficult because they

A can't be controlled just by programming.
B can't be programmed to recognise adults.
C don't respond to casual requests.
D will never be able to obey orders.

4 The example of a robot taking food to Africa is used to show that

A robots are capable of unselfish actions.
B Asimov's laws require robots to think.
C travel is a difficult concept for robots.
D robots can make moral judgements.

5 Many experts think that the dangers posed by the science of robotics are

A being covered up by experts.
B over-dramatised by pressure groups.
C overestimated by the public.
D worthy of more discussion.

5 Discuss these questions.

a What sort of jobs do you think we should use robots for? Think about:
• safety
• health
• human limitations

b Are there any jobs you think we should not use robots for? Why?

mean machines

ooking for a good domestic robot? According to one website, the world's first fully automated, life-sized domestic assistant is about to go on sale. There's just one catch: the website promoting this amazing gadget is just a tease, a clever bit of
5 advertising from 20th Century Fox to promote its movie, *I, Robot*. In this sci-fi action thriller, detective Spooner, played by Will Smith, investigates the murder of a scientist employed by a fictional robotics company. Despite the fail-safe mechanism built into the robots, which prevents them
10 from harming humans, the detective suspects one of them was responsible for the scientist's death. Further investigation leads him to believe that robots may even be planning to take over the world.

I, Robot is loosely based on a collection of short stories by
15 science-fiction writer, Isaac Asimov. Most of these revolve around the famous 'three laws of robotics' which he first drew up in 1940. In those days, barely two decades after the word 'robot' had been coined by playwright Karel Capek, other writers were still slavishly reworking Capek's narrative
20 about robots taking over the world. But Asimov's grasp of science fact – he gained a PhD in chemistry – lent rigour to his science-fiction and he was already asking what practical steps humanity might take to avoid this nasty fate. His solution was to program all robots to follow three laws:

25 **1** A robot may not injure a human being, or, through inaction, allow a human being to come to harm.

2 A robot must obey the orders given it by human beings, except where such orders would conflict with the First Law.

3 A robot must protect its own existence as long as such
30 protection does not conflict with the First or Second Law.

These three laws might seem like a good way to keep robots in their place, but to a roboticist they throw up more problems than they solve. Experts in the field of A.I. (artificial intelligence) have come to the sobering conclusion that
35 preventing intelligent robots from harming humans will require something much more complex than simply programming them. In fact, programming a real robot to follow the three laws would be a formidable undertaking. For a start, the robot would need to be able to recognise humans
40 and not confuse them with chimpanzees, statues and humanoid robots. This may be easy for us humans, but it poses considerable difficulty for robots. To follow rule two, the robot would have to be made capable of recognising an order and distinguishing it from a casual request – which is
45 beyond the capability of contemporary artificial intelligence.

To follow any of the three laws, the robot would have to determine whether and to what extent any of them applied to the current situation. This would involve complex reasoning about the future consequences of its own actions
50 and of the actions of other robots, humans and animals in its vicinity. But why should the robot restrict its actions to its own immediate vicinity? The first law, as stated above, includes no clause restricting its scope to the immediate surroundings of the robot. A robot standing in the Arctic
55 might reason that it could take food to Africa and thereby save a child from starvation. If it remains in the Arctic, the robot would, through inaction, allow a human to come to harm, thus contravening the first law. To enable robots to avoid getting caught on the horns of such dilemmas, they
60 would need some capacity for moral reasoning. Ensuring robots had such a capacity would be hideously complex compared to Asimov's three laws.

If these speculations seem far-fetched, the day when they become pressing issues may be closer than you suspect.
65 Computer scientist Bill Joy is not the only expert who has urged the public to start thinking about the dangers of robotics, and Greenpeace has brought out a special report urging people to debate the matter vigorously. We should not be too alarmist, however. While the field of robotics is
70 progressing rapidly, there is still some way to go before robots become as intelligent as Will Smith's fictional adversary. As Chris Melhuish, a leading British roboticist admits, 'The biggest threat our robots currently pose to humans is that you can trip over them.'

Vocabulary

Big issues

1 Discuss the answers to questions a–g.

a If a city is *overpopulated*, is it too big or are there too many people living there?

b What is the difference between a *famine* and a *drought*?

c What is the difference between a *natural resource* and a *financial resource*?

d Which one can erupt: a *tornado* or a *volcano*?

e Can soil erosion cause a *flood* or a *landslide*?

f Which is more serious: an *earth tremor* or an *earthquake*?

g Are epidemics caused by *contagious* or *controversial* diseases?

2 Match the words from each pair in 1–5 with definition a or b. Use your dictionary to check your answers.

1 vital/trivial
   a necessary or essential
   b not important or serious

2 controversial/critical
   a serious, uncertain and possibly dangerous
   b causing discussion and disagreement

3 momentous/momentary
   a lasting for a very short time
   b very important or serious

4 principal/principle
   a most important; main
   b moral rule or strong belief

5 antisocial/unsocial
   a harmful or annoying to others
   b outside normal working hours

Grammar

Conditionals GR p178–180

1 Match sentences a–d with descriptions 1–4.

a If a virus attacks a computer, it prevents it from working properly. (zero conditional)

b If their best side plays, Manchester United will probably come out on top. (first conditional)

c If I had enough money, I would buy a new digital camera. (second conditional)

d If you had told me that you needed some advice, I would have helped out. (third conditional)

1 a hypothetical statement about the past
2 a condition which is improbable/impossible in the present
3 a statement of general fact
4 a condition that is possible/probable in the future

2 Underline the correct verb forms in a–f.

a *I'll give up/I'd give up* my job and go backpacking round the world if *I'd have/I had* a bit more courage.

b Nobody *would find/would have found* the climbers if they *hadn't managed/didn't manage* to attract the mountain rescue team.

c If you *stayed out/stay out* all night without telling your mum, she *probably kills/will probably kill* you.

d If *I realised/I'd realised* the first prize in the raffle was a sports car, I *would have bought/would buy* a lot more tickets!

e If *you leave/you'll leave* metal objects in the rain, they generally *rust/will rust*.

f She *wouldn't crash/wouldn't have crashed* the car if a dog *hadn't run out/wouldn't have run out* in front of her car.

3 Explain the differences in meaning or function between these pairs of sentences.

1a If *you're finding* it difficult to do your homework, I'll give you a hand.
  b If you *find* it difficult to do your homework, I'll give you a hand.
2a Those swimmers *could have drowned* if passers-by hadn't raised the alarm.
  b Those swimmers *would have drowned* if passers-by hadn't raised the alarm.

3a Please let me know if *you need* any advice.

b Please let me know if *you should need* any advice.

4a If *you stayed* in this country a bit longer, we could spend more time together.

b If *you were staying* in this country a bit longer, we could spend more time together.

5a If we *offered* you the position, would you accept?

b If we *were to offer* you the position, would you accept?

4 Complete a–f by putting the verbs in brackets into the correct form.

a If the bridegroom's friends .... (not/tie) him to a lamp post on his stag night, he .... (not/end up) in a police station.

b If you .... (look) for something to do, ... (go) and dig the garden!

c As a rule, coloured clothes .... (fade) if you .... (leave) them in the sun for too long.

d If you .... (want) to get rid of your old football kit, ... (try) selling it on the Internet.

e We .... (arrive) sooner if the workmen .... (not/dig) up the road on our way here.

f .... (be) the manager to discover what has been going on in the office, he .... (be) horrified.

5 Complete sentences a–f with your own ideas.

a If I could spend a romantic evening with anyone I chose, …

b I will be really disappointed if …

c If I could change one thing about my life, …

d It would have been unbelievable if …

e I would feel absolutely ecstatic if …

f If I could change places for one day with anyone in the world, …

6 Underline the words used instead of *if* in these conditional sentences, then correct any mistakes you find.

a They would have ended up divorced unless the intervention of their friends.

b I'll marry you provided you don't expect me to get on with your mother!

c As long as you won the lottery, how would you spend the money?

d Jim will be allowed out of prison supposing he reports to the police station twice a week.

e Tonight's open-air concert will be cancelled provided the weather improves.

f I'll be raring to go tomorrow as long as I get a good night's sleep tonight.

g There's no hope of our team winning the League unless we start to play better.

7 Complete gaps 1–12 in the paragraph below, using the verbs in brackets in the correct tense.

I was kicked out of school at the age of 16 because I was bone idle. If anyone .... (1 tell) me then that I would end up making a living as a scriptwriter, I .... (2 never/believe) them. I admit that writing is one of the few things I've ever been good at. At school, if one of my mates .... (3 have) trouble writing up a project, I .... (4 do) it for them – provided they .... (5 pay) me enough, of course! But write for a living? That was never on the cards. After I left school, I drifted in and out of various jobs. I wanted to travel the world but I knew I .... (6 not/get) very far unless I .... (7 have) a few dollars under my belt. So how to earn it? A friend of mine came up with a brainwave. Why not try writing a TV screenplay? Supposing it .... (8 be) good enough, it .... (9 may/earn) me enough money to travel the world. I owe that friend a lot. If he .... (10 not/urge) me on, I .... (11 never/get) started as a writer. And instead of having homes in Paris, Brisbane, and Los Angeles, I .... (12 still/work) in a dead end job in my home town.

Listening Part 3 Multiple choice

1 **Look at the advertisement below and discuss these questions.**

a Which countries might volunteers be needed in?
b What resources might be lacking in places like these?
c What kind of professional skills would be useful in developing countries?
d Why would jobs like these be rewarding?

Volunteer jobs

Each year, hundreds of people start rewarding jobs as volunteers in developing countries. These countries need you to:

- use your professional skills to train and advise colleagues.
- live and work within the local community.
- work creatively and adapt to new surroundings – often with few resources.

2 🎧 **Listen twice to a radio interview with Tom Davies, who spent a year as a volunteer in Nepal, and choose the best answers for questions 1–6.**

tip
Make sure all the information in the option you choose is correct, not just some of it.

1 Why did Tom go to live and work abroad?
  A He was bored with his routine.
  B He wanted to do something useful.
  C He saw an advertisement in a newspaper he had bought.
  D He wanted to take advantage of every opportunity in life.

2 How did he regard his experience abroad?
  A He was worried about being away from home.
  B He was apprehensive about what lay in store.
  C He thought the time would pass all too quickly.
  D He knew he would have very little time to appreciate his surroundings.

3 What does Tom say was the most important thing offered by the organisation?
  A enough money to make ends meet
  B paid travel and accommodation
  C the opportunity to meet fellow volunteers
  D help to readjust on his return home

4 What does Tom say about the snow leopards?
  A Some hunting of the animals is allowed.
  B Larger numbers breed away from inhabited areas.
  C They are regarded as the most important animals in the Himalayas.
  D They have become more domesticated.

5 How has the programme Tom and his colleague devised helped?
  A Farmers can be compensated for lost animals.
  B The government runs an insurance scheme for farmers.
  C Farmers have the funds needed to buy more land.
  D Local groups have formed to protect the snow leopard.

6 What does Tom say he cannot do at the moment?
  A Give an example of a profitable local scheme.
  B Prove that fewer snow leopards have been killed by hunters.
  C Show that the number of snow leopards has increased.
  D Promise that profits from his scheme will go back into the community.

3 **Would you be interested in doing voluntary work abroad? If so, where and doing what? If not, why not?**

Speaking Parts 3 and 4

1 Look at the pictures and read the task below. What do the pictures represent?

> - How difficult is it to make decisions like these?
> - Which two decisions have the greatest long-term effects on our lives?

2 In pairs, do the Part 3 task in 1. After three minutes, stop and compare your decisions with those of another group.

3 🎧 Read the Part 4 questions a–c. Listen to six students' answers and decide which of the questions they are answering. How appropriate are their answers?

a What decisions in life do you consider the most difficult to make?
b Some people believe that a lot of important decisions are out of our hands. What do you think?
c What sort of decisions in life are influenced by money?

4 Discuss your own thoughts on the questions in 3. These words and phrases might help you.

at stake	short term
in the long run	out of the blue
on the spur of the moment	out of our control

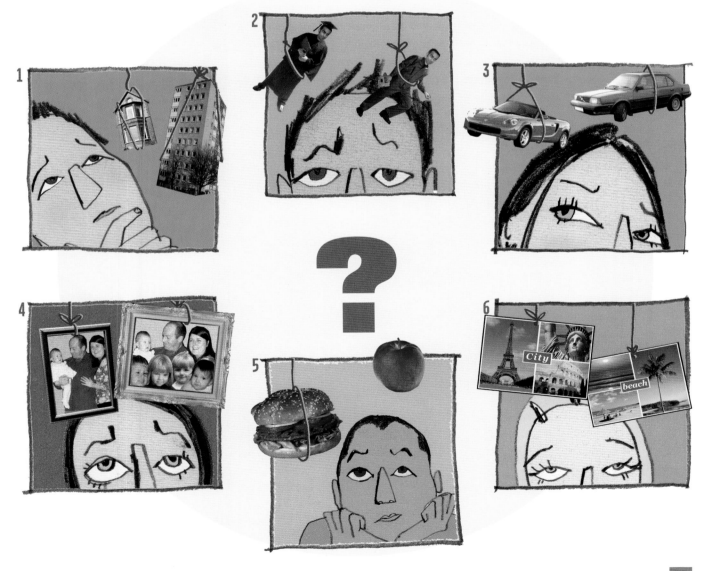

Use of English Part 1 Multiple-choice cloze

1 How important in life are the four things below?
Is there anything else that is more important?

- helping others
- enjoying yourself
- doing something to be remembered by
- passing on your genes by having children

tip

Look for:
- slight differences in meaning between A–D.
- words that look similar but have different meanings.
- fixed phrases and expressions.
- dependent prepositions.

2 Read the text below quickly. Is the writer's tone mainly

a humorous   b philosophical   c pessimistic?

3 Read the text again and the tip box and decide which word
(A, B, C or D) best fits each space 1–12.

It is often 0 ....C.... that a look at our origins will 1 .... us to the meaning of life. It certainly did not 2 .... that way for Dr Frankenstein's creation. Desperate to know where he had come from, unlike us he 3 .... the awful truth. Yet what he found out did not 4 .... life's meaning, it just upset him. Perhaps instead of answering the question of why we are here by looking backwards, we should look forwards. What future goal would 5 .... this life worth living? The problem with working towards goals was identified by the philosopher of common sense, Aristotle. His 6 .... was that we do many things for the sake of something else. We eat to live, work to pay the bills, study to pass exams, and so on. But unless at least one action is done for its own sake, there is no 7 .... in doing any of them. Not everything can be a means to an end: there must be ends which are valuable in their own right. There is much that makes life precious enough to 8 .... to and savour. So what gives people's lives value? It might be 9 .... the suffering of others, helping one's children 10 .... their futures, or overcoming a problem. But life is uncertain and we are often thrown off 11 .... The basic answer to the question of life's meaning is probably this: there are more 12 .... to live rather than die, and they are to be found in the living of life itself.

0	A	granted	B	grasped	C	assumed	D	assigned
1	A	influence	B	persuade	C	show	D	lead
2	A	work off	B	work out	C	turn up	D	turn down
3	A	discovered	B	recovered	C	delivered	D	directed
4	A	relate	B	exhibit	C	tell	D	reveal
5	A	value	B	judge	C	make	D	rule
6	A	argument	B	discussion	C	reason	D	debate
7	A	aspect	B	point	C	design	D	matter
8	A	hold on	B	hold up	C	reach up	D	reach over
9	A	relaxing	B	releasing	C	relieving	D	relenting
10	A	assemble	B	build	C	raise	D	erect
11	A	route	B	plan	C	way	D	course
12	A	purposes	B	excuses	C	ideas	D	reasons

Vocabulary

Expressions with *end*

1 Use 1–8 to complete the expressions with *end* in a–h.

1	in	4	up	7	meet
2	sight	5	means	8	at
3	loose	6	on		

a I'm at a .... end this week. Do you fancy doing something?

b I've been overwhelmed with work for weeks and there's no end in ....

c Helping my brother move house was just a .... to an end; I want him to do an even bigger favour for me!

d I'm struggling to make ends .... what with three children to feed and all the bills to pay.

e I got on the wrong train last night and ended .... in the middle of nowhere!

f The best thrillers have an unexpected twist right .... the end.

g My mum wasn't keen on lending me her car, but .... the end she gave in.

h We can make more space in the classroom by putting the tables .... end and leaning them against the wall.

2 Use your dictionary to check any unknown expressions in 1. Which word in the dictionary did you find expressions a–c under?

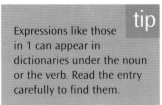

> **tip**
>
> Expressions like those in 1 can appear in dictionaries under the noun or the verb. Read the entry carefully to find them.

3 Match the expressions with *end* in 1 with meanings a–h.

a finally
b have nothing particular to do
c things are unlikely to change
d eventually arrived
e as something finishes
f upright
g manage financially
h something done to achieve something else

Review

1 **Write the missing words in sentences a–f. The first letters are given.**

a Heavy rain caused a l........... after many trees on the hillside had been felled.

b Coal is a n........... r........... which is often uneconomical to mine nowadays.

c A severe f........... in the south of the country left thousands starving.

d During the violent storm, a t........... was reported to have caused extensive damage to property in the city centre.

e A c........... d........... like tuberculosis can be life-threatening.

f The city has become o........... because of all the new housing estates which have sprung up over the last few years.

2 **Circle the correct word in italics to complete sentences a–f.**

a Your suggestion will provide only a short- *haul/term/stay* solution to our traffic problems.

b An all-round education always pays off in the long *run/way/time*.

c We must act on global warming now – the future of our planet is at *stake/hand/large*.

d Ted didn't plan his decision – he resigned on the *point/head/spur* of the moment.

e The announcement that the company was to be sold shocked everyone as it came completely out of the *question/blue/ordinary*.

f I regret that we can't help with your query. The matter is now out of our *reach/touch/control*.

3 **Decide which of these adjectives best collocate with the nouns in italics in a–g.**

principal	trivial	controversial
momentary	momentous	antisocial
unsocial		

a The accident is thought to have been caused by a *lack* of concentration on the part of the driver.

b There is no doubt that 'not guilty' was a *verdict* – there was widespread disbelief that that the accused was found innocent.

c A board of directors meeting is not the occasion to discuss such a *matter*. Details such as this can be dealt with at a much lower level.

d Ted made a *decision* when he resigned from his city law firm and relocated to a remote island.

e His new job is interesting but it will entail working *hours* and some night shifts.

f One of the *causes* of the declining bird population is the destruction of their natural habitat, but there are many other factors.

g The penalty for *behaviour* such as vandalism can be a short spell in prison.

4 **Replace the words in italics with a suitable expression with *end*. The words in brackets will help you.**

a If you find yourself *with nothing particular to do* (loose) this weekend, why not visit our new department store?

b Property prices have been rising for months and *things are unlikely to change*. (sight)

c It's difficult to *manage financially* (meet) when you're out of work.

d We were enjoying the film, but *as it finished* (at), there was a power cut and we never found out what happened!

e Paul didn't enjoy his job – it was *something he did to achieve something else*. (means)

f After driving for two hours, we *eventually arrived* (up) right back where we'd started from.

g Jack took his maths exam four times but *finally* (in) he passed it.

h If you put the desk *upright* (on), it will go through the door.

5 **Complete gaps 1–6 in the paragraph below, which gives advice about finding a job.**

There are lots of factors to .... 1 if you're young and looking for your first job. Before you .... 2 up your mind about what career path to take, get as much advice as possible, and be advised .... 3 rushing into a decision without careful research and consideration. Bear in .... 4 that you could be making a choice that will affect you for several years to come. .... 5 up the pros and cons of different jobs, how much they pay, where they are located, promotion prospects and so on. At the end of the day, remember that it's up .... 6 you to choose your own path.

It's a crime

Lead in

1 Read the information below about crime in the UK and explain the meaning of these words.

criminal damage	domestic violence
counterfeit	mugging
robbery	fraud

2 Discuss these questions.
a Are you surprised by any of the statistics? Say which and explain why.
b Why might the number of some crimes appear to have fallen whilst others have risen?
c How do you think crime statistics in your country might compare with these?

Crime in England and Wales

England and Wales have a combined population of around 53 million.

In 2006, the total number of crimes in England and Wales was around 10.9 million.

Total crime numbers peaked in 1995, and have since fallen by 44%.

In 2006, 23% of the population were the victims of crime.

Fraud

Plastic card fraud, in non face-to-face transactions, rose by 21% in 2005.

The rise in plastic card fraud comes from an increase in the use of counterfeit cards and the fraudulent use of card details – not through the misuse of stolen cards.

Violent crime

In 2006, the total number of violent offences in England and Wales was 2.4 million. These included:

357,000 incidents of domestic violence.

817,000 incidents where the offender was an acquaintance.

382,000 incidents of mugging.

Criminal damage

In 2006, the number of incidents of criminal damage in England and Wales was 2.7 million. More than half of these were against vehicles.

In 2006, around 8 in 100 households experienced some type of criminal damage.

After a peak in 1993 of 3.5 million incidents, criminal damage continues to fall every year.

Robbery

In 2006, the number of robbery offences in England and Wales for people aged 16 or over was 311,000.

A study of 2,000 police files found that:

22% of recorded robbery victims were between 11 and 15 years old.

23% were between 16 and 20.

5% were over 60.

Figures from www.crimestatistics.org.uk

Reading

Part 4 Multiple matching

1 Do you enjoy crime stories in books or films? What would you say are the elements of a good crime story?

2 Read the text opposite and suggest a heading or brief summary for each section to show you understand the development of the text. Compare your ideas with a partner's.

3 Read the text again and say in which section of the text (A–F) 1–13 are mentioned. The how to do it box will help you.

how to do it

- Read the text for general meaning.
- Highlight key words in the questions.
- Read the text again, looking for the key words from the questions expressed in a different way.
- Underline relevant sentences, write the question number next to them, and tick off the question; this reduces what you need to read each time.
- Do the same with each section, leaving the most difficult questions until last.

the importance of understanding how a character thinks	1 …
inventing an interesting profile for your character	2 … 3 …
the character's belief that he will go unpunished	4 …
the necessity of writing a convincing plot	5 … 6 …
well-written stories spoiled by an improbable storyline	7 …
using human emotions as a basis for a story	8 …
the risk of basing characters on reality	9 …
why killing makes a good story	10 …
not underestimating the difficulty of writing a crime novel	11 …
a crucial question to ask about your main character	12 …
the different ways that readers will see a novel	13 …

4 Complete these phrases with *of* or *for* and check your answers in the text.

a   to be capable …
b   a source …
c   a kind …
d   the result …
e   to allow scope …
f   compensation …
g   a view …
h   to blame …

5 Do you have a favourite fictional criminal and/or detective? What makes them so appealing?

a

Why do so many of us enjoy reading crime and suspense fiction? The predictable answers are that the books tell intriguing stories and are exciting and easy to read.
5 But if you don't read the genre or don't admire it, then you will find it very hard to write. Don't be misled into imagining that a detective story is a simple matter because there are rules to follow. In reality,
10 the crime writer achieves everything that an ordinary novelist does – but also has to ensure that the result is intriguing, exciting and easy to read. As far as content goes, all that distinguishes crime fiction is that the
15 novels feature criminality. And criminals make good characters for fiction because they are active, not passive. They are not the stupidest people, either. To commit a crime they have shown initiative and
20 intelligence in the planning and audacity in carrying it through. Their moral failing is in wanting to do it; their folly is in believing they can get away with it; and their arrogance lies in doing it again.
25 Whether stories centre on criminals or their victims, crime is rich ground for novelists.

b

The best way of learning about any kind of writing is to read good examples of it. As
30 you cut from one author to another, notice whether a writer who scores on story and atmosphere might be sloppy about prose, perhaps scattering adverbs and adjectives where one carefully chosen word would
35 provide more effect. Or whether one whose style is elegant confuses you by an unlikely twist of the plot. A writer who serves up all the rest in splendid fashion, may leave the principal characters too shady for your
40 liking. Obviously, your verdicts will be subjective. While you are muttering about situations not being fully explained, another reader may be enthusing about the subtlety of the novel. But you will be
45 learning what can be achieved within the genre and what perceived failings you wish to avoid in your own work.

Writing crime fiction

*Do you enjoy a good thriller or detective novel? Have you ever thought about writing one?
Lesley Grant-Adamson has some advice for aspiring writers.*

c

It is acceptable to take actual people and events as the basis for fiction but they must be distinctly altered. You wouldn't want to libel anyone by having him appear only transparently disguised as a murderer; and you certainly mustn't use genuine names. Besides, the fewer fetters on your creative powers the better. Even when you set out thinking you are going to use a real person, you will rapidly drift from him as you dream up ways to enhance the character. There might be more advantage for you as a plotter if the vet changes career and becomes a doctor; the semi-detached where he lives is so humdrum you might prefer him to move into the haunted mansion on the moor. By the time you have finished playing with him, you will hardly recognise the vet, and more to the point, neither will he.

d

Although they are as varied as the people who write them, all novels are based on conflict. Characters will be in difficulties; through the course of the novel they will struggle to cope; and, by the end, their position will have changed. In crime fiction the difficulty or challenge will be caused by, or result in, a crime. That crime is almost invariably murder because it's the extreme, the one for which there is no possible compensation for the victim and no expiation for the wrongdoer. To achieve a believable story, the method should be suited to the character who murders. Common methods of dispatching victims include shooting, stabbing, hitting with a blunt instrument, poisoning, drowning or contriving accidents. A habitual criminal might reasonably produce a gun, but an elderly housewife is more likely to brandish a heavy pan. As the genre examines human beings in extreme situations, the story you are developing must allow scope for this. At least one of your characters must be under pressure, and it will increase during the spinning of the yarn. The springboard for your story is most likely to be friction within a family, between neighbours or colleagues. Trouble in relationships, and the excesses that can result when someone becomes stubborn, jealous, obsessive or vengeful, is a bountiful source of story ideas.

e

For some writers, the idea for a whole book begins with the appearance in their mind of an insistent character. Whether he came to you as a gift out of nowhere or as the result of a real effort to create him, you should pose some searching questions about him. They boil down to this: is he strong enough? That doesn't mean he has to be physically or mentally robust, merely that he must be capable of interesting the reader for the length of the book. A good character always has an internal conflict. He might be burdened with guilt, say, or struggling to overcome a personal failing. Whatever it is, the problem colours his view of life. If your character does not interest you very much, you can be certain he will not interest anyone else. Get inside your character's head. Find out whether he enjoys his own company or is lonely. Check what he thinks about his parent, his siblings, his colleagues. Maybe he blames them for his problems?

f

If a character or story comes to you very easily, be wary. First ideas should always be challenged. If they are good, scrutiny won't damage them. When they don't come up to scratch, you will save yourself much disappointment by dropping them. Although a reader knows it's 'only fiction', he'll cringe when your hero is thumped and sigh when your heroine is sad. But he is no fool. He knows when you are telling the truth about human beings. When you are not, he may become impatient and close the book.

Vocabulary
Crime and punishment

1 Discuss the difference between:

   a murder and manslaughter
   b mugging and smuggling
   c bribery and blackmail
   d burglary and robbery
   e arson and assault
   f fraud and forgery

2 Complete the table with the missing words.

	verb	person	act
a	mug	....	....
b	rob	....	....
c	....	burglar	....
d	....	....	murder
e	steal	thief	....

3 Look up *murder* and *mug* in your dictionary. How many other sayings and meanings can you find in their entries?

4 Complete this paragraph about the British legal system with the missing prepositions.

   with   of   on   for   against   into   to

   If you are arrested 1 .... committing a crime, the police must caution you immediately. You will be taken to a police station and interviewed, and may then be charged 2 .... a criminal offence and taken 3 .... custody. For a serious crime, you will appear in court as a defendant and be tried by a jury. If you are found guilty 4 .... the crime, you can appeal 5 .... the verdict. You may be sentenced 6 .... a number of years in prison, but could be released 7 .... parole for good behaviour.

5 Is the legal system in your country similar to the description in 4?

Grammar
Passives GR p170–171

1 Underline the passive verbs in a–g.

   a Viewers were appalled to hear that the reality TV show is to be axed. Two soap operas are also said to be under threat.
   b The idea that Mars could one day be colonised by human beings is no longer fiction.
   c Local residents, annoyed about the siting of wind turbines near their village, complained that planning procedures are being broken.
   d Environmental issues are the focus for discussion at the conference to be hosted by the United Nations.
   e Although experts are convinced that robots can be made to think for themselves, their efforts have met with little success so far.
   f If governments want to clean up the planet, they must act now, and more funding for research will have to be made available.
   g All adults eligible to vote are required to complete and return the enclosed form.

2 Complete rules a–c for forming the passive.

   a We form the passive with the verb .... in an appropriate tense + the .... participle of the main verb.
   b The object of an active verb becomes the .... of the passive verb.
   c If the name of the agent needs to be mentioned, we put the word ' .... ' in front of it.

3 Match these uses of the passive (a–c) with sentences from 1.

   a when the agent is unknown, unimportant, or obvious, or is deliberately not mentioned
   b to make reports and official documents more impersonal, and to show that the actions are more important than the agent
   c to avoid the overuse of personal pronouns or vague words, e.g. *people, they*

4 Make this newspaper report more formal by putting the italicised sections into the passive.

> *They have recently discovered a 2,000-year-old shoe* in Britain in a disused well, on an area due to be quarried. The 30 cm piece of leather is still flexible because *something has kept it damp* and away from air for thousands of years. Experts are excited about the find but warn that *they need to do a lot more work* before *they know everything* about it. *They have never found anything like this* before. *They have found similar shoes* in bog sites in Ireland and on the continent but these are undateable. *Someone may have placed it* into the well as part of a ritual, or *someone could have simply lost it*. In the distant past, *people often buried shoes* in the foundations of new buildings as good luck charms.

5 Write the passive equivalents of these sentences.

a In a crackdown on antisocial behaviour, police are making teenagers remove neighbourhood grafitti.
b They heard the politician say under his breath that 'all journalists were troublemakers'.
c They wouldn't let anyone into the building until firefighters said it was safe to do so.
d On the CCTV footage, we clearly saw money change hands in return for a small package.

6 Complete sentences a–d with your own ideas.

a I would feel ashamed of myself if I was ever heard …
b As part of the act, the magician was seen …
c In many countries, until you are 18 you are not allowed …
d One thing many kids hate about school is being made …

7 Give advice for the situations in a–e, using *have/ get something done*. Try to vary the ways of giving advice.

Example

I've been having splitting headaches recently and can't read things clearly.

You should get your eyes tested./Why don't you get your eyes tested?

a Water has been coming in through your parents' bedroom ceiling.
b I bought a pair of trousers but they're too long for me.
c Your pet dog has lost his appetite recently.
d I want to sell my house but it's looking a bit shabby.
e Your sister's car has been making strange noises.

8 A reporter has gathered rumours and facts from sources who don't wish to be named in print. Rewrite the information more formally for his newspaper, using the reporting verb in brackets and beginning with the words in italics.

Example

'I hear *the Prime Minister* is really angry with his Foreign Minister.' (report)

The Prime Minister is reported to be furious with his Foreign Minister.

a 'Don't quote me on this, but I've heard that *a UFO* has crashed in Texas.' (rumour)
b 'I've been told that *Robbie Williams* is going to do another world tour.' (say)
c 'They reckon that *scientists* have found a new planet.' (believe)
d 'Apparently *factory bosses* are planning to make two hundred employees redundant.' (think)
e 'Everyone imagines that *the event* was cancelled because of the singer's poor health.' (assume)

Listening Part 1 Short extracts

1 Do you know any stories of daring robberies, real or fictional?

2 🎧 Read questions 1–6 below before you listen to the three different extracts. Then listen and choose the best answer (A, B or C) for each question. The tip box will help you.

tip

Use the question to decide 'how' to listen e.g. listen for specific information (q.4) or infer an opinion (q.6).

Extract one
You hear part of a radio programme concerning an attempted robbery.

1 What was the thieves' plan?
   A to carry out a raid on a local bank
   B to make off with a collection of priceless objects
   C to steal money from a national monument

2 The outcome of the attempted robbery was that the thieves
   A were tricked into stealing the wrong things.
   B were unable to break into their intended target.
   C found themselves caught in a trap.

Extract two
You hear a woman and a police officer talking about credit card fraud.

3 The woman was surprised because
   A someone had obtained her credit card details without her knowledge.
   B a hotel receptionist had refused to accept her credit card.
   C her credit card company had contacted her about some transactions.

4 What information does the police officer give?
   A It's difficult to use a credit card without knowing a PIN number.
   B Credit card companies accept the risk that fraud will occur.
   C The woman will be liable for any bills.

Extract three
You hear two people on a current affairs programme talking about crime and punishment.

5 The two speakers agree about
   A the support that even violent criminals deserve.
   B the need to ensure that prisoners do not reoffend.
   C the problem of preventing prisoners escaping.

6 What is the man's opinion of punishment for offenders?
   A Punishment can be turned into something that benefits society.
   B Community service is suitable for non-violent and violent criminals.
   C Offenders should be consulted about their punishment.

Speaking Part 2

1 Look at the photos opposite and discuss what topics you may be asked to talk about in the exam.

2 Think of a topic heading for each group of words A–C. Which photo does each phrase in A and B refer to? Which photos might the phrases in C match?

A a controlled parking zone
  a smoke-free environment
  a hard hat area
  an airport check-in queue
  a department store
  a quiet environment

B to prevent interruptions
  to prevent damage to goods
  to maintain a healthy atmosphere
  to prevent accident or injury
  to avoid congestion
  to protect passengers and crew

C having to pay a fine
  being given a verbal warning
  having your property removed
  being sacked
  being asked to leave the premises
  receiving a warning letter

3 Read the tip boxes, then in pairs, choose a different set of photos each and do this task.

‘These pictures show situations in which rules and regulations apply. I'd like you to compare two of these pictures, saying why the rules and regulations have been applied in these situations, and what the penalty might be if people ignore them.’

4 Look at each other's photos again and say in which situation you think the rules and regulations are the most important.

- Why have rules and regulations been applied in these situations?
- What might the penalties be if people ignore them?

tip

Use the prompts above the photos as a reminder to answer the complete task.

tip

Try to give reasons for your opinions.

Mobiltelefone gefährden die Sicherheit der Patienten.

NO PARKING

Writing Part 1 A report WG p160

1 Discuss which of a–f are true of a report.
   A report:
   a should begin and end like a letter
   b usually focuses on past events
   c should be chatty in style
   d is usually divided into sections with clear headings
   e may contain bullet-pointed lists
   f doesn't need an introduction or conclusion

2 Read the exam task and input. Then read the model answer opposite and discuss what the writer does correctly, and what he/she does wrong.

> While studying in Britain, you join a drama group. Recently you helped to organise a trip on a Murder Mystery Weekend. The secretary of the group has asked you for a report saying what the group enjoyed, outlining any problems, and recommending improvements for future trips. Read the comments on the Timetable below and write your report.

Timetable

Friday

5.30 am	Depart London Victoria Coach station.	
1.30 pm	Arrive Edinburgh, Scotland. Lunch at hotel.	
3.30 pm	Walking tour of fictional crime scenes of Edinburgh.	
7 pm	Murder Mystery Game with buffet dinner.	

8 hours on coach!! (why not fly?)

great! close to centre

interesting but tiring

great fun

Saturday

9 am	Visit a forensic crime laboratory – find out about the latest techniques used in detecting crime.	
1 pm	Lunch in hotel	
2 pm	Free time to explore city.	
7.30 pm	Return to hotel. Dinner.	
9 pm	Coach departs for London Victoria.	

needed more time there

Lovely city – lots to look at.

3 Complete a–f with one of the prepositions below, then say whether a–f introduce or conclude a report.

| in   into   up   to   of   on |

a The aim .... this report is to …
b .... conclusion, I would say …
c To sum ...., our group felt that …
d The following report relates ....
e Taking everything .... consideration, …
f .... balance, we are of the opinion that …

4 Which of these phrases would be suitable for making recommendations in your report? What is wrong with the others?

a If I were you I'd …
b I'd like to suggest …
c It might be a good idea to …
d How about … ?
e You could consider …
f Why don't you … ?
g One possible solution would be …

5 Read the task and input again and make notes for a–c.

a positive features of the trip
b negative features of the trip
c recommendations for future trips

6 Write your report in 180–220 words.

Dear Sir or Madam

I am writing this report about our recent visit to Edinburgh for a 'Murder Mystery Weekend'. I will outline the good and bad points of the visit and make recommendations for future trips.

There were many enjoyable aspects to the trip. For example, the hotel was excellent, being conveniently located near the city centre. The main event, the Murder Mystery Game itself, was really well organised and enjoyed by everyone. Edinburgh is such an attractive city, offering visitors plenty of sightseeing, so our free time for exploring was very welcome.

Unfortunately, there were a few problems with the visit. To start with, our departure time was extremely early, and to make matters worse, the journey by coach took eight hours. I would recommend that in future we go by plane instead. Additionally, while the tour of crime scenes was engaging, it was quite exhausting, and could therefore be shorter. On the other hand, the excursion to the crime laboratory was so fascinating that, in my opinion we had insufficient time there, so I would suggest extending this.

All in all, it was a positive experience, and I hope that my report will enable you to make even greater improvements for future trips.

Review

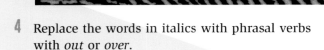

1 Join sentence halves a–h with 1–8 using *of* or *for*.

a Richard is a quiet man and certainly not capable
b Please accept this cheque as compensation
c I think there is scope
d You need to have a clear view
e When you see the result
f The audience was intrigued by the sudden appearance
g I'm afraid the children were to blame
h The writer's view

1 the damage to your property.
2 how your story is going to end.
3 any kind of violent behaviour.
4 eating all the ice-cream in the freezer.
5 improvement in this project.
6 all your hard work, you'll realise it was worth it.
7 one of the actors in their midst.
8 life at that time is rather interesting.

2 Divide a–m into three groups of crimes connected with:

1 violence.
2 obtaining money, goods or other advantage.
3 damage to property.

a arson   f fraud   j assault
b robbery   g burglary   k blackmail
c murder   h forgery   l mugging
d bribery   i smuggling   m theft
e manslaughter

3 Match sentence halves a–g with 1–7.

a A convicted criminal can appeal
b You must be read your rights if you are arrested
c If you are a suspect, the police may take you
d With enough evidence, you may be charged
e A prisoner released on the promise of good behaviour is
f If you're found guilty
g For serious offences you may be sentenced

1 into custody.
2 to several years in prison.
3 against their sentence.
4 of some offences you may get a suspended sentence.
5 for committing a crime.
6 on parole.
7 with an offence.

4 Replace the words in italics with phrasal verbs with *out* or *over*.

a When he got a burst tyre, Bob *drove* onto the hard shoulder of the motorway.
b After so many problems, we were delighted when our plans *were successful*.
c We *left the house* so late that we got caught in the rush hour.
d After working round the clock, the newspaper staff managed to *produce* the special edition.
e If you can *manage to wait* another ten minutes, we'll stop at the next service station.
f Don't forget to *switch off* the lights.
g The paintings in the exhibition were *arranged* in a circle round the room.
h Do you think Jason will ever *recover from* the shock of not being chosen to play in the match?
i The Prime Minister *extended* her hand to each member of the winning team.
j It's advisable to *investigate* all the facilities before deciding to join a gym.
k Didn't you get the factsheet that I *distributed*?
l By deducting the bottom figure from the top one, we can *calculate* how much money we've got.

5 Fill in the missing prepositions in these extracts from a report.

a The aim ...... this report is to ...
b The following report relates ...... the matter ...
c To sum ...... , everyone felt that ...
d ...... conclusion, I would have no hesitation in ...
e ...... balance, we are of the opinion that ...
f Taking everything ...... consideration ...

6 Use one word in each gap (1–10) to complete this extract from a report about a trip.

1 .... were many positive aspects 2 .... the trip. Firstly, the accommodation itself was excellent, 3 .... conveniently situated between the town centre and the beach. Unfortunately, a few 4 .... did occur. To start 5 .... , the hotel was situated next to a night club which was 6 .... noisy that it was difficult to sleep and, to make matters 7 .... , it didn't close until the early hours of the morning. 8 .... , the rather restricted mealtimes meant that we could not enjoy a leisurely meal beyond 10 p.m. However, all in 9 .... , my experience was a positive one. I hope that my report will 10 .... you to improve facilities for the future.

Buying and selling

Lead in

1 What ways of buying and selling are shown in the photos?

- from a catalogue
- online
- in a market
- second-hand
- through an agent
- at an auction
- charity shop

2 Answer these questions about the ways of buying and selling in 1.

- a What kinds of things can be bought and sold?
- b What do you already buy or sell in these ways?
- c What ways would you not use to buy or sell?

3 Discuss your monthly spending habits and put these in order of how much money you spend on each.

- cinema
- clothes
- accommodation
- books/magazines
- music
- eating out

4 Discuss these questions.

- a What else do you spend your money on?
- b Do you think you spend too much on anything?
- c Have you ever bought anything just because of an advert? What was it and how did the advert persuade you to buy it?

Reading Part 2 Gapped text

1 Quickly read the text below to find out how eBay was started, and what item the writer bought.

2 Discuss the meaning of these phrases from the text.

  a   media coverage (1.7)
  b   major corporations (1.16)
  c   unwanted stock (1.16)
  d   successful entrepreneurs (1.39)
  e   career advancement (1.58)

3 Read the text again, then match paragraphs A–G with gaps 1–6. There is one extra paragraph.

4 Have you or anyone you know bought or sold something on eBay? What was it? Is there anything you'd like to buy or sell on eBay?

the appeal

The history of the Internet is littered with tales of businesses that were set to take over the world and then failed to live up to the hype. With eBay it is the other way round. The online auction house is now the biggest e-commerce
5 business in the world, a staggering success story that just keeps on growing. Yet it was the grapevine that ensured its success rather than advertising or media coverage.

1 ☐

The stories that have got eBay talked about reinforce the message that when it comes to picking up a bargain, or
10 making a few quid out of something you thought was worthy only of the dustbin, the rich and famous are no different from the rest of us. Tony Blair's wife, Cherie, bought a Winnie the Pooh alarm clock on eBay for her son Leo; Robbie Williams' bed sold for £15,400 and millionairess Jemima Khan used the
15 site to acquire a second-hand designer dress.

2 ☐

Major corporations use eBay to shed unwanted stock but it's the private individual who really gives the site its character. Transactions put strangers in touch with each other. Emails are exchanged. There are online discussion boards and, crucially,
20 eBay operates a feedback system whereby buyers and sellers rate each other's honesty and efficiency. It pays to do right by your fellow eBayers. If your rating falls much below 100 per cent – 98 per cent is barely good enough – then you will find that people simply won't deal with you.

3 ☐

25 With such a range and speed of sales – and a commission on each – it is hardly surprising that the business is now a global giant. It was launched in 1995 and was the brainchild of Pierre Omidyar. Born in Paris to Iranian parents who emigrated to the US when he was six, he got a degree in computer sciences and
30 moved to California, where eBay was born. In those days it was called Auctionweb.

4 ☐

A revelatory moment soon followed. Omidyar owned a broken laser pointer, and rather than take it back to the shop, he decided he would try to sell it on the site he had set up. To his
35 amazement, a buyer came forward, who said that he liked playing around with things and fixing them. He paid $14. If a broken laser pointer could sell, what couldn't? Seeking to answer that question turned Omidyar into one of today's most successful entrepreneurs.

5 ☐

40 More typical, perhaps, are users such as Victoria Egan, a 30-year-old housewife who estimates that she makes £100 a month dealing on eBay, which is handy when you have a young family to support. 'I started e-Baying after we had our first child,' she says. 'To begin with, I sold a few things just to
45 free up space at home. I also bought but the selling is more addictive. For me and my husband, it's also an environmental thing. It's about recycling things.'

6 ☐

A friendly exchange of emails with the seller completed my entry into the eBay community. Now I plan to start selling, but
50 to do so I'm going to need a digital camera in order to post photographs of my items on the website. When I explained this to Paul Witten, he said to me, 'Well, you know where the best place to buy a digital camera is, don't you … ?'

A He is not alone in seeing the money-making possibilities that eBay offers. There are those who claim to make a healthy living just by selling on the site. In particular, women at home with young children – in circumstances otherwise incompatible with career advancement – seem to have picked up on the opportunities on offer. For example, Julie King, a 32-year-old former IT consultant, earns £70,000 a year buying shoes and bags wholesale and selling them on. Her 'Killer Heels' company has now taken off beyond her wildest dreams.

B This personal evaluation clearly works. Other online auction houses have tried to get in on the act, but eBay's statistics dwarf them. At any given time some 25 million items are up for sale, in more than 50,000 different categories – from cars and computers to antiques and books. It is listed in the top 250 companies on New York's Nasdaq exchange. On an average day on eBay UK, someone buys one mobile phone every minute; a football shirt every five minutes; a vehicle every four minutes; and a laptop every two minutes.

C As one inveterate observer of social trends put it: 'I hadn't seen it on the telly and wasn't aware of having seen it advertised. I only knew about it through friends when I first started using it.' Many of the millions of people who are registered users of eBay like to think of themselves as part of a community brought together by a shared love of buying and selling and of the items that really interest them, whether that's 1920s clothing or teddy bears.

D The inspiration behind the project came not from the company's founder but from his wife. She was an avid collector of sweet dispensers, commenting to her husband that it would be great if she were able to collect them via the Internet and interact with other collectors. As an early Internet enthusiast, he realised that people needed a central location to buy and sell unique items and to meet other users with similar interests.

E The beauty of the idea lay – of course – in its simplicity. 'It is in a complete class of its own,' says Witten. 'We have a very low cost base and unlike other online retailers we have no product of our own, so we have no storage. It's a virtuous circle. The more users come, the more follow.'

F The experiences related by these women were intriguing and so, in the interests of research, I registered on eBay. I was quickly hooked. After a while I began scrolling through a category of interest to me – cycling memorabilia. I soon spotted something I really wanted in the form of a vintage Soviet Union cycling jersey, bidding for which stood at £11. There was a day and a half to go until the conclusion of the sale and I started bidding. When I got the news that I had won the auction, I was elated. The jersey cost me £36.01, not an absolute bargain but a price I was very happy to pay for something I could never have found elsewhere.

G You probably wouldn't find any of those people standing next to you at a car-boot sale on a Sunday morning, but in the virtual auction house, social barriers disappear. 'To me, it's been like a great social experiment,' says Paul Witten, who joined eBay.co.uk a few years ago and became head of events and education. 'The challenge was, how do you bring people together in a venture like this and maintain a level playing field? I think we've succeeded, yet a lot of people find it hard to believe that we treat everybody equally.'

Vocabulary

Expressions with *business*, and words connected with shopping

1 Complete expressions a–e with the correct preposition below, then discuss what each of the expressions means.

> out   of   in   to   on

a I just need a few tools to fix the car, then we're .... *business*.
b I don't think you should interfere. It's *none* .... *your business* really.
c I'm afraid the Managing Director is away .... *business* until the end of the week.
d Our local shop *went* .... *of business* when a new out-of-town superstore opened.
e Right. Let's get *down* .... *business* and start making some decisions.

2 Read the definitions for the expressions in a–h to see if they are correct. If not, use your dictionary to give the correct definition.

a The star was arrested for *shoplifting* designer clothes. (stealing goods from a shop)
b In some countries, you are expected to *haggle over* the price of goods. (pay the full price)
c I'm going on a *shopping spree* at the weekend because Friday is payday! (buy one or two necessary things)
d My sister loves to *go window-shopping* when she's on holiday. (looking at goods in a shop without intending to buy anything)
e Sometimes it's a good idea to *shop around* before buying anything. (compare the price or quality of goods offered in different shops)
f It's advisable to keep the *receipt* when you buy something. (piece of paper that shows that goods have been paid for)
g I absolutely love shopping. I admit I'm a real *shopaholic*! (someone who likes to go shopping now and again)
h Have you seen Tom's new car? It was so expensive he had to buy it *on credit*. (an arrangement to pay later for something you buy)

Grammar

Mixed conditionals and wishes GR p179–180

1 Form mixed conditional sentences by putting the verbs in brackets into the correct tense.

a Our firm .... (not/be) in debt today if we .... (listen) to our accountant's past warnings.
b If our parents .... (not/lend) us the money, we .... (not/live) in our own flat now.
c I .... (be) a lot better off this year if my last tax bill .... (not/be) so high.
d If he .... (not have to) leave early tomorrow he .... (come) out tonight.
e He .... (not misread) that last road sign if his eyesight .... (not be) so poor these days.
f If you .... (not/listen) just now, you .... (have) trouble using the equipment later.

2 Add conditional clauses as shown in brackets to form mixed conditional sentences in a–e.

a We wouldn't know as much about the universe as we do now if … (3rd conditional)
b If email hadn't been invented … (2nd conditional)
c If we haven't discovered intelligent life on other planets by now … (1st conditional)
d I'd be a lot better off today if … (3rd conditional)
e Venice wouldn't have become such a popular tourist destination if … (2nd conditional)

3 Correct the mistakes with verbs in four of these sentences.

a I wish I had a bit more money. I hate having to borrow from my parents.
b My sister wishes her boyfriend will propose. She's crazy about him.
c Don't you wish English grammar would be a bit easier to understand?
d Is there anything in your life you wish you had done differently?
e I wish I would afford to buy a car.
f I wish the rain stopped.

4 Complete the rules below and find an example for each point from 3.

 a *wish/If only* + past simple is used for situations in the present which we would like to be different but which can't change.

 b *wish/If only* + ... is used for situations that could change in the future, and for criticising current situations.

 c When the subject of both verbs is the same we use .... instead of *would*.

 d *wish/If only* + ... is used for regrets about the past.

5 Talk about your wishes about the past, present and future, giving reasons.

Examples

I wish I hadn't stayed out so late last night. If I'd gone to bed a bit earlier, I wouldn't feel so tired this morning.

I wish I had a good voice. If I were a better singer, I could be in a band.

6 Complete the gaps in a–k in an appropriate way.

 a If only I .... go out tonight. The football Cup Final is on TV.

 b I do wish you .... more carefully. I've said the same thing three times already.

 c I bet your friend wishes he .... that girl his phone number. She just won't leave him alone!

 d If only someone .... me not to buy that mobile phone. It's been nothing but trouble since the day I bought it!

 e I wish the sun .... ! Then we could go to the park and play tennis.

 f If only plasma TVs .... so expensive. There's no way I can afford one.

 g Like most of the other students, I wish we .... exams at the end of this course.

 h If only you .... nearer! Then I could see you every single day.

 i Sue really wishes she .... go on the trip but she has too much work to do here.

 j I wish I .... all those prawns. They've given me stomach-ache.

 k I wish something exciting .... to me in the next few days.

7 Complete the text by putting the verbs in brackets into the correct tense.

As a child, Sue Matthews used to watch the birds in the sky and wish that she .... (1 be able to) fly like they did. 'If only I .... (2 have) wings,' she would sigh, 'then my life .... (3 be) perfect.' By the time Sue was 18, her childhood dream was long forgotten. She hated her job and wished she .... (4 stay) on at school. 'If only something .... (5 happen) to change my life,' she moaned to her friends. 'If things .... (6 continue) like this, I think I .... (7 go) crazy!' What happened next was a pure stroke of luck. Sue wasn't a keen reader and if she .... (8 not/be) forced to sit in the doctor's waiting room for an hour, she .... (9 may/never/pick) up the local paper and noticed the ad that was to change her life. A group of enthusiasts planned to set up a skydiving school at the tiny airport outside town and were looking for new members. If enough people .... (10 apply), the ad said, classes .... (11 start) in a fortnight's time. Fortunately, Sue was not the only person to rush to the phone that day and the skydiving school was soon in business. And as she stepped out of the plane for her first free fall and saw the rolling green hills below her, Sue knew that her childhood dream really had come true.

I wish I could fly.

Listening Part 3 Multiple choice

1 What, for you, makes an advert good or bad? Do you have any favourite adverts?

2 🎧 Listen twice to an interview with Paula Stuart, the managing director of an advertising agency, and choose the correct answer for 1–6. The how to do it box will help you.

how to do it

■ Read the task and questions for general meaning.

■ Remember that the questions follow the order of the listening text.

■ Mark your answers but check them on the second listening.

□ Check that the option you choose answers the question accurately.

1 Paula feels drawn to the world of advertising because she is

   A a hard-hitting business person.
   B a creative person.
   C a talkative person.
   D a persuasive person.

2 What comment does Paula make about her career in advertising?

   A It's been a long and difficult struggle.
   B She has succeeded despite the setbacks.
   C There have been more bad times than good ones.
   D She quickly got to the top of her profession.

3 What does she feel are the differences between working in advertising and working in other industries?

   A You can make your reputation overnight.
   B You can build on past successes.
   C Success depends exclusively on future achievements.
   D One inventive idea will guarantee your profitability.

4 Paula says that if you look back on past advertising campaigns, you find that

   A a campaign which lasts too long can be a disaster.
   B brand names benefit from high-profile campaigns.
   C people never forget a successful campaign.
   D a rejected campaign can be reinvented later.

5 What does she consider to be the secret of continuing success?

   A constantly searching for innovation
   B building up a reliable network of contacts
   C concentrating not on the past or future but on the present
   D having the courage to carry on with what you are doing

6 Paula sums up the advertising industry as being one in which

   A long-established brands are beginning to reassert themselves.
   B newcomers are finding it difficult to make a living.
   C the number of employees is constantly shrinking.
   D the average age of employees is younger than it used to be.

3 Do you agree that all adverts should be 'legal, decent, honest and truthful'? In what ways might they not be?

Speaking Parts 3 and 4

1 Discuss which of the different ways of advertising shown here and on page 122:

- should reach the widest audience.
- would be the most/least expensive.
- might irritate people.
- would have the most visual impact.

2 🎧 Listen to four pairs of students discussing adverts for a new range of leisurewear. In which conversation (1–4) does someone

a explain an opinion ....
b not expand on their answer ....
c disagree impolitely ....
d interact well with their partner ....
e ask an inappropriate question ....
f paraphrase unknown vocabulary ....

3 Look at the photos opposite and below and read the exam prompts. With a partner, do the task in four minutes.

- How successful might these ways of advertising be in persuading people to buy leisurewear?
- Which two ways of advertising would you choose to use for a promotion?

4 Discuss these Part 4 questions.

a What kinds of things do you think should not be advertised? Why?
b Some people say there is too much advertising nowadays. What's your view?

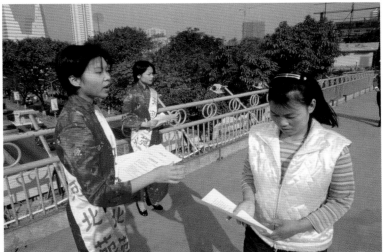

Use of English

Part 3 Word formation

1 Look at the photos and discuss what 'bling' means. Does it appeal to you? Why/Why not?

2 Read the text below, ignoring the gaps, to find out who is wearing 'bling' and who is making money from it.

3 Complete gaps 1–10 with words formed from those next to the text. The tip box will help you.

THE BUSINESS OF 'BLING'

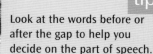

tip

Look at the words before or after the gap to help you decide on the part of speech.

It was a New Orleans rapper named 'BG' that first coined the term 'bling bling' to describe his taste in **0** ..flashy.. jewellery. Since then, it has certainly not gone **1** .... as a fashion statement. In fact, it has become the byword for a **2** .... , extravagant lifestyle. The term is so widespread that it's even entered English dictionaries. Bling means big money, so it's hardly **3** .... that people are keen on experimenting with bling including even the most **4** .... jewellery companies. When footballer David Beckham wanted a gift for his wife, he turned to a New York designer. Better known to his clients as 'Jacob the Jeweller', he sent a pink diamond ring to Spain so that Beckham could surprise his wife with the **5** .... present. It meant Jacob could add another celebrity to his list of customers.

0	FLASH
1	NOTICE
2	GLAMOUR
3	SURPRISE
4	TRADITION
5	EXPECT

But he isn't the only one catering for such high-profile people. Other New York jewellers have client lists that are **6** .... made up of hip-hop and R&B stars. The value of hip-hop as a music and lifestyle industry is put at an **7** .... $10 billion annually. As with the world of fashion, hip-hop stars are now joining in and **8** .... creating jewellery lines of their own. And they face fierce **9** .... from those in the rap world.

It seems jewellery is much more than a **10** .... accessory. Perhaps the era of bling is only just beginning.

6	INCREASE
7	CREDIBLE
8	FEVER
9	COMPETE
10	BASE

Part 4 Gapped Sentences

4 For questions a–e, think of one word only which can be used appropriately in all three sentences. All the words appear in the text opposite.

a There was a .... debate about the best way to tackle the issue.

Despite .... competition, Anderson won the contest with ease and style.

The property was guarded by two .... guard dogs.

b I have to admit that modern music is not really to my ....

Everyone thought the speech was in very bad .... and wholly unsuitable for the event.

The trip to Syria was our first .... of life in the Middle East.

c I know for a .... that something is going wrong at work.

Everything comes to an end – that's a .... of life.

The trip was terrible – as a matter of .... , I've never been very fond of travelling.

d There are times when I can't .... going into college.

The government has to .... up to the fact that they no longer have the people's support.

Let's .... it, our chances of winning the lottery are very small indeed.

e Our students have always taken a .... interest in current affairs.

The only person who is .... on fish in my family is my brother.

My sister has a .... eye for a bargain and loves going shopping.

Vocabulary

Easily confused words (2)

1 Use your dictionary to find the correct word in *italics* to complete each sentence.

a In some countries the *economic/economical* growth rate has been dramatic in recent years.
b It is company policy that the *personal/personnel* manager attends all interviews.
c One of my colleagues gets to work by walking or cycling on *alternative/alternate* days.
d At the monthly farmers' market they sell only locally grown *products/produce*.
e Most international businesses promote equal *opportunities/possibilities* for all employees.

2 Decide which of the words not used in 1 are defined in a–e. Use your dictionary to help you.

a something that is private to you
b goods that have been manufactured
c the chances that something may happen
d something that saves you money
e another way of doing something

3 Read the text and choose the most suitable word to correctly complete 1–10.

It is **1** *scarce/scarcity/scarcely* surprising that Tricia Black, one of the country's leading businesswomen, is now a multi-millionaire. She puts her success down to **2** *honesty/honest/honestly* and claims that people will simply stop dealing with you if you are **3** *trustworthy/untrustworthy/trusting*. And when it comes to her **4** *employment/employers/employees*, she is incredibly **5** *sense/sensible/sensitive* to their needs, and treats everyone **6** *fair/fairly/fairness*. She has also worked **7** *tirelessly/tiresomely/tiredly* for charity and has raised money for many good causes. Black tries to deal in products that are **8** *environmentally/environment/environmental* friendly. It seems that what she **9** *really/real/reality* wants in life is to become a **10** *height/highly/high* regarded member of the community.

Writing Part 2 A report WG p160

1 If you could choose to do work experience in any job for six weeks, what would you like to do and why?

2 Read the exam task and model answer. Make brief notes on who the writer worked for and what he did. How did he feel about the experience?

> You are studying abroad. Recently your college sent you to do six weeks' work experience. Now your college principal has asked you to write a report. You should say
>
> • who you were working for and how you spent your time there
> • whether your experience was positive
> • whether you would recommend the experience to other students.

3 Read the model answer and discuss questions a–e. Has the writer:

a included the important points?
b organised ideas into paragraphs?
c linked sentences and paragraphs?
d used the correct register?
e made a good impression through the layout of the report?

Introduction

The aim of this report is to describe and evaluate my six weeks' work experience with RPC Music and to make recommendations for the future.

About the company

RPC Music is one of the oldest record companies in the world, dating back to 1940. It employs around 5,000 employees worldwide and is represented in over 50 countries. The company records and publishes music of all types and represents many of the best-known recording artists in the world.

My work experience

During my six weeks with RPC Music, I was assigned to three different departments.

Publicity

My first placement was in the publicity department. Here I learnt how CDs are promoted and helped write promotional literature for music magazines. I also helped to set up a TV interview with one of RPC's best-known rock artists.

4 Think of a job you know enough about to base the exam task on. Make notes on:

a who you would work for and what they do.
b what tasks you might do as work experience.

tip

If you don't have any work experience, use your imagination to plan your answer with enough information.

5 Compare your notes from 4 with a partner, and discuss the positive and negative experiences you might have. Think about a–g below.

a working hours   e variety of tasks
b location   f colleagues
c facilities available g future career
d dress code

6 Plan your introduction and think about your headings. Decide whether you would recommend your experience to others or not and give your reasons. Then write your report in 220–260 words.

Sales

I spent two weeks in the sales department where I helped check stock and learnt how to process orders.

Design

During my final fortnight I worked in the design department where I helped to arrange photo shoots. I also helped design a cover for a new CD.

General comments

On the whole, I found my time with RPC Music extremely beneficial. The staff were very helpful and I obtained a good understanding of how each department functions. However, I believe I would have benefited more if my work experience had been for a longer period.

Conclusion

To sum up, RPC are an ideal company with which to do work experience. I have no hesitation in recommending that we send other students to the company in future.

Review

1 Complete the dialogues with suitable responses using expressions with the word *business*.

1 A: Do you know why the store closed?
  B: The number of people downloading music from the Internet put it ....

2 A: I haven't seen much of you recently – have you been away?
  B: I've been abroad for a couple of weeks ....

3 A: Why won't you tell me what happened?
  B: It's rather personal and ....

4 A: Have you got everything for the gym?
  B: I'll get my trainers and we're ....

5 A: Don't you think it's time we began our end-of-term project?
  B: Absolutely. Let's meet tomorrow afternoon and get ....

2 Write words which match the definitions in a–h. The first letter of each word is given.

a look at but not buy goods: w........... s...........
b buy a lot of things you don't really need: go on a s........... s...........
c someone who is always shopping: a s...........
d pay at a later date: buy o........... c...........
e argue over the price of something: h...........
f paper showing proof of purchase: a r...........
g compare the prices of goods in different shops: s........... a...........
h steal goods from a shop: s...........

3 For questions a–c, think of one word only which can be used appropriately in all three sentences.

a My cousin's just emigrated to Australia so I have a fantastic .... to spend some time there.

I'd like to take this .... to say how grateful I am for all the help you have given me.

We intend to bring in fundamental changes to the structure of the college at the earliest ....

b I have little respect for politicians because I think they tend to be .... with the truth.

The latest model, the X900, is said to be one of the most .... cars to run.

It's much more .... to buy in bulk than to purchase items individually.

c The birthday cake was very rich with .... layers of chocolate and cream.

I like the job but I don't like working .... Sundays, because I only have two full weekends off each month.

Profits proved unpredictable with the company going through .... periods of success and failure.

4 Complete sentences a–j with 1–10 below.

a I .... can't understand how you could do such an unkind thing!
b It takes an .... brave person to risk their life to save others.
c The law .... states that it is illegal to drive when drunk.
d None of us were .... dressed for a cold day.
e They were .... astonished to learn that their neighbour had been arrested for spying.
f It is .... surprising that Gemma became a scientist. She always loved science.
g In a recent survey, ... half those interviewed could correctly name the capital of the USA.
h Many thanks to all those who have worked .... to organise this very special event today.
i Mr Westfield, who died recently, was a .... regarded member of our community.
j He may be a strict teacher, but he treats all the students ....

1	plainly	5	barely	8	highly
2	hardly	6	fairly	9	adequately
3	utterly	7	exceptionally	10	tirelessly
4	simply				

5 Choose the correct words for 1–9 to complete this extract from a report.

The **1** *ambition/aim/goal* of this report is to evaluate the IT course I recently attended. Throughout the course, I was **2** *selected/assigned/chosen* to a personal tutor. As part of my studies, I was asked to **3** *turn/put/set* up and conduct an interview with other students. I **4** *passed/spent/filled* several hours doing this and **5** *on/in/over* the whole, I found it, and indeed the course itself, extremely useful. However, I would like to **6** *do/advise/make* one recommendation for the future. The course would have been of more **7** *good/benefit/advantage* if it had been for a longer **8** *period/interval/span*. Despite this, I have no **9** *doubt/hesitation/uncertainty* in recommending the course to others.

Entertainment or art?

Lead in

1 Which of these do you consider to be 'art'? Why? What do you think makes 'good' art?

2 Which of a–d do you think art should do? Does it have any other role? Give examples where possible.

a entertain   c provoke
b stimulate   d inform

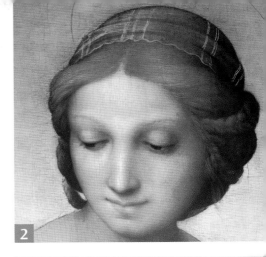

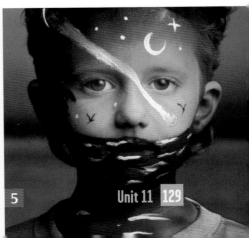

Reading

1 Quickly read the three extracts which are all concerned in some way with performing in public. What different types of 'performance' are mentioned?

2 Read the three extracts again and choose the best answer (A, B, C or D) for questions 1–6. The tip box will help you.

> **tip**
>
> If necessary, use the context to help you with unfamiliar words or phrases.

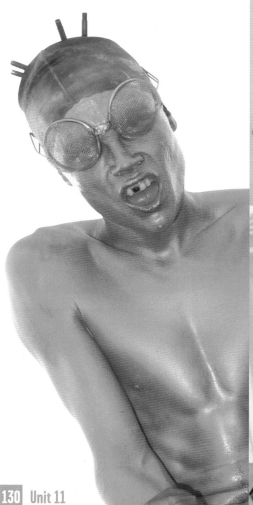

is it art?

The little boy on the bike is screaming: "He's a nutter! He's wearing tights on his head!" But Danny McCarthy walks on, his round glasses poking through the black stockings that cover his face, a battered suitcase in one hand, a brown paper parcel in the other. What the
05 screaming child doesn't realise is that he is witnessing performance art. McCarthy, who lives in Ireland, is walking around London as part of an ongoing performance entitled *What Do You Do When You Get There and There is No There There?* which centres on the Irish experience of emigration.

Performance art became accepted in the 1970's, when conceptual art
10 was in its heyday. Conceptual artists saw ideas as more important than the finished product. Performance became the execution of those ideas. Performance artists want to take their art directly to a public forum. They believe that looking at something on a wall in a gallery has an adverse affect on people because it puts them in a passive position. Performance
15 art, therefore, is live, is not for sale, has no rules, and may entertain or shock. It can include painting, dance, video, and much more. It is art because its creator says it is.

Unlike conventional art, performance art requires an audience to construct its own narrative from
20 the cues it gives. So perhaps that boy on the bike will make up a story about the 'nutter' with tights on his head. Maybe the story will impress a girl. Maybe he's already forgotten
25 about it. Maybe it'll stay with him for ever. Maybe that's the mystery.

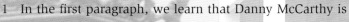

1 In the first paragraph, we learn that Danny McCarthy is
   A a successful artist.
   B down on his luck.
   C not what he seems.
   D a recent immigrant.

2 What does the writer suggest about performance art?
   A The effects are hard to predict.
   B It asks too much from an audience.
   C It promises more than it gives.
   D The appeal is a lasting one.

Giving a speech

You know the feeling. Your heart is running a marathon but the rest of you is standing still. There are butterflies in your stomach and you have an ominous feeling that something bad is going to happen. And the speech you've got to give is a few hours away! 30

If the idea of public speaking reduces you to a jelly, here are four steps you can follow to reduce your anxiety.

1 Be the first person to arrive at the venue.

2 Greet as many audience members as possible and exchange a few words with them. This will provide your audience with a vitally important initial impression; the speaker they have come to hear is interesting, accessible and warm. It will help you to know that here and there in your audience are listeners who already have a positive attitude towards you. 35 / 40

3 Picture in your mind a real two-way conversation. Don't stare blankly at the ceiling. Use gestures and facial expressions. You may think that there are 25 or 250 people watching you but, in terms of real communication, there are only two people in any room. The speaker and a single listener. 45

4 Ask questions during your speech, to individuals, to maintain a participatory feeling. One-quarter to one-half of your speech should literally be a discussion with the audience. That way it will not look or feel like a 'speech'. 50

Finally, remember that it isn't a 'speech' at all that you're delivering. It's an 'expanded conversation' with every person in the room. 55

3 What is one technique recommended for dealing with an audience?

A ask people who are well disposed towards you to join the audience
B find out in advance what kind of speaker the audience prefer
C get the support of the audience before you start
D do what you can to make your audience feel at home

4 According to the writer, public speakers should try to

A spend time answering questions.
B give a one-sided point of view.
C forget people have come to hear a speech.
D engage directly with the audience.

What I think of Shakespeare

A schoolchild watching a play by the Royal Shakespeare Company might think that a performance by such expert actors would be as good as it gets. But this is not always so. Because English is the first language of only some of the audience, no one – neither director nor actors – dare rely on Shakespeare's words. Instead they play the fool, doing anything to blur the line's delivery. In a production of Romeo and Juliet I once saw, the actors threw an orange to each other during the balcony scene. 60 / 65

Shakespeare's theatre must be got off the page to be experienced fully, but not as in the mannered performances of today's leading actors. I remember going, as a 16-year-old, to a performance of *Hamlet* at a nearby school. Hamlet was a tall, fair boy of excruciating thinness. He had no technique, but he had Hamlet's words. He seemed hypnotised by the poetry. He listened to himself, as actors rarely do. What came through him, like sunlight through glass, was the strenuousness of Hamlet's struggle with disgust and disbelief. We could have giggled at his knobbly knees in the dreaded tights – but we didn't. At home, I realised that I could be entranced again whenever I read Shakespeare aloud. After school, my mates and I took all the parts, noticing who spoke little and meant much, and who babbled and bleated. In later years we saw great actors play Hamlet. None of them was a patch on a gangling boy who did nothing but say the words as simply and as thoughtfully as he could. 70 / 75 / 80 / 85 / 90

5 According to the writer, the problem with the way some actors perform Shakespeare is that they

A speak with poor diction.
B might distract the audience.
C misquote the original Shakespeare.
D lack sufficient training.

6 What was the writer's reaction to watching the boy who played Hamlet?

A shock
B amusement
C approval
D disappointment

Vocabulary

Art and entertainment

1 Find the odd one out in word groups a–g. What is the theme of the new group?

a	soundtrack	subtitles	easel
b	canvas	plot	chapter
c	lyrics	tune	sketch
d	clip	premiere	gallery
e	stage	landscape	rehearsal
f	palette	cast	extra
g	performance	show	watercolour

2 Choose the most suitable word to complete a–f.

a This stunning self-portrait was painted in oil on *palette/canvas/easel*.

b Do you know who wrote the *extras/lyrics/chapter* for this musical?

c Some people aren't keen on films with *soundtracks/subtitles/special effects* because they find them distracting.

d A convincing thriller needs a strong *landscape/tune/plot*.

e A new *gallery/landscape/sketch* is planned to showcase local artists' works.

f A bad dress *show/rehearsal/performance* could foretell a successful opening night.

3 Use your dictionary to find definitions for words from 2. In pairs, give a definition to your partner and ask them to guess the word. Then swap roles.

4 Discuss the following questions.

a Which is more important, the lyrics or the tune of a song?

b How important to a film is the soundtrack?

c What kind of films often need extras?

d Would you consider a career in the entertainment industry? Why/Why not?

e What significant changes have already happened or are likely to happen in the entertainment industry?

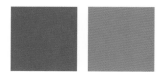

Grammar GR p180–182

Comparatives and superlatives

1 Correct the errors with comparatives and superlatives in sentences a–i.

a Michael Schumacher invariably drove more fastly than the other Grand Prix drivers.

b The longer I live in this city, more I like it.

c The Pyramids are among the ancientest structures in the world.

d My job interview wasn't nearly as rigorous than I had expected.

e What an awful film! It had by far the less convincing ending I think I've ever seen.

f Summers in Australia tend to be much more hot than in Britain.

g He did a great deal more badly in the athletics competition than his teachers had expected.

h You may think you know the answer but I'm afraid you couldn't be wronger.

i Both of my brothers are considerably elder than me.

2 Correct the spelling errors with the adjectives in a–e.

a Repairing my motorbike was slightly trickyer than I'd anticipated.

b Many of us would like to be a bit slimer but dieting too strictly can be dangerous.

c This year has already been much weter than the whole of last summer.

d Meteorologists say that this summer has been dryer than any other summer on record.

e Joshua was already feeling seasick and his face turned several degrees paleer when the boat left the harbour.

3 Discuss the answers to a–d, using comparative and superlative forms of the words in brackets.

a Put these planets in order of distance from the Earth: Mars, Venus, Jupiter (far/near)

b Put these inventions in order of age: transistor radio, electric guitar, portable calculator (old/recent)

c Put these oceans in order of size: Pacific, Indian, Atlantic (large/small)

d Put these in order of number of calories they contain: bread, chocolate, lettuce (little/much)

4 Match a–d with a sentence of similar meaning from 1–4.

a It's *slightly* safer.
b It's *far* safer.
c It's *just* as safe.
d It isn't *nearly* as safe.

1 It's *no more* dangerous.
2 It's *much* more dangerous.
3 It's *nowhere near* as dangerous.
4 It isn't *quite* as dangerous.

5 Which italicised words and expressions in 4 above could be replaced with a–e?

a a bit
b a great deal
c a little
d a lot
e nothing like

6 Complete these sentences using the expressions from 4 and 5.

a The standard of living in Northern Europe is .... higher than in most African countries.
b As you can imagine, crossing the continent in a bumpy old truck is .... as comfortable as travelling by plane.
c I thought things would be cheaper in the market but the trainers I bought there were .... as expensive as the ones in the shop.
d A five-star hotel should be .... luxurious than a four-star hotel.
e Temperatures in the south of my country are .... warmer than in the north but the difference isn't very great.

7 Choose the correct word to complete each of a–g.

a The film was *enough/so/too* scary that my little brother had nightmares after watching it.
b I like the idea of bungee jumping but I don't know if I'd be brave *so/such/enough* to do it.
c The painting had to be restored because it was in *enough/so/such* a bad state of repair.
d Elaine has *very/so/too* little talent for singing that it's no wonder she was dropped from the choir.
e Tim had *too/so/such* great a shock when lightning struck his plane that he swore never to fly again.
f My neighbour auditioned for a big musical but they said he was *enough/too/so* old for the part.
g Our local bus service is *very/such/so* unreliable that I prefer to walk.

8 Complete sentences a–e using *as* or *like*.

a I've been working .... a volunteer in the local hospital.
b What on earth's the matter? You've gone as white .... a sheet!
c You look .... a film star in that outfit.
d I'm not so much angry .... disappointed at what the council have decided.
e Mrs Lyons was built .... a bus but her son was small and rather weedy.

9 Compare two places in your country, using a variety of comparatives and superlatives. Use the prompts to help you.

- popularity with tourists
- weather
- which you would rather visit
- attractions
- cost

Listening

Part 2 Sentence completion

1 Why do you think animated films appeal to both children and adults?

2 Read the exam task below about Pixar, a film studio which makes animated films, and decide what types of words are missing, e.g. nouns, adjectives, numbers, etc.

3 🎧 Listen to the radio programme and complete sentences 1–8.

4 What do you think makes an Oscar-winning film? Is it always the 'best' films that win Oscars?

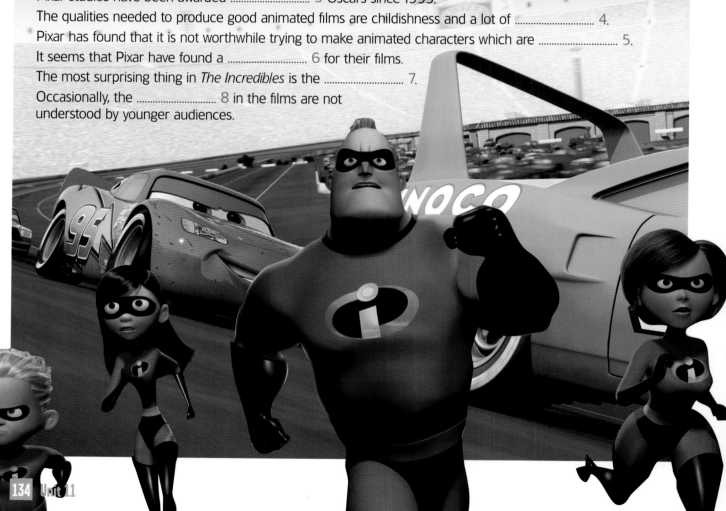

The PIXAR animated film studio

'Renderfarm' is the name of a .... 1 at the Pixar film studios in San Francisco.

Pixar's rivals have found the film studio's success .... 2.

Pixar studios have been awarded .... 3 Oscars since 1995.

The qualities needed to produce good animated films are childishness and a lot of .... 4.

Pixar has found that it is not worthwhile trying to make animated characters which are .... 5.

It seems that Pixar have found a .... 6 for their films.

The most surprising thing in *The Incredibles* is the .... 7.

Occasionally, the .... 8 in the films are not understood by younger audiences.

Speaking Part 2

1 Discuss what a–e have in common. Say which ones can be used to talk about each photo in 1–4, and when you would use each of the others.

   a spectator   c witness   e viewer
   b audience   d observer

2 🎧 Read the exam task above the photos, then listen to part of what one candidate said while doing the task and note down all the link words she uses.

> • Why might the people have chosen to watch these kinds of entertainment?
> • How different might the people's reactions to the entertainment be?

3 With a partner, each choose one pair of photos and take it in turns to do the task in 2, talking for a minute each. Then look at each other's photos and decide which people are most enjoying what they are watching.

Use of English

Part 2 Open cloze

1 Read the text opposite quickly, ignoring the gaps, to find out how music is being used at a railway station and with what results.

2 Read the text again and complete each of gaps 1–15 with one suitable word.

3 Would the idea described in the text work where you live? Why/Why not?

Part 5 Key word transformations

4 Rewrite the second sentence in a–d keeping the meaning the same. Use three to six words including the word given.

a I'm afraid I now find myself unable to attend the meeting tomorrow.

   LONGER

   Unfortunately, I am .... to attend the meeting tomorrow.

b If listening to music is forced on people, they react against it.

   MADE

   If people .... music, they react against it.

c Eliminating a problem is difficult if you don't know what's causing it.

   RID

   It's not easy to .... a problem when you don't know what's causing it.

d Perhaps he has forgotten about the rehearsal again.

   SLIPPED

   Maybe the rehearsal .... again.

MUSIC TO THEIR EARS

The experience of standing at a bus stop or on a railway station platform and feeling intimidated 0 ...by..... a group of noisy youths is not uncommon. A variety of expensive solutions to this problem have been tried but now the idea 1 .... playing classical music is gradually becoming adopted 2 .... a low-cost answer. All that's needed is the required licence to play music and 3 .... few speakers – and the problem seems to just disappear.

One railway station had 4 .... experiencing problems with youths hanging around, 5 .... getting up to criminal activities but engaging in anti-social behaviour, 6 .... using bad language and annoying passengers. Passengers complained 7 .... the authorities responded by introducing classical music, a solution 8 .... completely eliminated the problem. Music makes 9 .... an important part of our identity. If we are forced to listen to music that we don't like, we will react and move 10 .... from it. Predictably, the youngsters loathed the music and very quickly gave 11 .... and left.

Now the passengers not 12 .... say they don't see youths hanging around, but they also no 13 .... feel uneasy when travelling. The trouble-makers may have disappeared, 14 .... the music continues by popular demand, because passengers say it brightens the time spent waiting for trains. For the time 15 .... then, music seems to be the answer.

Vocabulary

Three-part phrasal verbs GR p182–183

1 Complete the three-part phrasal verbs in a–g with the missing particle, then match them with similar meanings 1–7.

a I don't want to *fall* .... *with* you but I really can't agree with what you're doing.

b I think the reason the car's stopped is that we've *run* .... *of* petrol.

c We had to *put* .... *with* the noise in our hotel because nowhere else had any rooms available.

d Sam bought me a bunch of flowers to *make* .... *for* hurting my feelings.

e My father doesn't *get* .... *with* his new boss so he's looking for another job.

f One of the marketing team has *come* .... *with* a good idea for a new advertisement.

g The factory has decided to *do* .... *with* the old computers and install a new system.

1 tolerate
2 get rid of
3 have a good relationship with
4 argue
5 compensate for
6 use all of something
7 think of

2 Form three-part phrasal verbs in a–f using *out*, *up*, *in* or *on* and complete the sentences appropriately. Use your dictionary to help you.

a You'll have to walk .... I can't *keep* .... *with* you.

b What's got into Clare? She *came* .... *with* a very .... remark at breakfast this morning.

c If Jack's wife keeps *going* .... *at* him all the time he's likely to ....

d If you don't *stick* .... *for* your rights, people will .... you.

e His wife *walked* .... *on* him, leaving him to .... on his own.

f The reason Tina's so .... is that her parents *give* .... *to* her all the time.

3 Correct any mistakes with the phrasal verbs in these sentences.

a Ben fell down with his father some years ago and they haven't spoken to each other since.

b Do you know which writer first came away with the term 'robotics'?

c Could you talk more slowly please? I can't keep up to what you're saying.

d I'd like to find a solution but I'm afraid I've run away of ideas.

e Don't let anyone bully you – stick up to yourself!

f My parents keep going on with me to study harder.

Writing Part 2 A review WG p159

1 What is the most recent film you have seen? What made you decide to see it?

2 Which of a–e might be included in a film review?

   a a summary of the plot
   b comments on special features
   c a biography of the lead actors
   d a description of the costumes
   e a recommendation about whether or not to see the film

3 Read the exam task and the model answer below and answer these questions.

   a Does the answer address all parts of the task?
   b Does the information given help you decide whether you would want to see the films?

You write for an international student magazine. The editor has asked you for a review recommending two films, one for adults and the other for a younger audience. You should comment on the plot and the acting and explain why the films are suitable for each age group. Write your review in 220–260 words.

Pirates of the Caribbean: Dead Man's Chest and *Sin City* are both highly enjoyable movies. However, they will appeal to very different audiences.

Dead Man's Chest is a gripping adventure story, packed with laughs. Ruthless pirate hunter Lord Beckett (Tom Hollander) sets out to retrieve the fabled Dead Man's Chest. This will give him power over Davy Jones, the heartless villain who rules the seas. It will also allow him to destroy the Pirates of the Caribbean. But pirate captain Jack Sparrow (Johnny Depp) and his courageous companions Will (Orlando Bloom) and Elizabeth (Keira Knightley) are out to stop him. The acting is superb. Bill Nighy gives a haunting performance as Davy Jones, his face sprouting octopus tentacles. But Johnny Depp steals the show, with his rolling eyes, flashing gold teeth and mischievous grin.

4 Find adjectives in the model answer which mean the same as a–j. There may be more than one answer.

a very exciting
b heartlessly determined
c cruel
d brave
e extremely good
f hard to forget
g naughty/playful
h violent
i extremely attractive
j strong and independent

5 Tell a partner what you thought of the last film you saw, using some of these ideas.

a It's a gripping/slow-moving/action-packed story.
b The plot is far-fetched/intriguing/predictable.
c The final scenes are thrilling/spine-chilling/ spectacular.
d The script is witty/natural/awkward.
e The acting is wooden/uninspired/unconvincing.
f The lead actor/actress gives a tremendous/ mediocre/fantastic performance.
g The special effects are amazing/stunning/ disappointing.

6 Decide whether adverbs a–i are strong, 'medium', or weak adverbs. Then say which of the adjectives you chose in 5 they can modify.

a rather
b slightly
c utterly
d extremely
e really
f absolutely
g completely
h totally
i fairly

7 Choose two suitable films to review for the exam task. For each one make notes on:

• the plot and the acting
• any other notable aspects
• who they are suitable for and why.

8 Write your review including:

a an introduction naming the films and their genre
b a conclusion summarising who they are suitable for.

Sin City is a much more bloodthirsty affair. Set in a crime-infested city, the plot has three storylines. Street fighter Marv (Mickey Rourke) is searching for the murderer of a seductive woman, killed while sleeping beside him; ex-photographer Dwight (Clive Owen) has accidentally killed a cop and is trying to cover it up; and tough cop Hartigan (Bruce Willis) is framed for a crime he did not commit. The cast is wonderful, especially Rourke, who delivers one of the most outstanding performances of his career.

Either of these films would make a great evening's entertainment. *Dead Man's Chest* is a family film with something for everyone, but *Sin City*, with its adult themes, extreme violence, and bad language, is definitely not a film for the kids!

Review

1 Complete sentences a–g using the verb in brackets in the passive form and an appropriate ending from 1–7.

Example

A plot is thought up by an author.

a ~~A plot (think up)~~
b A soundtrack can (hear)
c Extras (often/hire)
d Tunes and lyrics (write)
e An easel can (find)
f A premiere (organise)
g Rehearsals (always/hold)

1 on a film
2 for crowd scenes in films
3 ~~by an author~~
4 to publicise a film
5 before a show's first night
6 for musicals
7 in an artist's studio

2 Complete the words in a–f which refer to people looking or watching. The first letter of each one is given.

a A crowd of curious o.......... had gathered around the street performer.
b I didn't actually take part in the debate as I'd simply been sent along as an o.......... .
c Police are appealing for w.......... to the accident to come forward and give statements.
d At the end of the match the players thanked the s.......... for the fantastic support they had given throughout the tournament.
e I gather there's some a.......... participation in this play, so if you don't want to join in, don't sit near the front of the stage!
f TV controllers desperate to win back v.......... have vowed to cut the number of repeats as ratings reach an all-time low.

3 Rewrite the second sentence in a–e keeping the meaning the same. Use three to six words including the word given.

a Is the government considering getting rid of low-level income tax?
   DOING
   Is the government thinking .... low-level income tax?

b Brian and Susan have surely had an argument because they aren't speaking to each other.
   FALLEN
   Brian and Susan .... because they aren't speaking to each other.

c The Smiths lived with the noise of traffic in the city for years before they moved to a small village.
   PUTTING
   After years .... the noise of traffic in the city, the Smiths moved to a small village.

d He forgot my birthday and I couldn't forgive him, because he did nothing to show he was sorry.
   MAKE
   I would have forgiven him if he'd tried .... my birthday, but he did nothing to show he was sorry.

e We couldn't think of a better idea for improving the traffic problems.
   COME
   We were not .... a better idea for improving the traffic problems.

4 Rearrange the letters in brackets (1–7) to form adjectives to complete this article.

When Alexandre Dumas wrote his (thingrill) ....1 classic, *The Man in the Iron Mask*, he said it combined two driving forces of life: love and action. The musical based on the novel, however, captured none of its charisma and turned a (pingprig) ....2 story into a (spaceratcul) ....3 failure. The critics hated it. In addition to slamming its (wardkaw) ....4 lyrics and (ringspinuni) ....5 music, they criticised members of the cast for their (nedoow) ....6 acting. Visually, the production may have looked attractive and no doubt entertained some of the audience, even if for all the wrong reasons. The show's producers blamed (pointingpasid) ....7 attendance figures throughout theatreland, but the real reason for its sudden end, just two days after its premiere, were some of the most scathing reviews of recent times.

A changing world

Lead in

1 Read the extract below and discuss these questions.

  a What arguments do you think those in the energy industry and environmentalists would use for and against opening up the Wildlife Refuge?

  b Do you think decisions like these are inevitable in the long run?

  c What threats are there to other areas of outstanding beauty?

It is described as the last great American wilderness and has been the battleground between America's most powerful oil interests and environmentalists for more than two decades. But the giants of the energy industry are celebrating a significant victory and looking forward to the chance to move into one of the most lucrative oil fields left in the US, following the decision to open up the pristine Arctic National Wildlife Refuge in northern Alaska.

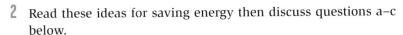

2 Read these ideas for saving energy then discuss questions a–c below.

- Turn down your thermostat by one degree.
- Replace an ordinary lightbulb with a low energy one.
- Turn off TVs instead of leaving them on standby.
- Turn off lights in unoccupied rooms.
- Only boil enough water in a kettle to meet your needs.

  a Which of the above have you ever done, or do you do regularly?

  b Do you think the suggestions could make a significant difference?

  c Who should be responsible for protecting our resources – governments or the individual?

Reading Part 4 Multiple matching

1 Read the text opposite about five places under threat (A–E), and match them with areas 1–5 on the map below.

2 Underline the key words in questions 1–12 in the exam task below. Where possible think of other ways of expressing the same information.

Example *increase in plant life = flourish of vegetation* (line 20).

In which section, A–E, are the following mentioned?

a possible *increase* in *plant life* in certain places   1 ....
an area that was once entirely under water   2 ....
a system which relies on the direct effect of temperature on water   3 ....
the potential disappearance of huge numbers of plants and animals   4 ....
a geographical feature that may face almost total destruction   5 ....
a substance which provides vital nourishment for sea creatures   6 ....
an area where extreme temperatures protect the earth   7 .... 8 ....
a harmful effect equivalent to decades of man-made pollution   9 ....
the damaging effect that rainfall could have on temperatures   10 ....
a possible increase in the number of destructive insects   11 ....
an area where evidence of its past can be seen at certain altitudes   12 ....

3 Read each section A–E carefully one at a time. Identify which of 1–12 are mentioned in each, leaving any difficult ones until last.

4 Do you think we have a duty to preserve the earth as it is? Why/why not?

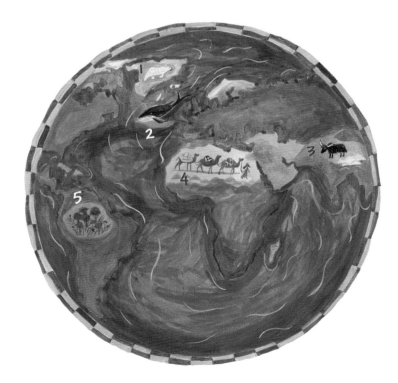

CHANGING PLACES

Five parts of the world where global warming could have dramatic consequences for the environment.

A The Amazon Forest

The size of western Europe, the Amazon forest is one of the most biodiverse regions on Earth. Models suggest that with global warming will come a drop in Amazonian rainfall, leading to
5 the gradual death of the forest and subsequent collapse of the myriad ecosystems it supports. The extinction of species is only one consequence of a warmer planet. Carbon dioxide is a greenhouse gas and scientists have
10 long warned about the levels produced when we burn fossil fuels. As the trees of the Amazon die off, they will fall and rot, and they too will release carbon dioxide. In the worst-case scenario, the quantities of gas emitted could be
15 of the same order of magnitude as from the twentieth century's total fossil fuel output.

B The Sahara Desert

Occupying some 3.5 million square miles of northern Africa, the Sahara desert is expected to shrink with global warming as more plentiful
20 rain brings a flourish of vegetation to its southernmost reaches. For those on the edge of the desert, the fertile land will undoubtedly be a boon, but the Sahara plays a broader role in the health of the planet. The dry dust that is
25 whipped up from the desert by strong prevailing winds contains crucial nutrients that seed the Atlantic and may even help fertilise the Amazon. As the Sahara turns from brown to green, the flux of these nutrients into the ocean
30 is expected to drop, restricting food available for plankton, the smallest of links in the marine food chain. As the number of plankton falls, so does food for aquatic creatures further up the food chain. That's not the only knock-on effect.
35 Plankton lock up the greenhouse gas CO_2 from the atmosphere and so help counter global warming. With fewer plankton, the oceans will take less of the gas from the Earth's atmosphere. When and if rains return to the
40 Sahara, disease and crop damage from pests could soar too.

C Greenland

The Greenland ice sheet holds about 6% of the planet's supply of fresh water and it is imperative that this water remains frozen. If global warming sees temperatures rise by more than about 3°C,
45 Greenland ice is likely to begin to melt, steadily releasing all that water – currently resting on land – into the North Atlantic Ocean. Climate models suggest that a more drastic temperature increase of some 8°C could see the Greenland ice sheet all but disappear, causing a dramatic rise in sea level. And this is not the only
50 danger posed by the melting of the world's frozen wastes. The Arctic tundra is a storehouse for decaying vegetation that has been buried for thousands of years. If the permafrost melts, carbon and methane stored in this vegetation will be released. As these are greenhouse gases they will cause a further acceleration
55 in the increase of temperatures.

D The North Atlantic

The North Atlantic current is one of the strongest ocean currents in the world. It works like a conveyer belt. Surface water in the North Atlantic is first cooled by westerly winds from North America, making the water more dense and salty so it sinks to
60 the ocean floor before moving towards the equator. Driven by winds and replacing the cold water moving south, warm water from the Gulf of Mexico moves upward into the Atlantic. The effect of the current on climate is dramatic. It brings to Europe the equivalent of 100,000 large power stations' worth of free
65 heating. Global warming could change all that. Computer models predict that as global warming increases, so will rainfall in the North Atlantic. Gradually, the heavier rains will dilute the sea water and make it less likely to sink, a process that could bring the whole conveyer belt to a gradual halt. Collapse of the North
70 Atlantic current would hit Iceland, Scotland and Norway most, where temperatures could drop 10°C or more.

E The Tibetan Plateau

The Tibetan plateau spans one quarter of China's entire landmass and reaches 6,000 metres above sea level. Four of the world's 10 highest mountains straddle its
75 southern border. Many millions of years ago the entire region lay beneath the sea – fossils of marine animals can be found in mountain ridges now standing more than 4,000 metres above sea level. The area is of global ecological importance, being the highest ecosystem on the planet as
80 well as one of its last remaining great wildernesses. Permanently buried under snow and ice, the region acts as a giant mirror, reflecting the sun's rays back into space. The effect is to keep a lid on global warming, at least locally. In a warmer world the white of the Tibetan plateau
85 will slowly turn to brown and grey as the snow retreats to reveal the ground beneath. As well as contributing to a rise in global temperatures, these changes could effect global jet streams, disrupting weather patterns right across the world.

Vocabulary

Expressions with *earth*, *world* and *ground*

1 Complete sentences a–i with *earth*, *world* or *ground*.

  a Carmen's designer shoes must have cost the ....! Where did she get the money, I wonder?

  b Now I've passed my driving test, I feel on top of the ....

  c The government hoped a lot of people would vote in the election but they were very thin on the ....

  d My grandfather is always telling me that if I graduate from university, I will have the .... at my feet.

  e I fell behind at college last term and now I have a lot of .... to make up.

  f Nothing on .... would persuade me to swim with a shark.

  g My sister's boyfriend's a bit boring – I don't think he's going to set the .... on fire.

  h Now that my dad's new business has got off the ...., it's bringing in good profits.

  i Politicians are always trying to set the .... to rights.

2 Complete sentences a–f to illustrate the meaning of the phrases in italics.

  a The food in that hotel is *out of this world*. I really …

  b A break will *do him the world of good*. He's …

  c Jane's *in a world of her own* today so …

  d Believe me, I wouldn't hurt you *for the world*. On the contrary, …

  e Her husband *thinks the world of her*. Recently …

  f Where *on earth* have you been? You …

3 Discuss questions a–d below. Your dictionary will help you.

  a Have you ever bought anything that cost the earth? Was it worth it?

  b If you were a politician for a day, what would you do to set the world to rights?

  c In a perfect world, what would your town be like?

  d Do you know anyone without a care in the world?

Grammar

Emphasis GR p182

1 Use an appropriate word to complete the inversions in a–h.

  a *No sooner* .... the firemen extinguished one forest fire than another started.

  b *Never before* .... I been so petrified as when I did a parachute jump.

  c I suspect that *only* much later from now .... we find out the cause of the explosion.

  d *Little* .... we know at the moment where the ability to clone humans might lead.

  e *Under no circumstances* .... passengers permitted to smoke on the flight.

  f *At no time* .... you leave your luggage unattended at airports.

  g *Rarely* .... anyone have witnessed such an amazing sight as the view from space.

  h *Not until* they were sure that everyone was safe .... the soldiers leave the building.

2 Correct the errors with word order in a–h. You may need to change more than one aspect of the sentence.

  a Scarcely the band had announced their world tour when they were forced to cancel it.

  b The planet not only is becoming polluted but it is getting warmer too.

  c In no way the lorry driver was to blame for the crash.

  d No sooner the prince arrived in the ski resort than he was besieged by reporters.

  e Little Shakespeare's contemporaries can have guessed how enduring his plays would prove to be.

  f Nowhere in the world they serve such delicious food as in Italy!

  g Not until a few years ago anyone knew about the existence of the buried treasure.

  h Botanists only by chance discovered the rare plant growing under a rock.

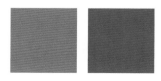

3 Rewrite the information in a–h using the emphasising structures from 1 and 2.

a We drove off to the coast and got a puncture almost immediately.

b I couldn't find a pencil anywhere in the house.

c When she went to work that day she didn't know what lay in store.

d It was pure luck that we were passing by as the boy fell down the cliff.

e The mistake wasn't your fault at all.

f This flat is damp and draughty as well.

g It's only recently that we found out his true identity.

h They'd only just got to the summit when a thick fog descended.

4 Talk about things currently in the news, using a–g for emphasis.

a It's a real shame …

b It came as something of a shock …

c It wasn't much of a surprise …

d It will be interesting to see …

e It isn't the first time …

f It angered a lot of people …

g It was embarrassing …

5 Join the pairs of sentences in a–h starting with the information shown.

Example

I love visiting foreign countries. I particularly like trying out exotic food.

What I particularly like about visiting foreign countries is trying out exotic food.

a I know you went to the disco last night. I'm curious to know who you went with.
What I'm curious to know is …

b I don't like gardening in general. The job I hate most is mowing the lawn.
Mowing the lawn …

c I think John and Clare are too young to get married. I've suggested that they wait for another year.
What …

d Of course a cruise would be wonderful. I'm just worried about how much it would cost.
All …

e You told me English was a useful language. You didn't tell me the grammar would be so hard.
The thing …

f It wasn't me who upset your mother. It was you.
The person …

g I had to leave work early today. I'm holding a dinner party for twenty people tonight.
My reason …

h You need a gorilla suit for the fancy-dress tomorrow? You won't get one anywhere but a joke shop.
The only …

6 Complete dialogues a–e with your own ideas.

a I really like getting out and about at weekends.
Really? All I …

b My favourite films tend to be romantic comedies.
Actually, what I …

c I'm learning languages because I want to travel.
Are you? The reason …

d I'm going to visit some old friends this evening.
That sounds good. What I'm …

e I quite enjoy doing homework.
Really? Doing homework …

Listening Part 4 Multiple matching

1 Discuss the advantages and disadvantages of producing energy in the four different ways shown. Think about:

- cost
- renewable energy
- safety
- local residents

2 🎧 Listen to five people talking about nuclear power. Which of the advantages or disadvantages you discussed in 1 do they mention?

3 🎧 Listen again twice and do the exam tasks below.

For 1–5, choose from A–H how the people felt initially about the building of nuclear power stations.

A I was determined to fight to stop them building one.
B I felt that research had proved it was a cleaner form of energy.
C I felt I knew too little about it to form an opinion.
D I regarded it as an unavoidable necessity.
E I believe the alternatives would not produce enough energy.
F I wasn't bothered where my power supply came from.
G I felt we already had more nuclear power stations than we need.
H I strongly objected to it.

Speaker 1 ☐ 1
Speaker 2 ☐ 2
Speaker 3 ☐ 3
Speaker 4 ☐ 4
Speaker 5 ☐ 5

For 6–10, choose from A–H what concerns the people have now about nuclear power stations.

A Local people aren't kept up to date with developments.
B They put people off moving into an area.
C They create very few jobs in an area.
D They are too costly a method of providing energy.
E They pose a threat to the very existence of the planet.
F We still don't know what their long-term effects might be.
G There are alternatives we should explore first.
H They eventually become a health and safety hazard.

Speaker 1 ☐ 6
Speaker 2 ☐ 7
Speaker 3 ☐ 8
Speaker 4 ☐ 9
Speaker 5 ☐ 10

4 What action could you take to protest against something you disagreed with?

Speaking Part 3

1 Imagine that there is a large disused area of land in your town. Look at the photos, then suggest three more ways to develop the land to benefit the local community. Think about:

- young people
- families
- the elderly

2 Look at the photos on page 154 to see how they compare with your ideas in 1.

3 Use a–h and 1–8 to comment on the benefits and drawbacks of the ideas here and on page 154.

a	provide more	1	different tastes
b	worsen	2	use of public transport
c	create	3	visitors to the area
d	encourage	4	business opportunities
e	generate	5	residential accommodation
f	promote	6	traffic congestion
g	cater for	7	a wildlife area
h	cause	8	noise pollution

4 🎧 Listen to two candidates doing part of the Part 3 task, and comment on their performance.

5 In pairs or small groups, do the exam task in 4, then decide which two ideas would be the least effective. Try to use some of the phrases below.

Suggesting alternatives

You have a point but …

That's true, but don't you think … ?

I'm not sure I agree with you. What about … ?

I can see what you mean but …

Yes, but on the other hand …

I agree with you up to a point …

Use of English Part 1 Multiple-choice cloze

1 What do you think the pieces of art shown are made from?

2 Read the leaflet below about a recycling project, then decide which answer (A, B, C or D) best fits each gap.

	A	B	C	D
0	increase	lift	raise	multiply
1	distributing	discarding	disposing	dumping
2	disagreement	trouble	dispute	problem
3	immediately	instantly	currently	directly
4	producing	erecting	fixing	renovating
5	share	assist	enter	participate
6	bearing	cutting	holding	backing
7	loss	suffering	damage	injury
8	levels	grades	layers	stages
9	direction	course	attempt	aim
10	transmitted	transformed	translated	transported
11	communicated	informed	instructed	acquainted
12	affair	venture	speculation	offer

Turn trash into treasure

The facts

The amounts of household waste produced annually are on the ...A... **0**. As a result, ... **1** of such large amounts is rapidly becoming a serious .... **2** we have to address.

How to recycle ... with a difference

Our recycling for art programme 'Turning trash into treasures' is .... **3** one way of tackling this problem. This is a great way of .... **4** original works of art such as mosaics and collages, which are not expensive to make. Projects may vary from area to area, but everyone is eligible to .... **5**.

Why recycle?

Recycling has many advantages, such as .... **6** down on landfill space and limiting environmental .... **7**. This leads to a reduction both in energy use and in pollution .... **8**, but it can also encourage people to be creative. Paper, magazines and broken pottery and glass can all be recycled. Our main .... **9** in recycling materials like these is that they can be .... **10** into exciting new creations.

FURTHER INFORMATION

Our website will keep you .... **11** of the progress of our new and exciting .... **12**.

Part 4 Gapped sentences

3 For questions a–e, think of one word only which can be used appropriately in all three sentences. All the words appear in the text opposite.

a Eating too much fast food can .... to problems later in life.

If you would all like to go on a tour of the palace gardens, I'll .... the way.

I'm not sure if I would really want to .... a life of luxury.

b Thanks for a .... day. I really enjoyed myself and we must do it again.

The matter is of .... importance and requires immediate attention.

I don't read many books, I've never really been a .... reader.

c My .... concern is that whatever decision we make, we have to stick by it.

The .... street in town is called the London Road.

In some countries, the .... meal of the day is eaten in the late evening.

d You will receive a bill for the full .... which is to be paid within 24 hours.

It's difficult to estimate the precise .... of time necessary to complete the course by distance study.

No .... of persuasion would change Jim's mind about the trip.

e It's a .... of time trying to help Jane, she never listens to any advice.

Take some cake home with you – I hate to see good food go to ....

Do you know how much .... is created annually by this country?

Vocabulary

Adverbs and their meanings

1 Put the adverbs below into pairs with similar meanings. Choose one adverb from each pair and use it in a sentence to illustrate its meaning.

Example
a annually   j yearly
Glastonbury is a famous music festival held annually in Britain.

a annually   f rarely
b increasingly   g occasionally
c infrequently   h presently
d currently   i progressively
e irregularly   j yearly

2 Which of b–i in 1 have the same meaning as a–f below? There may be more than one possible answer.

a now and then
b from time to time
c hardly ever
d more and more
e almost never
f at the moment

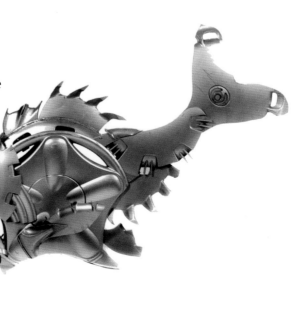

Writing

Part 1 A proposal WG p162

1 How 'green' is your school or workplace? Does it encourage recycling or energy-saving measures?

2 Read the memo and notes below, then complete these instructions for the writing task.

> You work for a large company which the ....1 wants to be more environmentally aware. Read his ....2 and your notes with suggestions below. Using the information given, write a ....3 for the managing director in 180–220 words.

> **MEMO**
>
> We are anxious to ensure that our company shows more concern for the environment. Could you write me a proposal? Describe the problems, suggest what improvements we should make, and make some recommendations for encouraging the staff to be more environmentally aware.
>
> Thomas Davies
>
> Managing Director

> Lights and photocopiers get left on – it's a waste of energy!
> Put up posters?
>
> Traffic is bad. Parking is difficult.
> Car-share scheme? More room for bikes?
>
> Cans, bottles and paper thrown out with rubbish.
> Remind staff about recycling bins. Provide more.
>
> Windows and doors get left open when the heating's on. Heating bills are high!
> Solar panels in roof?

3 Decide which of the phrases is suitable for the proposal, and what is wrong with those you reject.

a The purpose of this proposal is to …
b What I'm going to do in this proposal is …
c The aim of this proposal is to …
d I advise you to …
e I recommend …
f Why don't we …
g You really must …
h I suggest we …
i If you do what I say …
j It would be good if you …

4 Read the model proposal and answer the questions below. The how to do it box will help you.

a Could the format be improved?
b Have set phrases been used appropriately?
c Has the word limit been followed?

5 Rewrite the information from a–c, included in another student's proposal. Try to use as few words as possible without losing any key information.

Example

A car-share scheme would be a great help when it comes to reducing the environmental impact caused by all the people who work here. (24 words)

A car-share scheme would greatly reduce our impact on the environment. (11 words)

a If we encouraged staff to use the recycling bins that are provided, we could cut down on the amount of unnecessary waste that is produced.
b We could put up some posters. These could remind staff that they ought to be more energy-conscious.
c Solar panels, which we could install in the roof, would provide an ideal solution to the problem of our bills, which are extremely high.

6 Write a first draft of the proposal in your own words, then cut out any unnecessary information until it is the right length.

The purpose of this proposal is to highlight the areas where we are not sufficiently environmentally aware, to suggest steps to improve the situation and to make recommendations for greater staff involvement.

Although we already have recycling bins, not enough use is being made of them at present. I recommend installing more such bins, in prominent positions. A memo could then be sent to all members of staff drawing their attention to the new facilities and reminding them of the importance of recycling all waste articles.

Currently, we are wasting a great deal of energy. Lights and photocopiers are left on unnecessarily, in some cases even overnight. We are also failing to conserve heating. Windows and doors are left open when temperatures get too high and this clearly impacts on our heating bills. I suggest we put up posters reminding staff to turn off machinery when not in use. I also propose that we install solar panels to reduce our energy consumption and, consequently, our heating bills.

The level of traffic around our premises is becoming intolerable. Introducing a car-share scheme could help reduce the problem. In addition, I recommend providing more space for bike parking as this would encourage more of our staff to cycle to work.

If the recommendations contained in this proposal are carried out, I am confident that our company can reduce our negative impact on the environment significantly. I therefore propose that the steps outlined above are carried out in full, and that they be put in place in as short a time as possible.

how to do it

- Read the input information and make a list of the key points you must cover.
- Check who will read the proposal and use the correct register.
- Use the correct format, e.g. separate into sections with headings.
- Include some appropriate set phrases.
- Keep referring to your list of key points as you write, to check you haven't missed anything.

Review

1

Complete the phrases in sentences a–l with *earth*, *world* or *ground*.

a That new restaurant was excellent but the place never really got off the ....

b That outfit I bought for the wedding was stunning but it cost the ....

c The studio's latest film is uninspiring. It's certainly not going to set the .... on fire.

d After my illness last month I had a lot of .... to make up at work.

e The mountain walks in this area are out of this .... You'll love them.

f Everyone had hoped for a huge turnout at the film premiere but fans were thin on the ....

g I suffer from vertigo, so nothing on .... would make me go bungee jumping!

h A few days' rest will do you a .... of good. You haven't been your usual cheerful self lately.

i I felt on top of the .... when I got engaged but the wedding day was a disaster!

j It's the tennis final this weekend and I wouldn't miss it for the ....

k What on .... have you done to your hair? It looks absolutely dreadful!

l What's on your mind? You seem to be in a .... of your own at the moment.

2

Replace the words in italics in a–h with verbs 1–8 below in the correct form.

a Police are hoping the witness will *make available* more information about the robbery.

b A radical change of image is needed if we are to *help sell* the rock band's new tour.

c Does anyone know what *led to* the accident last night?

d Thanks to their new advertising campaign, they have *produced* huge interest in the product.

e Susan's parents made every effort to *persuade* her to go to university.

f Will scientists ever really find out how the universe *was formed*?

g What was already a difficult situation was *negatively affected* by media interference.

h We need to *provide material to be used by* people with different learning styles.

1 cause   4 worsen   7 generate
2 provide   5 promote   8 encourage
3 cater for   6 create

3

For questions a–c, think of one word only which can be used appropriately in all three sentences.

a By limiting the number of cars on the road, we may achieve a .... in the consumption of petrol.

Job creation schemes have resulted in a significant .... in the unemployment figures.

In off-peak periods we offer a considerable .... in prices for families with children.

b The climate in winter .... completely from one part of the country to another.

Medical opinion .... as to the best way to treat this condition.

Some languages have genders for nouns, others do not. Italian .... from English in this respect.

c We should be in no doubt that pollution causes serious .... damage.

There are many .... groups dedicated to ensuring the long-term future of our planet.

The .... impact of increased air travel is a cause for concern.

4

Write adverbs with the same meaning as phrases a–e. Some letters are given to help you.

a more and more: inc...   pro...
b from time to time: irr...   occ...
c hardly ever: ra...   in...
d every twelve months: an...   y...
e at the moment: pre...   cur...

5

Rewrite the information in a and b using as few words as possible, beginning with the words shown.

a It would be a very good idea to try and persuade people to recycle things like old mobile phones they do not want any more.

People ...

b It would really make a lot of difference to create some parks and it would make the whole area a much more pleasant place for local inhabitants to live in.

Creating ...

Appendix

Unit 1

What are you like?

Lead in

2 Add up your points for each separate section: a = 1, b = 2, c = 3.
Then look below to see which category you are in.

Head or Heart: If you got 3–5 points you're Head; 6–9 points you're Heart.

Extrovert or Introvert: 3–5 points you're Introvert; 6–9 points you're Extrovert.

Facts or Ideas: 3–5 points you're Facts; 6–9 points you're Ideas.

Now find your combination of answers in the table (e.g. Head, Introvert, Ideas)
to see what it says about your personality and the careers that might suit you.

Combination	Personality type	Possible careers
Heart, Introvert, Facts	methodical, conscientious, friendly and sensitive	nurse, teacher, doctor, librarian
Heart, Extrovert, Facts	energetic, fun-loving, sociable and caring	teacher, designer, child-care worker, office manager
Heart, Introvert, Ideas	committed, faithful, sceptical and inventive	psychiatrist, writer, artist, entertainer
Heart, Extrovert, Ideas	fun-loving, optimistic, passionate and facilitative	writer, musician, editor, designer
Head, Introvert, Facts	dependable, practical, realistic and analytical	accountant, IT, engineer, mechanic
Head, Extrovert, Facts	adventurous, high-energy, tough, ambitious	marketing manager, supervisor, purchasing agent
Head, Introvert, Ideas	independent, clear-thinking, logical and insightful	architect, lawyer, judge, manager
Head, Extrovert, Ideas	flexible, innovative, decisive, energetic	photographer, journalist, doctor, administrator

Unit 6

Would you believe it?

Lead in

1 a T

 b F The word simply comes from 'new'.

 c T

 d F It takes no longer to digest than anything else, i.e. a few hours.

 e F The number of people alive today is estimated at 6.5 billion. 6 billion are estimated to have lived since the building of the Pyramids, and probably about 60 billion in total in the 40–45,000 years humans have been around.

 f T A 20 cm stalk contains about six calories. More are burnt off during digestion – not chewing – but you would have to eat a lot of celery to make any real difference to your weight.

Unit 12

A changing world

Speaking

2

Writing Guide

Formal letters

An international TV company is planning to make a series of programmes, in English, about issues of interest to young people around the world. Could you help to present it? If so, write and tell us

- which three issues you think we should include, and why

- why we should choose you to present the series.

Write your **letter of application**.

1 Begin with 'Dear …' and use 'Sir/Madam' or 'To whom it may concern' if you don't know the person's name.
2 Give your reason for writing.
3 Use linking phrases where appropriate.
4 Close your letter with a set phrase.
5 Finish with 'Yours faithfully' if you don't know the person's name or 'Yours sincerely' if you do.
6 Start a new paragraph when you change topic.
7 Letters of application require a formal style.

phrase bank

Starting your letter
Dear Sir/Madam
I am writing to apply for …
I am writing to you about/with regard to …

Giving personal information
I've been studying … for the past two years.
I currently work as a … so I am used to …

Concluding
I hope my application will meet with your approval.
I look forward to hearing from you.
I hope you will find this information of use.
Yours faithfully/Yours sincerely

Dear Sir or Madam (1)

I am writing to apply for the post of presenter for your forthcoming series. (2)

I am twenty years old and for the past two years I have been working as a journalist for a local newspaper. As the writer of the 'Youth Today' section, I spend a lot of time interviewing young people on issues they find important. In my free time, I belong to a drama group and have played major roles in various shows so I would be very much at ease in front of an audience. Language would not be a problem since (3) my mother is English and I am bilingual.

The three issues I believe we must cover in this series are relationships, health, and careers. In the relationships programme, we could deal with possible areas of conflict such as with family and friends, as well as (3) girl or boyfriends. Most young people have difficulties with relationships at some time, therefore (3) I am sure they would enjoy a focus on this issue. As regards (3) health, most young people worry about how they look, guaranteeing that a programme giving advice and suggestions in this area would go down well. Finally (3), on the issue of careers, I know a lot of young people worry about what kind of profession they should enter, so a programme that gives them advice and information about this would, I think, have a strong appeal.

I hope you will see me as a suitable presenter and that you like my ideas for the programmes.

I look forward to hearing from you. (4)

Yours faithfully (5)

Miranda Jimenez

Contributions

You work for the local tourist information centre and have been asked to write a contribution, in English, for a guide book to your town or city. You should describe some of the major cultural and leisure attractions, and highlight any special events taking place over the summer months.

Write your **contribution.**

introduction (2)

Barcelona is one of the most exciting and cosmopolitan cities in Europe. Situated on the coast, there are beaches and large areas of forest nearby. Summers here are warm so life is conducted in the open air. Although it is a large city, it is easy to get around because of the excellent metro, bus and taxi services.

what to visit (2)

Las Ramblas is one of the most famous boulevards in the city. Stroll under the trees, listen to the buskers and admire the amazing living statues and street theatre. (1) There are colourful market stalls selling flowers and vegetables, galleries, terraced cafés and famous theatres. The boulevard leads to the harbour, dominated by the statue of Christopher Columbus, which can be climbed for a fantastic view over the city. (3)

El Ensanche is the modern centre of Barcelona, where you can find the awe-inspiring cathedral of Sagrada Familia, designed by the modernist architect Antoni Gaudí. Elsewhere you can find works by other great names in modern art and architecture, such as Salvador Dalí, and Picasso.

leisure attractions (2)

Maremagnum is a popular shopping and leisure centre close to Las Ramblas. Here you can find shops, the Imax cinema, and a wide variety of restaurants, bars and discos. Night life begins at around 11 pm and goes on until the early hours.

special events (2)

The Festival of 'el Grec', which begins at the end of June, has something for everyone, including music, theatre and dance, jazz, flamenco and contemporary music.

There are also sports tournaments and competitions throughout the season.

---

1 Use imperatives to give instructions or strong advice.
2 Divide your contribution into sections with clear headings so that it is easy to follow.
3 Divide sections into paragraphs where appropriate.
4 Information leaflets are usually written in a fairy formal style.
5 Keep the information clear by avoiding very long and complicated sentences.

Articles

You read this notice in a student magazine.

> Are cities the best places to live or is life in the countryside a better option? If you could choose, where would you prefer to settle down? Write us an article outlining your preference and giving the reasons for your choice.

Write your **article**.

Urban jungle or country retreat – which is best? (1)

Imagine the scene. (2) You wake up every day to the sound of birdsong. Throwing open your bedroom window, you look out on a vista of green fields and rolling hills. There are no housing estates, no shops, no cinemas – in fact, apart from a few cottages, there is nothing but open countryside. (4)

Does this sound idyllic? (3) Well, not to me. Of course, living in the middle of nowhere might appeal if you're elderly, or if you're a writer looking for inspiration. And 'getting away from it all' can be quite relaxing in the short term. But if you think life is for living, the last thing you should do is go and live in the countryside.

So what makes city life any better? Well, let's start with the people. Where else can you meet such an interesting mix of races and nationalities? Then think of the job opportunities. Where but in a city will you find such a range of choice? And when you want to relax, just think how much culture and entertainment is waiting for you, often just a short bus ride away.

I've spent most of my life in the city and I wouldn't live anywhere else. I've been able to meet an incredible mix of people, see the best shows and entertainers, and keep up with the latest trends and fashions. Life is never dull – in fact there's too much to do. Would I exchange all that for life in the country? Never in a million years! (6)

1 Give your article an eye-catching title.
2 Start your article in an interesting way to make the reader want to read on.
3 Ask questions and address the reader to involve them.
4 Appeal to the reader's imagination.
5 Start a new paragraph when you change topic.
6 Finish with an interesting conclusion.
7 Use an informal, lively tone for most magazine articles aimed at young adult readers.

Competition entries

You have seen this competition in an international lifestyle magazine.

> Are you addicted to your mobile phone? Could you survive without your computer and your digital camera? Write and tell us which *two* items of modern technology you find most indispensable and why, and win yourself an iPod.

Write your **competition entry.**

Over the past century, technology has changed people's lives beyond recognition. Who, now, can imagine life without a television? How on earth, we wonder, did our grandparents cope without microwaves or dishwashers? (1)

Now, of course, we have a new generation of technology. Plasma TVs and top-of-the-range portable media centres have joined the 'must-have' list for those who can afford them. Although (2) I regard some of these new gadgets as luxuries, there are two that I just couldn't do without – my computer and my mobile phone.

Let's start with the computer. As a student, I need to access a lot of information. What better way (2) is there to do this than on the Internet?(1) I need to write essays and projects too, which I also do on my computer. And when I want a break, I can use the same computer to play games, download music, go to a chat room, or email my friends. And all in the comfort of my bedroom.

The second item I absolutely rely on is my mobile phone. I use it all the time – to hear what my friends are up to, to text them jokes and messages, and to let them know I'm running late. With my latest model (2) I can even take photos and make short videos.

There are many items of modern technology that I could manage without, but without a computer and a mobile phone, I'd be really lost. These, for me at least, have become an indispensable part of modern life.

1 Use questions to hold the reader's interest.
2 Vary your sentence patterns by using a range of linking words/phrases.
3 Divide your entry into paragraphs, with a clear introduction and conclusion.
4 Use a lively tone but don't be too informal – remember who will read your entry!

Reviews

The editor of a local newspaper has asked you to write a review of *two* quite different places where young people can meet up for a drink or a meal in your town.

Write your **review**.

review

There are many places for young people to eat together and socialise in our town but two have become very popular. Keen to discover whether they live up to their reputation, I went along this week to sample what was on offer.

The first on my list was *Hollywood Rock*. Step inside this restaurant and you feel as if you've been transported into the past. The interior is a series of small rooms, each dedicated to legendary rock performers like Elvis or the Beatles. The walls are decorated with rock guitars and record covers and other memorabilia. (3) As you eat, rock music booms out around you. The menu is predictable (1) – the usual choice of pizzas, burgers and fries – but it offers good value for money.

My second visit was to *Gigi's*, a riverside café in the student quarter. This is a very cosmopolitan venue, attracting students from all over the world. In good weather, customers can eat outside and enjoy the marvellous river views. The menu is limited (1), with an emphasis on seafood, but it is reasonably priced and the quality is good. There is live music at weekends, but noise levels are kept low.

So which of the two restaurants should you choose? While *Hollywood Rock* is original and will appeal to certain music fans, it is noisy, which makes conversation difficult. (1) If you prefer to socialise outdoors or in a slightly quieter setting, I suggest you try *Gigi's*. (4) But go early – tables fill up quickly, especially at weekends.

1 Remember that reviews can include criticism as well as praise.
2 Divide your review into paragraphs with a clear introduction and conclusion.
3 Give a clear, concise description of the place you are reviewing.
4 Keep your opinions/recommendations for the final paragraph.

Reports

You are on the student committee at your college. This year you helped the English Department organise a study trip to Britain. The Principal of the college has asked you for a report on the trip. Read the brochure about the trip, with the comments from students and your notes. Then write your **report** saying what was successful about the trip, and what wasn't, and suggesting improvements for future trips.

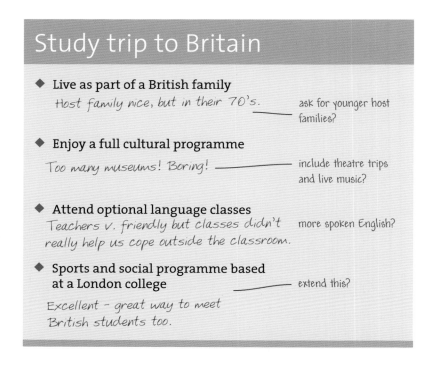

Study trip to Britain

◆ **Live as part of a British family**
  Host family nice, but in their 70's. —— ask for younger host families?

◆ **Enjoy a full cultural programme**
  Too many museums! Boring! —— include theatre trips and live music?

◆ **Attend optional language classes**
  Teachers v. friendly but classes didn't   more spoken English?
  really help us cope outside the classroom.

◆ **Sports and social programme based
  at a London college** —— extend this?
  Excellent – great way to meet
  British students too.

1 Use appropriate linking words.
2 Use appropriate phrases to make recommendations and suggestions if appropriate (also see page 163).
3 Organise your report into sections with headings.
4 Include a clear introduction and conclusion.
5 Write clear and concise sentences.
6 Use a formal style.

Introduction (4)
The aim of this report is to assess the success of this year's study trip to Britain and to recommend any changes.

Accommodation (3)
Although (1) the families that students stayed with were very hospitable, they were rather elderly. It would be preferable (2) if younger host families could be found for our next trip.

Culture (3)
The cultural programme had a very serious emphasis and included a large number of visits to museums. Students found there were too many such activities. I suggest that (2) the next trip should offer a wider variety of cultural visits and include visits to some of the top shows in the theatre, rock and pop events and other types of popular culture.

Language classes (3)
While most students got on well with their teachers, they didn't find the classes very relevant to their stay. For next year, I suggest we request that more class time is spent on oral work.

Sports and social programme (3)
Students were highly enthusiastic about this side of the trip so (1) I propose (2) we extend the programme next year.

Conclusion (4)
To sum up, (1) this year's trip appears to have been enjoyed by most students despite the reservations mentioned above. If the suggested changes are implemented, I have no hesitation in recommending (2) that we send other students on the trip next year.

phrase bank

Introductions
The aim of this report is to …
This report describes/outlines/deals with …
This report is based on …

Making recommendations
It would be a good idea to …
It might be advisable to …
It would be preferable to …
I suggest/propose/recommend that we (should) …

Conclusions
To sum up, …
In conclusion, …
I have no hesitation in recommending …

Proposals

Your college has been awarded a large sum of money. The college Principal
has asked the student committee to consult staff and students and then
write her a proposal. Read the comments you have gathered and your
notes. Then write your **proposal** describing what people are unhappy with,
and why, and suggesting how the money should be spent.

- The computers are ancient and
  they're always breaking down!   *new computers?*

- It's scary walking round the grounds
  at night – it's so dark.   *better lighting?*

- The whole place looks so shabby.
  There's graffiti everywhere.   *redecorate?*

- Why have we still got blackboards?
  They're so old-fashioned!   *replace with whiteboards?*

- The drama studio is minute! We can't
  stage any big productions.   *new building?*

1 Use appropriate language for making suggestions and recommendations
   (also see page 161).
2 Use linkers to sequence points.
3 Set out your text so that it looks like a proposal and not a letter.
4 Divide your proposal into sections with headings.
5 Include a separate introduction and conclusion.
6 Be clear and concise.
7 Use an impersonal tone.

Introduction (5)

The purpose of this proposal is to outline areas which need improving and to make recommendations as to where money should be spent.

Equipment (4)

Many students pointed out that the computers currently in use are becoming dated and are apt to break down quite frequently. I would therefore recommend (1) that we buy new, state-of-the-art computers. Additionally, (2) it was felt that blackboards were very outdated. I therefore propose that we invest in modern whiteboards.

Buildings (4)

Many students are unhappy with the size of the drama studio which is too small to house major productions. I suggest (1) we consider a new building as this would allow us to provide much better facilities and to stage much bigger shows.

Decoration and Lighting (4)

Several students pointed out the fact that the college is badly in need of redecoration. Others were worried about their personal safety due to the fact that the college is poorly lit. My recommendation is (1) that we redecorate the entire premises, inside and out, and that we install effective lighting in the college grounds.

Conclusion (5)

In conclusion, (2) I believe that the areas identified in this proposal are the ones that are most in need of improvement. If the recommendations above are followed, I believe they would have the support of all our students.

phrase bank

Introductions
The aim/purpose of this proposal is to …
This proposal relates to …
This proposal describes/outlines …

Suggestions and recommendations
I recommend/propose/suggest/
believe   (that) we (should) …

We could also …
If we … , we could …

Conclusions
To sum up, I believe that …
In conclusion, I would say that …
On balance, we are of the opinion that …

Essays

In class, you have been discussing the statement 'It is important to be honest in life.' Your teacher has asked you to write an essay saying whether or not you agree with the statement.

Write your **essay** giving your opinion.

> There is an old saying that 'honesty is the best policy', but sometimes it seems we're far more inclined to bend the truth or just tell bare-faced lies. In this essay, I'm going to explain why I think honesty is an important part of life. (1) (2)
>
> Let's begin with (5) personal relationships. Lack of honesty here leads to all kinds of problems. Take, for example, the relationship between parents and children. If you lie to your parents about what you have or haven't done, you could be in trouble if they find out. The result is that you will have to work hard to win back that trust. It's the same with friends. If you can't depend on them to tell you the truth or if you let them down, then your friendship is unlikely to last. (4)
>
> Honesty at work is just as important. In the first place, (5) a dishonest worker can cost a business dearly. It might start with calling in sick when there is nothing wrong or taking office stationery home. Not so serious you may say, but it is my belief that this shows a person who does not value honesty. Secondly, an untrustworthy worker makes for a bad colleague. Most people work in teams and if you cannot trust a colleague, the team will break down. (4)
>
> In sum, (5) it is my belief that honesty in our lives is absolutely crucial. Take it away, and our lives would become extremely unpleasant and this may affect others too. (1)

1 Include a clear introduction and conclusion.
2 Rephrase the question to avoid repeating the task.
3 Depending on the essay task – either present both sides of the argument or support a single argument with ideas/examples.
4 Use paragraphs to organize your ideas and points.
5 Use linkers and appropriate phrases to develop points clearly and logically.

phrase bank

Introductions
In this essay, I'm going to/I would like to …
Let's begin with …

Organising points
Take, for example …
In the first place/To start with, …
Secondly, …
Finally, …

Conclusions
In sum/To sum up, …
In conclusion, …
It is my belief/opinion that …
It seems to me that …

Set texts

Questions on set books are optional. Do <u>not</u> answer this question in the exam unless you have read the set book at least twice and have studied it very carefully.

What to do when reading your set book

Keep a special notebook with separate headed pages. When you finish each chapter, make brief notes about:

- the plot/key events
- the main themes (e.g. love and revenge)
- the characters (e.g. physical appearance, personality, behaviour, attitudes, motivation, development)
- the setting.

Use headings, like these below.

KEY EVENTS

Chapter 1
• We find out that …

CHARACTERS

Name of character: Mr X
• cool-headed in a crisis (in the text, it says " … ")
• very independent (in the text, it says " … ")
• has never been in love before (in the text, it says " … ")

Name of character: Miss Y
• wants to marry the hero (in the text, it says " … ")

Try to learn some of the key quotations that you have noted.

What to do in the exam

Follow the advice in the how to do it box and try to include some phrases from the phrase bank.

how to do it

- Plan your answer according to whether you have to write an essay, a review, an article, or a report.
- Use present tenses to describe the plot. Don't make things too complicated or you will confuse your reader!
- Quote from the text to support your points – but make sure your quotations are relevant.
- Answer the question fully and avoid irrelevant information.

phrase bank

Introductions
The main events of the novel happen in the course of one day/year.
The story is set /in a small town in America/on a deserted island.
One of the main themes of the book is childhood.

Characters
The hero of the novel is a man/woman called …
The villain of the piece is called … . The writer portrays him/her as a lonely/tormented figure.
I found/didn't find the main characters very convincing.

Comments
I thought the plot was excellent/exciting/disappointing.
I liked/didn't like the writer's style.
The ending of the book was exciting /rather disappointing.
Each chapter ended on a cliff-hanger.
There was a really strong sense of suspense.
The book was so exciting, I couldn't put it down
I found the pace a bit slow.

Grammar Reference

Present and past tenses

Present simple

Use the present simple:

1   to talk about habitual events and fixed truths:

   Most authors write about 1000 words a day.

   Violins have four strings.

2   to talk about how often you do something. Frequency adverbs (*always, usually, often, sometimes, never*) are often used:

   Carla checks her text messages every few minutes.

3   for states that imply permanence or for those that are true for a long time:

   The President of the United States works in the White House.

Present continuous

Use the present continuous:

1   for temporary states:

   He is acting as manager while his boss is away.

2   to talk about an activity that is taking place when you speak or around the time of speaking:

   Listen! This computer is making a strange noise.

   He's studying at evening class at the moment.

Past simple

Use the past simple to express an event that took place at a definite past time. Past time words are often used to fix the action or state in the past. For example, *when, yesterday, last week, three months ago*, etc:

   – When did you last write a letter by hand?

   – I think it was about a year ago.

When there are no past time words, the context often places the action or event in the past (either the recent past or the more remote past):

   Where did you learn to do those magic tricks?

   Karl Benz invented the first motor car.

The action can either last for a period of time in the past or finish at a fixed time in the past:

   Henry ran 15 kilometres every day for sixty years.

   He gave up running in June and died in July.

Past continuous

Use the past continuous:

1   to talk about things that were in progress in the past. They may or may not be finished:

   Last week, the police were watching the house on the corner.

2   to talk about a background activity:

   We were lying on our backs looking at the stars.

A single past event often interrupts the background activity, so the past continuous and the past simple are used together:

   We were lying on our backs looking at the stars when a comet flew across the sky.

But when two or more past events happen consecutively, the past simple is used for both:

   The Titanic hit an iceberg and sank a few hours later.

Note: Don't use the past continuous to talk about past habits or to say how often something happened in the past. Use the past simple:

   They phoned the zoo three times yesterday.
   (Not: They were phoning …)

Present perfect simple

Use the present perfect simple:

1   when there is a connection between the past and the present. The connection can either be implied or obvious. The exact timing is not important:

   The explorers have just reached the North Pole.

   He's lost a lot of weight in the last few months.

2   for things that have just happened or when the event is still relevant or is still 'news':

   Oh, no! The wheel has fallen off!

You must use the present perfect simple form when you mention the number of times:

That train has broken down three times so far this week.

The event might have started at some time in the past and still continues:

I have known about the problem for a long time, but I haven't done anything about it yet.

3 to give general news or information. This is followed by more detail using the past simple:

A new zoo for endangered species has opened in the Lake District. It took five years to build and runs entirely on solar energy.

Present perfect continuous

Use the present perfect continuous:

1 for events that began in the past and continue into the present. Like the present perfect simple, it is often used with *since* (+ starting point), *for* (+ period of time) and *how long*:

They have been going out with each other since Christmas.

That dog has been chasing its tail for about ten minutes.

2 to talk about long or repeated actions that have just finished, but where the consequence is still clear:

– *You're late for the meeting!*

– *Sorry! I've been trying to park my car.*

Past perfect simple

Use the past perfect to talk about what happened before a certain point in the past:

The robber had run away by the time the police arrived.

Past perfect continuous

Use the past perfect continuous to emphasise a longer action. This action continues up to the time of the main action (expressed by the verb in the past simple):

I wasn't surprised that Dave and Amy emigrated. They had been thinking about it for years.

But use the past perfect simple to say 'how many times':

By the time he was twenty-five, he had already been married twice.

Used to and *would*

Use *used to* (+ infinitive) to talk about past habits:

Believe it or not, but people used to write letters by hand and send them to their friends.

To ask questions, use *did* + name/pronoun + *use to* (not *used to*):

Did your parents use to allow you to ride a motorbike?

The negative form is *didn't use to* (not *didn't used to*):

Policemen didn't use to carry firearms.

It is sometimes possible to use *would* instead of *used to* when talking about past personal habits, but usually only in the positive. *Would* is quite a literary style and is often found in continuous narrative:

When we were young we would go to the river and throw stones in the stream, then go to a little teashop and buy some cakes.

Use *used to* for past situations and states that no longer exist or are no longer true. (*Would* cannot be used.)

In the 1930s that bar used to be a very famous little theatre.

Did Shakespeare use to live in London?

Note: Don't use *used to* to say how long something lasted in the past. Use the past simple:

I did the national lottery for a long time, but I didn't have any luck. (Not: I used to do …)

Future forms

Present simple

Use the present simple to express future events that are timetabled or part of a calendar:

The Directors' meeting starts at 3 o'clock on Friday.

Hurry up. The plane leaves in half an hour.

The present simple is used when the timetabling or arrangement is impersonal (someone else has made them or they are part of a natural law):

The next college term starts on 8th September.

For personal arrangements, where the speaker or another person has made the decision, the present continuous is usually used:

I'm starting a new course in biology next term.

Present continuous

The present continuous is used to express the future when definite plans or arrangements have been made:

- *What are you doing next Saturday?*
- *I'm taking my driving test.*

You can use the present continuous tense with verbs of motion, even if no fixed arrangements have been made:

You had better hurry up and get ready, because we're leaving very soon.

Going to and *will*

Use *going to*:

1 when you have made a decision to do something:

   Could you please let me know if you are going to accept the job?

2 when you have made some *basic* plans:

   I'm going to buy an old barn and do it up.

But when more definite plans are in place, use the present continuous:

   We've signed the contracts and we're moving into the building on Monday.

3 to say what someone is just about to do:

   I won't be a minute. I'm just going to say goodbye to my colleague.

4 for predictions when there is clear evidence that an event is about to take place:

   Based on the first page, I think I'm going to enjoy reading this book.

For 'neutral' predictions that are based on personal belief, rather than clear evidence, see *will* below:

Use *will* and *won't*:

1 to ask for and give information about the future, which is often a simple matter of fact:

   The train standing at platform 3 will stop at Oxford.

   'The work won't take long,' the builder said.

2 to express the near future when there has been no conscious planning or premeditation. For example, on-the-spot decisions:

   I'll have a mushroom omelette and a green salad.

   – *Will you marry me?*

   – *No, I won't.*

3 to predict what you think will happen in the future, based on what you believe or guess will happen:

   Soon, we will all pay our bills by mobile phone.

   Video machines won't be available in a few years.

But when there is clear evidence about what is going to happen, use *going to*:

   The builder looked at the old house and said, 'I'm sorry, but it's going to fall down.'

Future continuous

Use the future continuous to talk about an event that will be in progress at a certain time in the future:

   This time next week I'll be lying on a beach.

Future time phrases are common with this tense:

In a few months' time	
Before long	*we'll be travelling*
This time next year	*around South America.*
By December	

The question form of the future continuous is often used for polite requests as it avoids the urgency of other tenses:

   Will you be checking out of your room by noon?

Future perfect simple

Use the future perfect to talk about things that will have happened by a certain time in the future. It is often used with a phrase starting with *by* to emphasise completion before a certain future time:

By Monday	
By lunchtime	*he will have finished*
By this time next year	*his report.*
By the time you read this	

Future perfect continuous

Use the future perfect continuous to talk about how long things will have been happening by a certain time in the future (and perhaps beyond that time). It is often used with a phrase starting with *for* to emphasise duration:

   Next month he will have been working at the factory for twenty-five years.

The future in the past

Use the following 'future in the past' structures when you are talking about the past, and want to say that something was still in the future at that time:

1   past continuous or *was/were going to* (+ infinitive)

    Danny waited outside the station. He was meeting his daughter at 2 o'clock and they were going to watch the Cup Final.

    The planned or expected future action often doesn't happen:

    He was planning to sell the house, until it caught fire.

2   *would* (+ infinitive)

    None of us thought the exam would be so easy.

3   *was/were to* (+ infinitive)

    A politician was to give a speech, but she didn't turn up.

    Use *was/were just about to* in the same way:

    They were just about to disappear round the corner when they saw me waving.

Time clauses in the future

Use the present tense in many future subordinate clauses. Use a future form in the main clause:

He is going to Barcelona, when he gets a ticket. (Not: 'when he will get')

As soon as he arrives he's going to buy a weekly travel ticket. (Not: 'As soon as he will arrive')

Conjunctions that introduce these clauses include:

as soon as	when	once	by the time

Use the present perfect after *as soon as* or *when* to express completion:

James is going to have a party as soon as his parents have gone away.

I'll check your work for you when you have finished.

Use the present continuous after *while* to show that the action still continues:

I'll stop drilling while you are trying to work.

Non-continuous verbs

Many English verbs express a state rather than activity, so they are not normally used in any of the continuous tenses. These verbs fall into several groups:

1   Verbs that describe wants and likes and preferences, e.g. *want, like, prefer, hope, wish.*

2   Verbs that describe thought processes and opinions, e.g. *think, believe, know, remind, understand.*

3   Verbs for the senses, e.g. *hear, see, taste, smell, touch, feel.* But 'sense' verbs that describe an active, deliberate use of the senses are used in the continuous tenses, e.g. *watch, look, stare, listen.*

4   Verbs for belonging and containing, e.g. *own, possess, belong.*

Many of the verbs above and other 'stative' verbs can sometimes describe 'actions', with a change of meaning. With the new meaning it is usually possible to use continuous forms. Remember that continuous forms imply a temporary action:

She is usually quite honest. (a permanent characteristic)

She isn't being very honest. (a temporary condition)

I think you're unreliable and over-ambitious. (= have the opinion)

I'm thinking of changing my solicitor. (= consider)

He appears to be quite mature, but he's actually quite the opposite. (= seem)

Several comedy acts will be appearing at The Palace Theatre during the summer. (= take part in)

I don't expect you'll like this, but I'm leaving the company. (= think)

I've been expecting you to arrive since 8 o'clock this morning. (= anticipate)

I don't have much experience of negotiating prices. (= possess)

I'm having dinner with the Prime Minister after the meeting. (= eat)

This is how you should present your CV. Do you see what I mean? (= understand)

How long have you been seeing a psychiatrist? (= consult)

Passives

Form and structures

Most active sentences have a corresponding passive. All transitive verbs (verbs that take a direct object) can have a passive form. Intransitive verbs like *die, arrive, sleep,* etc. cannot have a passive form.

The object of an active sentence is the subject of the corresponding passive sentence:

Active: *We have counted all the votes, and we can now announce the winners.* (all the votes and the winners are the objects)

Passive: *All the votes have been counted and the winners can be announced.* (all the votes and the winners are the subjects).

You can form passives from all tenses, future forms and also modal such as *can, must,* etc. A passive is formed with the appropriate tense of *be* + the past participle:

present simple: *People who want a visa are required to complete long application forms.*

present continuous: *The plane is being prepared for take-off.*

present perfect: *I can't phone you. My phone has been stolen.*

past simple/past perfect: *The man wasn't allowed to see his solicitor until after he had been interviewed by the police.*

past continuous: *The children were being taught how to use a computer.*

the future: *You are going to be taken to prison, where you will be given a haircut and overalls.*

modals: *Credit cards can be used to confirm the hotel booking.*

The evidence mustn't be touched after it has been put into the plastic bags.

The prisoners should be allowed to make a phone call to their solicitors.

All the rules here have to be obeyed.

There are various passive structures that use the infinitive and are often used in news reporting. For example:

*The ringleader of the gang **is thought** to be Spanish.*

*Plans for the new sports centre **are said** to be under threat.*

*Negotiations **are believed**/**rumoured** to be coming to a conclusion.*

Use *have* + past participle in the past:

The ringleader of the gang is thought to have fled to Spain.

Plans for the new sports centre are said to have been shelved.

Use *to* + infinitive in the passive structure after the verbs *see, hear, make* and *allow*:

Three very suspicious men were seen to leave the building carrying black sacks.

A young boy at the back of the hall was heard to laugh during the Prime Minister's speech.

One thing he hated about prison life was being made to peel potatoes.

The passengers were not allowed to get off the plane.

Note: When the verb *let* is used in an active sentence, *allow* must be used in the equivalent passive sentence:

(active) *The police didn't let him phone his lawyer.*

(passive) *He wasn't allowed to phone his lawyer.*

When more than one verb is used in the passive, the auxiliary verb *be* does not have to be repeated:

Forensic evidence will be collected, sent to a laboratory and analysed.

You can change the subject of a passive sentence midway through the sentence. Again, the verb *be* does not have to be repeated:

Fingerprints are taken and the results (are) fed into a computer.

When to use the passive

Passive structures are used when the action is more important than who did it (the 'agent'). The most important information in English often comes at the beginning of a sentence, and new information or more details come at the end.

The passive is often used:

1 in advertising, because the product becomes the focus of attention:

Our sportswear is tested by robots and worn by world champions.

2 in formal, impersonal texts:

Your application has been received and you will be informed of our decision in due course.

3 in scientific texts, official writing and newspaper headlines:

Many breakthroughs in the fight against cancer have been made over the past few years.

4 when the agent is unknown or is not important or is obvious from the context:

The wheel was invented about 5000 years ago.

5 to avoid the overuse or repetition of personal pronouns or vague words such as people:

The M25 motorway is being repaired and should be avoided for the next two weeks.

You can mention the agent in a passive structure if it is important. Use *by* + name or noun:

The boxer was knocked out in the first round. (The agent is not named, so we assume it wasn't anything remarkable.)

The boxer was knocked out in the first round by a rock thrown from the spectator's area.

have/get something done

Use the structure *have* + noun/pronoun + past participle when someone else does something for you. For example, your car needs a service, your eyes need to be tested, etc:

Sorry, I can't talk. I'm just having my hair cut.

You can use this structure to refer to things that are done by someone else and are beyond your control:

The boy had his locker broken into and his camera stolen.

You can often use *get* with the same structure, but it is often more informal or more urgent:

I must get those documents signed.

Gerunds and infinitives

verb + *to* + infinitive

Certain verbs are often followed by *to* + infinitive of another verb:

deserve	expect	hope
manage	offer	promise
refuse	threaten	want

It's a pity he lost the race, because he deserved to win.

What did you expect to find when you opened the box?

To can stand alone to avoid repeating the verb or phrase:

I'm not sure I'm going to pass my driving test first time, but I certainly hope to.

With many verbs, an object comes before *to*:

The Sales Director asked the Editor to give an outline of the proposal.

verb + object + *to* – infinitive

The verbs that use this construction fall roughly into two groups:

1 Verbs that convey the idea of asking, telling, compelling, allowing, forcing:

advise	allow	ask	expect
forbid	force	permit	persuade
teach	tell	warn	

2 Verbs that convey the idea of wanting, needing, etc:

want	need	prefer	would like

Note that 'that clauses' are not possible with the verbs in this group:

I really don't want ~~that anyone misunderstands~~ me.

verb + infinitive

The infinitive without *to* is used after:

1 *had better* and *would rather*

There's a storm coming. We had better go home.

I would rather not sit in the back of the car.

2 the verbs *make* (meaning 'force') and *let* (meaning 'allow'):

You can't make me do anything that I don't want to do.

If you let me borrow your car, will you expect me to pay for the petrol?

Note that *make* in the passive is followed by *to* + infinitive:

The soldiers were made to stand for hours in the sun.

3 the objects of verbs of perception (*see*, *hear*, etc.):

When she was walking through the car park, she heard someone call her name.

verb + *-ing* form

Certain verbs are only followed by the *-ing* form of another verb. (That is, the *-ing* form of the second verb acts as a gerund, the object of the first verb.) Verbs that take *-ing* forms often convey likes and dislikes:

can't stand	detest	don't mind
fancy	feel like	enjoy

Other verbs convey the idea of saying, thinking, describing:

admit	consider	deny	describe
imagine	suggest		

Other common, miscellaneous verbs are also followed by an *-ing* form:

avoid	deny	finish
miss	practise	risk

Note that verbs that follow prepositions are always in the *-ing* form:

> *Don't apologise for arriving early. It's great to see you.*

> *He would probably get more done if he was better at working at night.*

verb + infinitive/*-ing* form

A few verbs can be followed by an infinitive or an *-ing* form, with little or no change of meaning. For example:

begin	continue	start

> *When the limousine drove past the crowd, some people began to throw/began throwing flowers onto the roof.*

Some common verbs can be followed by an infinitive or an *-ing* form, but with a change of meaning, e.g.

> **remember**: *I don't care how busy you are, you must remember to pay your credit card bill.* (= remember to do something in the future)

> *I remember going fishing a lot when I was a boy, but I don't remember catching many fish.* (= remember doing something in the past)

> **regret**: *I regret to inform you that I am resigning as company secretary.* (= be sorry for a present or future action)

> *Neither of my parents regret getting married when they were so young.* (= regret doing something in the past)

> **stop**: *'Come on,' said the man in the museum. 'If you stop to look at all the paintings, we'll never get round.'* (= stop one thing to do another)

> *He went to China last month and he hasn't stopped talking about it since.* (= give up doing something)

> **try**: *She tried to reach the book on the top shelf, but it was too high.* (= make an effort)

> *Have you ever tried doing a martial art?* (= try out as an experiment)

> **mean**: *Oh, I meant to tell you something. But I've forgotten what it was.* (= intend)

> *Buying this house means paying a higher mortgage.* (= become necessary)

Relative clauses

Defining relative clauses

Defining relative clauses are a vital part of the meaning of a sentence. They identify the subject or object or add vital information about them. Therefore you can't leave them out. They define *who* or *what* you are talking about. The vital information can come in the middle of a sentence or at the end:

> *The children that he knew would succeed were those who were motivated.*

> *Can you give me a good reason why you need to borrow so much money?*

Relative pronouns:	
who/that for people	*when* for time
that/which for things	*where* for place
whose for possession	*why* for reason

Who, that, which are often omitted when they refer to the object of the sentence (not the subject).

> *Have you ever had one of those days that starts bad and gets worse?* (*that* refers to the subject: 'one of those days')

> *Have you ever thought (that) things couldn't get worse?* (*that* refers to the object: 'things')

You can't omit *whose*. You can omit *when* if it refers to the object:

> *Sit down and tell me the exact time (when) it happened.*

You can omit *where*, but only if you add an appropriate preposition:

> *The old fisherman's hut (where we stayed) we stayed in was small and warm and it smelt of fish.*

You can omit *why* when it refers to the object:

> *Tell me the exact reason (why) you want to leave.*

You can omit the relative pronoun and the auxiliary verb, but only when the relative pronoun refers to the subject:

> *Buildings (that were) constructed before 1960 will be demolished.*

Non-defining relative clauses

'Non-defining' relative clauses are quite formal and mostly found in written or literary styles. They add extra information that is not vital to the meaning of a sentence. They can usually be omitted without losing the sense of the main sentence. This extra information can come in the middle of a sentence or at the end:

> *Manatees, which are sometimes called 'sea cows', can be found in the warm waters around Florida.*

> *The trees were full of large, black birds, all of which made a tremendous noise.*

Relative pronouns:

who for people
which for things (not *that*)
whose for possession

when for time
where for place

Whom is a formal relative pronoun that refers to the object:

> *The young artist, whom we had heard so much about, stumbled onto the stage to collect the prize.*

To identify a certain number of people or things from a group use: *none/one/two/most of whom which*:

> *She walked into a room that was full of teenagers, none of whom looked up from their work.*

You cannot omit relative pronouns in non-defining relative clauses.

Direct and indirect speech

Tense changes

When you report what someone said, you often 'move back' the speaker's verb tense:

'I feel dreadful.'	➡ *He said he felt dreadful.*
'I am swimming about 10 kilometres a week.'	➡ *The girl said she was swimming about 10 kilometres a week.*
'I was the athletics captain at school.'	➡ *He said he had been the athletics captain at school.*
'I have just become a vegetarian.'	➡ *She said that she had just become a vegetarian.*
'We have been planning the trip for a long time.'	➡ *He said they had been planning the trip for a long time.*
'I was travelling in Thailand when I heard the news.'	➡ *She said she had been travelling in Thailand when she heard the news.'*

If you move back the tense, then the speaker's words were true when they were spoken but not necessarily true when they were reported. Don't move back tenses if the situation is still true or still relevant:

'Bob and Anna are learning Russian,' he said.	➡ *He said that Bob and Anna are learning Russian. (they are still learning it)*
	He said that Bob and Anna were learning Russian. (they may have stopped)

A reporting verb can be in the present tense (e.g. *says*), in which case the speaker's verb tense does not change:

'The medicine is working.'	➡ *My doctor says the medicine is working.*

Modal verbs

These modal verbs change for reported speech:

will	➡	*would*
may	➡	*might*
can	➡	*could*
must	➡	*had to*

'You will feel better by Friday.'	➡ *The doctor said I would feel better by Friday.*
'You won't lose weight unless you do some exercise.'	➡ *She said I wouldn't lose weight unless I did some exercise.*
'You must train every day if you want to be a champion.'	➡ *He said I had to train every day if I wanted to be a champion.*

These modal verbs do not change for reported speech:

would	could	might	should
ought to	used to	had better	

'You should/ought to see a good sports psychologist.'	➡ *He said I should/ought to see a good sports psychologist.*

Other changes

When reporting, make logical changes to pronouns and possessives:

'My personal trainer has helped me build up my confidence.' ⇒ She said her personal trainer had helped her build up her confidence.

'I sometimes speak to myself.' ⇒ He said that he sometimes spoke to himself.

Make logical changes to 'place' words:

'I'm coming over there to see you.' ⇒ She said she's coming over here to see us.

The words this, that, these, those are usually reported as 'the':

'This diet doesn't seem to be working.' ⇒ She said the diet didn't seem to be working.

When this or that, these or those are used as subjects, they usually change to it or they:

'This/that is an incredible amount of money.' ⇒ He said it was an incredible amount of money.

'These/Those are very difficult problems to solve.' ⇒ He said they were very difficult problems to solve.

Make logical changes to 'time' words:

an hour ago	⇒	an hour before/previously
last year	⇒	the previous year
yesterday	⇒	the day before
tomorrow	⇒	the following day
in a week's time	⇒	a week later
next month	⇒	the following month

'I had a heart attack a couple of years ago.' ⇒ He said he had had a heart attack a couple of years before.

'I'm going to take up yoga sometime next month.' ⇒ He said he was going to take up yoga sometime the following month.

Questions

Reported questions are not real questions. The word order is the same as for statements. They do not have question marks. Verb tenses, modals, etc. change in the same way as reported statements.

Yes–No questions are usually introduced by if (or sometimes whether):

'Have you ever worked abroad?' ⇒ He asked me if I had ever worked abroad. (not: He asked me had I ever …)

'Would you like a hand with your luggage?' ⇒ The taxi driver asked me if I would like a hand with my luggage. (not: The taxi driver asked me would I like …)

To report wh-questions, use the wh-word followed by the reported clause:

'How long have you been working in the sports centre?' ⇒ He asked me how long I had been working in the sports centre. (not: He asked me how long had I been …)

'When did you first feel a pain in your back?' ⇒ The doctor asked me when I had first felt a pain in my back. (not: The doctor asked me when had I …)

Summarising verbs

There are a large number of verbs which summarise what people say, rather than report the exact words. These verbs are followed by various constructions. Some verbs have more than one construction. For example: suggest is not used with an object (I suggested him to go). It is followed by an -ing form or a that clause:

He suggested training hard and running the London marathon.

His coach suggested that she should rest for a couple of days.

verb + that

admit	mention	protest	complain
realise	explain	suggest	

verb + object + that

advise	warn	remind
persuade	tell	

verb + object + to-infinitive

beg	order	advise
forbid	warn	ask
remind	persuade	tell

verb + to-infinitive

threaten	refuse	agree
promise	offer	

verb + -ing form

deny	recommend	suggest
admit	propose	

verb + preposition + -ing form

apologise (for)	insist (on)	speak (of)
boast (about)	congratulate (on)	

verb + object + preposition + -ing form

accuse (of)	blame (for)
praise (for)	discourage (from)

Modals

There are ten modal verbs:

can	could	should	ought to
must	will	shall	would
may	might		

These five verbs and expressions act in the same way:

be able to	have to	need to
had better	used to	

Ability: can/could/able to

Use *can* to describe an ability in the present:

Professor Smith can speak five languages but he can't remember his name.

Don't use *can* to describe ability in the past or future. Use *could* or a form of *be able to* for the past and *be able to* for the future:

Use *could* for general ability only in the past:

Max could write before he could read.

Use *was able to/were able to* for one particular action concerning ability in the past:

They had to travel first class because they weren't able to get cheap tickets.

Use *couldn't* for specific or general lack of ability in the past:

When I asked Professor Smith what his name was, he couldn't remember.

Use *will be able to* for ability in the future:

After six months of intensive training you will be able to fly a helicopter.

Note: You have to use a form of *be able to* after verbs or phrases that are followed by the infinitive or *-ing* form:

I would like to be able to swim every day, but I don't have time.

Permission: can/could

Use *can* to ask for and give permission in the present. In formal situations, *may* can also be used:

Can I ask you a personal question?

You can now turn over your examination papers and you may start.

Could is also a polite way of asking for permission. But *can* is used in replies:

– *Could I use your dictionary for a moment?*

– *Yes, of course you can.*

Could and *was/were able to* are used to talk about permitted activities in the past:

The schoolchildren could/were able to wear casual clothes on the last day of term.

Will be able to is used for the future:

I'll be able to drive without 'L' plates when I pass my test.

Possibility: might, may

Use either *might* or *may* to express possibility in the future:

If we leave before midnight, we might/may arrive in time for breakfast.

Present possibilities can also use *might/may* when you are making a deduction based on current knowledge:

Due to the heavy defeat in the recent election, some party members might/may now be unhappy with their leader.

Use *might/may* + past participle to talk about a possibility in the past. It implies some uncertainty about whether the action happened or not:

> *I'm not sure, but I might/may have read this book when I was young.*

Necessity: *need (to)*

Although *need* is often used as a normal verb, it can also act like a modal verb to express a necessity (usually one that the speaker feels). In the present positive *use need to* + infinitive to express present or future necessity:

> *You need to apply for a new passport, if you've lost yours. You can't simply get a replacement.*

Use *needn't/don't/doesn't need to* to say that something is not necessary in the present or future or wasn't necessary in the past:

> *You needn't/don't need to put your seatbelts on yet. We have to wait for one more passenger.*

In the past, there are two negative forms.

didn't need to (+ infinitive)

> *I didn't need to send my CV. (perhaps I did send a CV, but it wasn't necessary, or I didn't send it and it didn't matter.*

needn't have (+ past participle)

> *I needn't have sent my CV. (I sent it, but it wasn't necessary.)*

Obligation: *must/have to*

Use *must* or *have to* to express a positive obligation in the present or future. *Must* is often used when the speaker feels an obligation himself/herself:

> *I must lose a bit of weight before I go on holiday.*

Have to is used when the speaker feels an obligation from outside (a rule, law, regulation) or is just expressing a fact:

> *We have to put the paper to be recycled in the green box.*

Mustn't is used to express negative obligation (an obligation not to do something):

> *You mustn't park on the side streets during normal working hours.*

Advice and recommendation: *should/ought to*

Use *ought to* and *should* for strong advice and recommendations. They are very similar in meaning:

> *When you go skiing on your own you should/ought to tell someone where you're going, in case you have an accident.*

> *If you're not a strong swimmer you shouldn't/ oughtn't to go out of your depth.*

Assumptions/Deductions: *must be/can't be*; *must have/can't have*

Use *must* for a logical deduction about the present, when you want to express certainty:

> *It must be very boring to live in a small village where nothing happens.*

The opposite of *must* in this case is *can't*:

> *The letter can't be from your Aunt Harriet. It's got a Chinese stamp on it.*

Use *must have* + past participle and *can't have* + past participle to make logical deductions about the past:

> *The burglars must have got in through the little kitchen window.*

> *Dave can't have played football yesterday. He broke his leg last week.*

Use *may have/might have/could have* + past participle to make assumptions that you are not entirely sure about:

> *I was expecting a package today, but it hasn't arrived. I suppose it may/might/could have got lost in the post.*

Participle clauses

Use participle clauses:

1 to simplify sentences:

When the runner finished the race he was gasping for breath.

The runner finished the race gasping for breath.

2 to reduce two sentences to one sentence:

He's broken his arm. He'll have to watch the match from the sidelines.

Having broken his arm, he'll have to watch the match from the sidelines.

Sentences with participle clauses can often sound quite formal. Some uses would not normally be used in everyday spoken English:

Being the richest person there, Fiona paid for the meal. (formal)

Fiona was the richest person there, so she paid for the meal. (informal and usual)

When you use participle clauses like adverbs they give more information about the *main verb*. For example: they may describe *the way* someone walked, *how* someone acted, someone or something's general manner or behaviour, etc. The main clause would normally come first:

The marathon runner came into the stadium waving at the crowds.

3 in written dialogues:

'You're just in time to check in,' he said, looking at the clock on the wall.

4 to talk about two things happening at the same time:

Sam and Millie sat on the jetty talking about their future.

If one long action is 'interrupted' by another shorter action, the longer action usually comes at the end of the sentence. The word *while* (meaning 'when' or 'at the time') can often be used:

The aid worker died peacefully in a remote African village, (while) doing the job he loved most.

5 to talk about two actions that happen within a short time period:

The fire swept through the Australian town, leaving burnt out houses behind it.

Often the second action is a direct consequence or *result* of the first action:

The film has been a runaway success, paving the way for five or six sequels.

Sometimes there is an obvious sequence – one action then another action. The participle clause would normally come at the beginning:

Taking off his heavy overcoat, he sat down on the red leather sofa.

6 to imply a reason:

Not knowing where he was, he stopped and checked the map. (= because he didn't know where he was)

Note: verbs that can't normally be used in continuous tenses can have a present participle form.

Prepositions are always followed by the present participle:

On hearing the news, they started to celebrate.

Before getting on the plane, the President and his wife waved and smiled at the small crowd.

Participles after a *noun* give more information about the noun. They are like shortened relative clauses in which the relative pronoun and the auxiliary verb have been omitted:

Ruby Stone, smiling and waving to the crowds, got out of the limousine. (who was smiling and waving ...)

Note that the structure noun + present participle indicates an activity in progress:

The man sitting over there wearing ...

If there is no activity in progress, you can't use a participle clause:

The scientist ~~inventing~~ the robotic washing machine will win a prize. The scientist who invented the robotic washing machine will win a prize.

With passive relative clauses, use the past participle:

The meeting, scheduled for 10 o'clock, has been cancelled. (that was scheduled)

These can often imply a condition:

Watered once a day, the plant will grow really well. (if it is watered)

Conditionals

Zero conditional

If-clause	Main Clause
Present Simple	Present Simple

Use the zero conditional to talk about scientific facts, constant laws of nature, unchangeable rules, customs and personal routines. Either *if* or *when* can be used in the *if*–clause.

If/When it is lunchtime in London, it is breakfast time in New York.

First conditional

If-clause	Main Clause
Present Simple	will/won't + infinitive

In the first conditional the **present** tense usually refers to possible/probable conditions in the **future**:

If there is much more rain, the whole village will probably get flooded.

If Real Madrid's captain doesn't play, they won't win the game.

Don't use *will/won't* in the *if*–clause:

If there will be much more rain, the whole village will probably get flooded.

Use the first conditional for threats or warnings involving direct action:

If you don't go away, I'll call the police. (= Go away or I'll call the police.)

You can use an imperative in the main clause:

If you hear the fire alarm, walk quickly to the nearest fire exit.

If you are frightened of heights, don't go up there.

You can use the present continuous or the present perfect instead of the present simple:

If you are doing your violin practice, I'll phone later.

If you have read my CV, you will know all about me.

Second conditional

If-clause	Main Clause
Past Simple	would/wouldn't + infinitive

In the second conditional the past tense refers to 'unreal' or 'hypothetical' conditions in the present or future:

If I had a daughter, I would teach her Russian. (unreal present)

If I started my own business, I wouldn't work on Friday afternoons. (hypothetical future)

Don't use *would/wouldn't* in the *if*–clause:

If I would start my own business, I wouldn't work on Friday afternoons..

Use the second conditional to give advice to other people:

If the solicitor was rude to you, I'd complain to his manager.

You can use the past continuous instead of the past simple:

If they were looking our way, they would see us.

The past tense in second conditionals distances meaning from reality (in the same way that the past is distanced from the present). Compare first and second conditionals:

First conditional: If I become President, I will increase taxes for high earners. (spoken by a Presidential candidate)

Second conditional: If I became President I would spend more money on after-school clubs. (spoken by a schoolgirl)

Third conditional

If-clause	Main Clause
Past Perfect	would have/wouldn't have + past participle

Use the third conditional for past events that are untrue:

If you had listened to the instructions, you would have known what to do.

If there hadn't been an earthquake, there wouldn't have been a tsunami.

Don't use *would have/wouldn't* have in the *if*–clause:

If there wouldn't have been an earthquake, there wouldn't have been a tsunami.

You can use the past perfect continuous instead of the past perfect:

If they had been looking more carefully, they would have seen the signpost.

You can use *could (not) have* instead of *would have* to express possibility:

> *If Sally had been a centimetre taller, she could have become a police officer.*

You can use *might (not) have* instead of *would have* to express 'perhaps/perhaps not':

> *If he had known the film wasn't very good, he might not have gone to see it.*

Formal forms

In first conditionals, you can use *should* before the infinitive in the *if*-clause to add uncertainty or increase politeness:

If he has a problem with his visa,	*I'll sort it out for him.*
If he should have a problem with his visa,	
If you need any help,	*I'll be in that office.*
If you should need any help,	

In second conditionals, you can use *were to* like *should*, above:

If we complained about the lack of clean water,	*what would you do about it?*
If we were to complain about the lack of clean water,	

Alternatives to *if*

You can usually use *provided* (or *providing*) and *as long as* instead of *if*:

> *Jim will land safely on the ground provided/as long as his parachute opens.*

Supposing (or *suppose*) means 'what if'. It can replace *if* in questions and comes first in the sentence:

> *Supposing you missed the plane, what would you do?*

Unless can be used to mean 'if … not':

You can't join the swimming team	*if you can't/ unless you can*	*swim 100 metres in less than 75 seconds.*
Don't sell your shares	*if there isn't/ unless there is*	*a sharp fall in prices.*
You can sit in a first class seat	*if nobody else/ unless someone else*	*wants it.*

Mixed conditionals

Mixed conditional sentences are formed from two clauses with different time references. The most common 'mixed' conditionals involve a clause from a second conditional and a clause from a third conditional. The *if*-clause can state the 'cause' or 'reason' and refers to the past (third conditional), with the 'result' in the main clause referring to the present (second conditional):

	(3rd)	(2nd)
1	*If Sally hadn't tuned her violin …*	*it wouldn't sound very nice.*

	(3rd)
2	*If Tom had read the instructions more carefully, …*
	(2nd)
	he would know what to do.

These conditionals answer the question 'why?'

1   *Why does Sally's violin sound okay? Because she tuned it.*
2   *Why doesn't Tom know what to do? Because he didn't read the instructions very carefully.*

Mixed conditionals of this type often express regret (or satisfaction) in the present for something that happened in the past:

> *If I hadn't married Tom, I wouldn't be living in Australia.*

They can express present possibilities based on past events:

> *If you had kept the receipt, we would give you your money back.*

The modals *might* or *could* can be used:

> *If I had started my own business ten years ago, I might be better off by now.*

> *If she had studied languages at university, she could be a translator.*

The time reference of the clauses can be reversed. The *if*-clause (the cause or reason) can refer to the present (second conditional), the main clause (the result) can refer to the past (third conditional):

(2nd)	(3rd)

> *If his eyes weren't so bad, he would have seen the road sign.*

(He didn't see the road sign because his eyes are bad.)

(2nd)	(3rd)

> *If Anna wasn't so clever she wouldn't have known how to take my blood pressure.*

(Anna knew how to take my blood pressure because she is clever.)

In mixed conditionals of this type, the reference to the present makes it clear that the situation exists now. In 'pure' third conditionals, the time reference only refers to the past.

(2nd)   (3rd)
If Jack wasn't interested in people, he wouldn't have studied sociology at university.

(Jack was and still is interested in people)

(3rd)   (3rd)
If Jack hadn't been interested in people, he wouldn't have studied sociology at university.

(Jack was interested in people, perhaps he still is, but we are not sure)

Wishes and regrets

Use *wish* + past simple for situations in the present that you would like to be different:

I wish I didn't get so many unwanted emails.

You can often use *were* instead of *was*, particularly in formal English:

The young man is so unhappy that he often wishes he were somewhere else.

Use *wish* + the past modal *could* (not *would*) to express a regret about a personal lack of ability:

I wish I could swim further without taking a rest.

Use *wish* + the past modal *didn't have to* to express lack of enthusiasm about an obligation:

I wish I didn't have to carry my identity papers with me everywhere I go.

You can use *wish* + *would* to criticise other people or an aspect of the present situation that you are unhappy with:

I wish she wouldn't keep talking about her children.

I wish this computer would stop crashing.

You can also use *wish* + *would* to talk about future situations that you want to change:

I wish someone would fix the central heating..

You can use *wish* + past perfect to express regrets about the past:

I wish the advertising agency had thought of a better brand name.

You can often use *if only* instead of *I wish*. But the result is more a thought than a voiced regret:

	I didn't have to commute to work every day.
I wish/	*I could get a job in advertising.*
If only	*English spelling was easier.*
	credit card companies wouldn't keep sending me their offers.

Comparatives and superlatives

Comparatives

Use *as … as …* to say that two elements are equal in some way. There are several structures you can use. The words *just* and *nearly* often come before the first *as*:

	adjective	
as	*adverb*	*as*
	much/many + noun	

He plays tennis nearly as well as his girlfriend.

I get paid just as much money as you.

There are just as many cafés in London as (there are) in Paris.

Object pronouns, nouns and clauses can follow the second *as*:

That car is nearly as old as me.

The food in Le Select is just as good as it was ten years ago.

Walking in London is often just as fast as taking a bus.

Use the opposite structure *not as … as …* to talk about two elements that are unequal in some way. The words *nowhere near*, *nothing like* and *not quite* often come before the first *as*:

The sports car was nowhere near as fast as I had expected it to be.

I can play the piano, but not quite as well as (I can play) the guitar.

Flying in a hot air balloon was nothing like as frightening as I thought it would be.

Use comparatives to compare people, groups and things. Use a comparative adjective (*healthier, more exciting,* etc.) or adverb (*earlier, more carefully,* etc.):

> You won the silver medal but Emma Dean beat you with a much faster time.
>
> Would you like to have your interview where there is a greater degree of privacy?

Use *than* to make comparisons between two different things of the same type:

> The weather in many countries is now warmer and wetter than it used to be.
>
> Fiats are less expensive than Ferraris.

You can qualify the comparative with these words and expressions:

a bit	a little	much	a great deal
slightly	a lot	far	

> Driving in a Mercedes is a great deal more comfortable than riding a scooter.
>
> Book 2 in the series is slightly longer than Book 1.
>
> She always does a bit better at English than maths.

You can also use the expression *no (more) ... than* in the same way as *just as ... as*:

> The film was no more frightening than the book.
> The book was just as frightening as the film.

You can use the following structure to talk about two things that happen together:

the + comparative clause + *the* + comparative clause

> The bigger the waves the better it is for surfing.
>
> The heavier the boxer the slower he moves round the ring.

Superlatives

Use superlatives to compare one member of a group with the whole group. Always use *the* with a superlative:

> the best film   the most exciting journey

You can qualify a superlative with these words and expressions:

among	one of	two of

> Shane Walker is among the best young writers in the country.
>
> Crossing the icy ridge was one of the most difficult parts of the expedition.

Degree: *enough, too, so, such, as, like*

enough

Use enough (with the meaning of 'sufficient/ sufficiently') after adjectives and adverbs:

> His exam results were okay, but they weren't good enough to get him his university place.
>
> You're playing well enough to be in the team, but not well enough at the moment to be team captain.

You often use *to* + infinitive after *enough*:

> I know you're physically fit but are you resilient enough to keep going?

too

Use *too* (with the meaning 'more than enough') before adjectives and adverbs:

> Sally auditioned for a part in a Broadway play, but they said she was too small for the part.
>
> He tried to take a photo of the Tour de France riders, but they rode past far too quickly.

You often use *too ... to* + infinitive:

> It was 38 degrees in the shade yesterday. Far too hot to sunbathe.
>
> I ran out of time. I wrote too slowly to finish all the questions.

so and *such*

Use *so* before adjectives or adverbs, but not when a noun follows:

> There probably are other planets, but they are so far away that astronomers can't see them.
>
> The trains are so unreliable (that) it's no wonder commuters get angry.

Note that you can use *so much* or *so many* with a noun:

> 'You've got so many problems,' said the psychologist, 'I hardly know where to start.'

Use *such* before a noun (with or without an adjective):

> I haven't been to the cinema for such a long time (that) I can hardly remember the last film I saw.
>
> Advertisers always want us to think they have such wonderful products, whereas most of it is such rubbish.

as and *like*

Use *as* as a preposition to mean 'in the role of':

> Mr Potter has been working as an accountant for twenty years.

But use *like* as a preposition when it means 'similar to':

> Mr Potter doesn't look like an accountant. He's built more like a professional athlete.

You also use *as* with adjectives to make comparisons:

> *Nothing seems as frightening the second time you do it.*

Emphasis

Inversion

Use the word order you use for questions to give emphasis:

> *I have never heard such a frightening noise.*
> *Never have I heard such a frightening noise.*

You can use inversion:

1 after certain 'negative' adverbials:

never	hardly	scarcely
rarely	little	not for one minute
not since	not until	never before

> *Hardly had he sat down when he started to talk.*
> *Scarcely had she got home when the phone rang.*
> *Little did they expect so many supporters to write to them.*

2 after expressions with *only* or *no*:

only when	not only
the only	in no way
on no account	under no circumstances
at no time	no sooner

> *The only way to get anywhere quickly is to fly.*
> *Although the trip wasn't very pleasant, at no time did I feel in any danger.*

You can use inversion to replace *if* in conditional sentences that include *should*, *were* or *had*:

> *If you should need any help with your bags, please let the receptionist know.*
> *Should you need ...*
> *If you were to stop messing around with your mobile phone, you might learn a bit more.*
> *Were you to stop ...*
> *If you hadn't tried to do three things at once, this would never have happened.*
> *Had you not tried ...*

Emphatic structures with *it* and *what*

You can use *It is ... . It was ...*, etc. to emphasise a particular part of a sentence:

> *There were five members of the climbing team, but it was Bill who reached the summit first.*
> *It was very disappointing that I didn't reach the top.*

Use *What is ..., What was ...* to emphasise the subject or object of a sentence:

> *What they saw when they reached the summit was a French flag fluttering in the wind.*

There are various other expressions that can be added to the start of a sentence for emphasis:

> *The reason I'm here today is to tell you about our new products.*
> *The thing I like most about Harry is his generosity.*
> *All he could talk about was his work.*

-*ing* forms as subject of a sentence

You can use an –*ing* form as the subject of a sentence to give emphasis:

> *Arguing with traffic wardens is a waste of time.*

Phrasal verbs

Adverbial phrasal verbs

Adverbial phrasal verbs are made from a verb + an adverb. Some phrasal verbs are intransitive (they have no object):

> *The witness broke down when he was asked about her husband.*
> *He packed his rucksack and set off.*

Transitive phrasal verbs (those with objects) are 'separable'. If the object is a noun, it can go:

1 between the verb and the particle:

> *The police broke the demonstration up.*
> *Can you set your ideas down in writing?*

2 or after the particle:

> *The police broke up the demonstration.*
> *Can you set down your ideas in writing?*

But if the object is a pronoun, you must put it between the verb and the particle:

> *The police broke it up.*
> *Please set your ideas down in writing.*

Prepositional phrasal verbs

Prepositional phrasal verbs are made from verbs + a preposition. The verb and the preposition are 'inseparable', so all objects whether they are nouns or pronouns must follow the particle:

You should turn off the motorway at junction 2.

We've received your complaint and we'll look into it.

Adverb particles can have several different meanings. For example, *off* can suggest:

1 a beginning of some kind:

    Go to bed early because we are setting off at dawn.

2 finishing or delaying:

    We're going to finish off the lesson with a quiz.

    I'm busy. I'll have to put the meeting off until tomorrow.

3 some kind of separation or disconnection:

    Workmen closed off the road to do maintenance work.

    Come in and take off your wet jacket.

    My phone has been cut off because I didn't pay the bill.

The particle *in* can suggest:

1 some kind of participation:

    Bob never joins in the fun.

2 some kind of deception

    She was too clever to be taken in by the salesman's smooth talk.

3 some kind of collapse/retirement due to pressure

    'Do you give in?' asked the wrestler, twisting the man's arm.

Some phrasal verbs change their meaning when used with or without an object. For example, the particle *out* can suggest:

1 failure:

    My old car made a horrible noise and gave out five kilometres from the garage.

2 distribution

    She stood in the market and gave out leaflets about her new shop.

Three-part phrasal verbs

A few phrasal verbs have three parts: verb + particle + preposition. You cannot separate the verb from the other parts. All objects must come after the preposition:

– *'He's going to do away with all his old mobile phones.'*

– *'Is he going to completely get rid of them?' I've just run out of time.*

OXFORD
UNIVERSITY PRESS

Great Clarendon Street, Oxford OX2 6DP

Oxford University Press is a department of the University of Oxford.
It furthers the University's objective of excellence in research, scholarship,
and education by publishing worldwide in

Oxford New York

Auckland Cape Town Dar es Salaam Hong Kong Karachi
Kuala Lumpur Madrid Melbourne Mexico City Nairobi
New Delhi Shanghai Taipei Toronto

With offices in

Argentina Austria Brazil Chile Czech Republic France Greece
Guatemala Hungary Italy Japan Poland Portugal Singapore
South Korea Switzerland Thailand Turkey Ukraine Vietnam

OXFORD and OXFORD ENGLISH are registered trade marks of
Oxford University Press in the UK and in certain other countries

© Oxford University Press 2008

The moral rights of the author have been asserted

Database right Oxford University Press (maker)

First published 2008
2012
10 9 8 7

No unauthorized photocopying

All rights reserved. No part of this publication may be reproduced,
stored in a retrieval system, or transmitted, in any form or by any means,
without the prior permission in writing of Oxford University Press,
or as expressly permitted by law, or under terms agreed with the appropriate
reprographics rights organization. Enquiries concerning reproduction
outside the scope of the above should be sent to the ELT Rights Department,
Oxford University Press, at the address above

You must not circulate this book in any other binding or cover
and you must impose this same condition on any acquirer

Any websites referred to in this publication are in the public domain and
their addresses are provided by Oxford University Press for information only.
Oxford University Press disclaims any responsibility for the content

ISBN: 978 0 19 480039 6

Printed in China

This book is printed on paper from certified and well managed sources

ACKNOWLEDGEMENTS

*The authors and publisher are grateful to those who have given permission to reproduce the following
extracts and adaptations of copyright material*: p9 'What are you like?' by Rachel Porter, *Daily
Express* 1 September 2004. p10 Based on an article by Maureen Rice entitled 'What are
you like?' © Maureen Rice, The Guardian 28 March 2004. Reproduced by permission of
Maureen Rice. p22 'The remotest festival on earth' by Sue and Patrick Cunningham,
Geographical, June 2004. p38 'Raiders of the Lost City' by Jonathan Glancey, *The Guardian*,
21 February 2005 © Guardian Newspapers Limited 2005. p40 'Shh…your real age is an
open secret' by Sarah-Kate Templeton, *The Sunday Times*, 24 October 2004 © NI Syndication
Limited. p46 'More than just a pretty face' by John Elliott and John Gerritsen, *The Sunday
Times*, 28 November 2004 © NI Syndication Limited. p50 'Do you want to be a professional
wildlife photographer?' by Hans Martens' by Hans Martens, Wildpicture.com. p53 'Will
these creatures one day stalk the Earth?' by John Triggs, *Daily Express*, 26 August 2004.
p57 '100 ways to get fit' by Andy Darling, *The Guardian*, 15 January 2005 © Guardian
Newspapers Limited 2005. p59 'Is it possible to be too fit?' by David Adam and David
Munk, *The Guardian* 10 June 2003 © Guardian Newspapers Limited 2005. p62 'How to put
your back into a blissful night's sleep' by Jo Revill, *The Observer* 28 March 2004 © Guardian
Newspapers Limited 2004. p64 'Do we need to worry about malaria?' by Alok Jha, *The
Guardian*, 18 September 2004 © Guardian Newspapers Limited 2004. p70 'The Science of
Superheroes' by Mark Peplow from http://www.bbc.co.uk/science/hottopics/superheroes/
index.shtml. Reproduced by permission. p76 'What's Left? Not These Whoppers, April
Fool' *Los Angeles Times*, 2 April 1998. Reproduced by permission. p83 adapted extracts from
A Short History of Nearly Everything by Bill Bryson, published by Black Swan, a division of
Transworld Publishers © Bill Bryson. All rights reserved. Reprinted by permission of the
Random House Group Ltd. p95 'Mean machines' by Dylan Evans, *The Guardian* 29 July
2004 © Guardian Newspapers Limited 2004. p98 Youth volunteering from www.vso.org.
uk. Reproduced by permission. p100 'Revealed – the meaning of life' by Julian Baggini, *The
Guardian* 20 September 2004 © Guardian Newspapers Limited 2004. p110 'The Millennium
Dome Heist' from www.bbc.co.uk. Reproduced by permission. p112 'It's all for your own
good' by Paul Lashmar, *The Guardian*, 25 September 2004 © Guardian Newspapers Limited
2004. p118 Everything must go by Simon O'Hagan, *British Airways Business life*, October 2004.
Reproduced by permission. p122 'Don't brand us with heritage' by John Hegarty, *The
Guardian*, 24 January 2005 © Guardian Newspapers Limited 2005. p124 Bling-bling by Ekow
Eshun, *British Airways Business life*, October 2004. Reproduced by permission. p130 adapted
extracts from 'An exhibition of yourself' by Libby Brooks from *The Guardian* 27 October
2001 © Guardian News and Media Ltd 2001. p131 adapted extracts from 'Got Stage Fright'
section of the website www.gsb.org. p131 adapted extracts from 'Today's actors are
Shakespeare's worst enemies' by Germaine Greer from *The Guardian* 20 November 2006
© 2006 Germaine Greer. p134 'How Pixar conquered the planet' by Oliver Burkeman, *The
Guardian*, 12 November 2004 © Guardian Newspapers Limited 2004. p136 'Music to deter
yobs' by Melissa Jackson from www.bbc.co.uk. Reproduced by permission. p141 'The oil
under this wilderness will last the US six months. But soon the drilling will begin' by John

Vidal, *The Guardian*, 18 March 2005 © Guardian Newspapers Limited 2005. p143 'Pressure
points' by Ian Sample, *The Guardian*, 14 October 2004 © Guardian Newspapers Limited 2004.

Sources: p28 *Geographical*; p34 'Holiday 2010? One small step for man, several nights self-
catering for mankind' by Mark Hodgson from *The Sunday Times* 3 October 2004. p35 'Your
Second Life is Ready' by Annalee Newitz from *Popular Science Magazine* 2005. p105 www.
crimestatistics.org.uk

*Although every effort has been made to trace and contact copyright holders before publication, this
has not been possible in some cases. We apologize for any apparent infringement of copyright and if
notified, the publisher will be pleased to rectify any errors or omissions at the earliest opportunity.*

The publisher would like to thank the following for their kind permission to reproduce photographs:
AAP (Australian Associated Press) p79bc (Dave Hunt); Alamy pp14r (Chris Leschinsky/
Glasshouse Images), 26b (Alex Segre), 28b (Sue Cunningham Photographic), 33bl (Mike
Hill/Image State), 33tl (Frank Krahmer/Image State), 33tr (Paul Gibbs), 38l (Mark Baigent),
39b&bc (Jacky Chapman/Janine Wiedel Photography), 44 (Mike Hill/Image State), 45bc
(David Fleetham), 45cl (Steve Bloom Images), 45tr (Profimedia.CZ s.r.o.), 51cl (Paul Doyle/
Photofusion Picture Library), 51cr (pixel shepherd), 51tl (Jeff Greenberg), 54bl (Robert
Slade), 54tl (Bildagentur Franz Waldhaeusl), 54tr (Martin Ruegner/Image State), 55c
(Christian Bauer/flonline), 55r (Jan Baks), 56 (Steve Bloom Images), 59 (Ranulph Feinnes/
Royal Geographical Society), 63cl (John Powell Photographer), 63tl (Dennis MacDonald),
75br (Popperfoto), 82b (Jochen Tack), 87cr (Ian Miles/Flashpoint Pictures), 98 (Jeff Morgan),
105 (Dennis Hallinan), 111br (Dennis MacDonald), 111tl (plainpicture/Combifix), 111tr
(T.Grimm/plainpicture), 112tl (David Stares), 116 (Dennis Hallinan), 117ac (Peter Adams
Photography), 123l (Ace Stock Limited), 123t (V&A Images), 128 (Peter Adams Photography),
135bl (Ron Sutherland/The Garden Picture Library), 143l (Jim Zuckerman), 146r (GP
Bowater), 147br (AT Willett), 149c (Craig Lovell), 154b&c (Justin Kase); Aquarius Library
p134 background; Bridgeman Art Library pp82, (Palazzo Corner Ca'Grande), 86 (Yale
Center for British Art, Paul Mellon Collection); Camera Press pp22–23 & 23l (Yann
Latronche/Gamma); Corbis UK pp14cr (George D Lepp), 19b (Steve Prezant), 19t (Rick
Gomez), 21b (Reuters), 27t (Reuters), 27tc, 30bc (Paul A Sounders), 30bl (Free Agents
Limited), 30br, 31 (Paul Steel), 33bc (Pat Jerrold/Papilio), 33br (Michael Pole), 33tc (Steve
Boyle/NewSport), 38r (Lindsay Hebberd), 39t (DiMaggio/Kalish), 39tc (Philip Gould), 45bl
(Paul A Sounders), 45br (Steve Kaufman), 45cr (W Perry Conway), 45tl (Martin Harvy/Gallo
Images), 51b (Earl & Nazima Kowall), 51tr (Tom & Dee Ann McCarthy), 55l (Niall Benvie),
58c (Douglas Peebles), 58l (Rick Doyle), 58r (Lucy Pemoni/Reuters), 63bl (Tom Stewart),
63br (David Pollack), 63cr (Eric KK Yu), 63tr (James Leynse), 67 (Simon Taplin), 70t (Marvel
Characters Inc), 71b (Marvel Characters Inc), 75bl (KM Westermann), 75tc (Helen Atkinson/
Reuters), 75tl (Frank Trapper), 78tl (Michael a keller/Zefa), 79b (Patrik Giardino), 81br
(Kazuyoshi Nomachi), 81bc (Archivo Iconografico, SA), 81bl (Roger Wood), 81c (Alinari
Archives), 81cr (Tim Page), 81t (Mimmo Jodice), 87br (Michael Freeman), 87cl (Richard T
Nowitz), 87bl (Jim Cornfielj), 87tr (Roger De La Harpe/Gallo Images), 88b (Bojan Brecelj),
88t (Charles & Josette Lenars), 90br (Najlah Feanny SABA), 91l (Bettmann), 107 (Images.
com), 111cl (Alan Schein Photography), 112tr (Varie/Alt), 114–115 (Derek Croucher), 118b
(eBay/Jens Wolf/dpa), 119r (Kim Sayer), 122 (Bruce Connolly), 123 acr (Robert Holmes),
123bcr (Caroline Penn), 124b (Julio Donoso/SYGMA), 126b (Enrique Marcarian/Reuters),
126t (Gary Houlder), 127b (John Gress/Reuters), 127t (Sam Sharpe), 129br (Bob Sacha),
129ac (Queen Elizabeth II of the United Kingdom from the Reigning Queens series, 1985/
Andy Warhol/The Andy Warhol Foundation for the Visual Arts), 129bc (Tony Gentile/
Reuters), 129l (Images.com), 129t (Francis G Mayer), 130–131b (Rune Hellestad), 131r
(Robbie Jack), 135bl (Mimmo Jodice), 135cr (Gunter Marx Photography), 135cr (Greg
Fiume/NewSport), 140 (Images.com), 141b (Lowell Georgia), 141c (Paul A Sounders), 141t
(Lowell Georgia), 141tc (Paul A Sounders), 142 (Robert van der Hilst), 143r (Craig Lovell),
146c (Owaki-Kulla), 147bl (Richard Chung/Reuters), 147tl (Ricki Rosen SABA), 147tr (Kelly-
Mooney Photography), 152 (Lowell Georgia), 154t (Terry W Eggers); Ecoscene p47; Empics
pp27b, 111cr, 130t (EPA/Paolo Aguilar), 135br; Getty Images pp21tl (Robert Earnest/Stone),
26 (Hiroshi Watanabe/Taxi Japan), 35 (Fredrik Skold/ Image Bank), 65 (James Endicott/
Stock Illustration Source), 78bl (Toshifumi Kitamara/AFP), 78tr (Richard Kolker/Photonica),
79 (Ryuhel Shindo/Photonica), 79c (Andrew G Hobbs/Stone), 117t (Michael Kelley/Stone),
117bc (jens Lucking/Stone),131 (Lester Lefkowitz/Stone),136 (MacDougall/Photographers
Choice), 141 (David Trod/Image Bank), cover_br (Digital Vision), cover_c (Pierre-Yves
Goavec/The Image Bank), cover_cl (Nick Daly/Photonica), cover_cr (Michael Banks/Stone),
cover_tc (Jac Depczyk/The Image Bank), cover_tl (Photodisc Collection/Photodisc Blue);
Hemera Technologies pp76, 118, 119c, 119l; Image.net (Peter Mountain/Disney Enterprises
Inc) Illustration Library/ Andrew Selby p89; iStockphoto p141bc (David Freund); Linden
Research Inc p35; Moviestore Collection pp134t (Walt Disney Pictures/Pixar), 134b (Walt
Disney Pictures/Pixar), 139 (Dimension Films) NASA p90bl; Nature Picture Library pp28tl
(Premaphotos), 28tr (Premaphotos); Oxford University Press cover_bc; Photolibrary.
com pp16–17 (Mike Lorrig), 26 background (Bernd Römmelt/Dauritius Die Bildagentur
GmbH); Punchstock/PhotoDisc Green p64, 78br (Photodisc), 117b ; Rex Features pp14bl
(Image Source), 14cl (Sipa Press), 21tr (Christophe Potigny), 54br (Ted Blackbrow), 66
(Sipa Press), 70bl (c.Columbia/Everett), 70br (Everett Collection), 90t (Sipa Press), 91r
(Markus Zeffler), 94–95 (c.20th C Fox/Everett), 111bl (Nicholas Bailey), 112b (Action Press),
123br (Andrew Drysdale), 124t (Jim Smeal/BEI), 146br (Sipa Press), 148l (Jim Wright),
148r (Tony Kyriacou), 148ac (Chris Hellier)149c (Tess Peni); Ronald Grant Archive pp71t
(Universal Pictures), 87tl, 95t (20th Century Fox), 134t (Disney Pixar), 134b (Buena Vista),
138 (Disney); Science Photo Library pp34 (Victor Habbick) 35 (Victor Habbick Visions), 82t
(Tom McHugh); Superstock p14tl; The Future is Wild pp52b, 52t,
53b, 53t, Tickle Inc pp10–11, 11t & b.

Illustrations by: Gill Button pp13, 49, 72, 99, 100, 121; Jo Goodberry/NB Illustration p142;
Brian Grimwood p69, 80; Sarah Nayler/NB Illustration p17.

Researched illustrations by: Rod Clark/The Art Market pp93, 104, 151; Melvyn Evans p101;
Oliver Gaiger pp41, 77, 96; Stephane Gamain/NB Illustration p57, 68; Brain Grimwood
pp9, 20; Tim Marrs p74; Sarah Nyler/NB Illustration pp29, 42–43; Ali Pellatt pp15, 25, 37,
61, 85, 97, 103, 109, 133, 145; David Tazzyman/PVUK pp113, 137.

Grammar reference by: Ken Singleton.